Architecture's Historical Turn

Architecture's Historical Turn
Phenomenology and the Rise of the Postmodern

Jorge Otero-Pailos

University of Minnesota Press
Minneapolis • London

This book is supported by a grant from the Graham Foundation for Advanced Studies in the Fine Arts.

Chapter 4 was previously published as "Photo[historio]graphy: Christian Norberg-Schulz's Demotion of Textual History," *Journal of the Society of Architectural Historians* 66, no. 2 (June 2007): 220–41; reprinted with permission from Society of Architectural Historians.

Every effort was made to obtain permission to reproduce material in this book. If any proper acknowledgment has not been included, we encourage copyright holders to notify the publisher.

Published by the University of Minnesota Press
111 Third Avenue South, Suite 290
Minneapolis, MN 55401-2520
http://www.upress.umn.edu

Printed in the United States of America on acid-free paper

Library of Congress Cataloging-in-Publication Data

Otero-Pailos, Jorge (1971–).
Architecture's historical turn: phenomenology and the rise of the postmodern/ Jorge Otero-Pailos.
p. cm.
Includes bibliographical references and index.
ISBN 978-0-8166-6603-4 (hc: alk. paper)—ISBN 978-0-8166-6604-1 (pb: alk. paper)
1. Architecture—Philosophy—History—20th century. 2. Postmodernism.
I. Title. II. Title: Phenomenology and the rise of the postmodern.
NA2500.O77 2010
724'.6—dc22
2009047050

The University of Minnesota is an equal-opportunity educator and employer.

17 16 15 14 13 12 11   10 9 8 7 6 5 4 3 2

For Laurence

Contents

Acknowledgments

When I entered Cornell University's undergraduate architecture program in the 1980s, an older student handed my classmates and me a copy of Christian Norberg-Schulz's *Genius Loci* and told us to read it if we wanted to get through school. I naively followed her advice and continued to read about architectural phenomenology for years. Later, I decided to write this book in order to critically assess architectural phenomenology's contribution to the wider intellectual development of postmodern thought in architecture. I was fortunate to come into contact with a number of mentors and colleagues who generously offered their insights at various stages, and to them I am indebted. While I was a doctoral student at the Massachusetts Institute of Technology, Mark Jarzombek, along with Daniel Bertrand Monk and John Rajchman, helped me lay the foundation for much of this project. I am grateful to my colleagues at Columbia University, first to Kenneth Frampton, who graciously allowed me to interview him on countless occasions, and also to all those who commented on drafts and presentations, especially Mark Wigley, Gwendolyn Wright, Barry Bergdoll, Mary McLeod, Reinhold Martin, and Felicity Scott. At other critical junctures, I benefited from the frank assessments of Stanford Anderson, Henry Millon, Vikramaditya Prakash, Hélène Lipstadt, Hilde Heynen, John Macarthur, Susan Buck-Morss, and Briankle Chang.

Postdoctoral fellowships from the Canadian Centre for Architecture and the American Scandinavian Foundation afforded me the necessary time to write. In Montreal, conversations with Joseph Rykwert, Marco de Michelis, Phyllis Lambert, Kent Kleinman, and Louis Martin helped sharpen the text. I am thankful to Anna María Norberg-Schulz for granting me unimpeded access to her late husband's papers and for her generous hospitality while in Oslo. Ulf Grønvold was very helpful in locating Norberg-Schulz's manuscripts, drawings, and extant buildings. In the context of the Fehn Symposium in Hamar, I had illuminating discussions with Alberto Pérez-Gómez, Mari Hvattum, Thordis Arrhenius, and Grö Lauvland.

A grant from the Henry Luce Foundation for the Study of American Art allowed me to travel to the archives of various universities in the United States. The research was made especially pleasant thanks to the efficient cooperation of librarians and archivists, notably Janet Parks at Columbia University's Avery Library Archives; Nancy Sparrow at the Alexander Architectural Archive at the

University of Texas, Austin; Paul Chénier at the Canadian Center for Architecture; Don C. Skemer at the Department of Rare Books and Special Collections of Princeton University Library; and Eva E. Madshus and Birgitte Sauge at the Norwegian National Museum of Art, Architecture and Design. I thank my research assistants Tania Goffe-Nuñez, Joselito Corpus, Catherine Gavin, Greta Hansen, Janusz Dylla, and Lian Chang.

Pieter Martin at the University of Minnesota Press was an ideal editor; he believed in the project and shepherded it intelligently.

The publication of this book would not have been possible without generous awards from the Graham Foundation for Advanced Studies in the Fine Arts and the New York State Council on the Arts: Architecture Planning and Design Program.

Architectural Intellectuality at the Dawn of Postmodernism

By the early 1960s, a young postwar generation of architects had seized the idea that architecture should participate in the liberation of human experience from the constraints of the social status quo. Raised during the ascendancy of postwar modernism in the West, they viewed its austere institutionalized aesthetics as the emblem of an oppressive and closed social order. They thought individual experience had been impoverished by the process of industrialization and became disillusioned with the modernist faith in technology as the driver of emancipation. In a radical break from modernist ideology, some members of that generation sought to reground the future of modern architecture in the premodern past. To accomplish this change of direction, they had to replace the piloting concepts of modernism, from the abstract ideas of space and form, toward new notions of history and theory. Out went the conviction that technology drove history, and in came the sense that architectural history was driven by the search for authentic, original human experiences. They replaced the belief that architecture would become more sophisticated as technology moved toward the future teleologically, with the notion that architecture would become more advanced as human experience returned to its origins ontologically. They conceived contemporary experience in terms of historical continuity rather than rupture. The protagonists of this intellectual shift were not a self-identified group armed with an emblematic manifesto, but rather a series of independent architects whose collective achievements are understandable only retroactively as constituting a new intellectual formation—architectural phenomenology— which recast history as the experiential content of modern architecture. This collective discourse achieved the greatest coherence in the United States, in the academic circles that formed around the figures of Jean Labatut (1899–1986), Charles Moore (1925–1993), Christian Norberg-Schulz (1926–2000), and Kenneth Frampton (b. 1930), whose teachings and writings made their impact on architectural culture slowly and deliberately, over decades rather than years. As some of the most influential pedagogues and international best-selling authors, they led the transformation of Western architectural culture during the so-called postmodern period, changing how architects learned and understood the relationship of modern architecture to its history. Their ability to produce such a discourse helped legitimize the recuperation of historical architecture as an inspiration for modern design and underpinned the emergence of the postmodern style. But more importantly, their ingenious construction of new experiential protocols for researching and writing architectural history had an intellectual impact that lasted long after the postmodern style went out of fashion. They made the study of architectural history the hallmark of the intellectual architect or, as we say today, the architect theorist. Yet, however staunchly committed to the intellectualization of architecture, they were also firm believers in the primacy of lived experience over detached mental analyses as a means to understand the history of architecture. They were thus caught in the paradoxical position of having to intellectualize their resistance to the emergence of theory as something separate from practice. Their ambivalence sowed the seeds of anti-intellectualism into contemporary architectural theory.

Postmodernism in architecture was both a stylistic movement and an intellectual sea change that germinated in the postwar period, took root in the 1970s, and flourished in the 1980s. While postmodernism is easy to identify stylistically, its intellectual contours are not as straightforward to discern. This book aims to clarify the nature of architectural phenomenology as one of the major unexamined intellectual sources of postmodern architectural thought. The name obscures as much as reveals its derivations, making them seem primarily philosophical, when in fact they were also aesthetic and included practices like camouflage, graphic design, and photography. It is difficult for us today to look at a camouflage pattern, a supergraphic paint scheme, or a carefully framed picture of a construction joint as anything more than various aesthetizations of theory, that is, as ex post facto representations of intellectual work. Yet before the rise of what we now call architectural theory, these practices were included in what was considered legitimate intellectual work in architecture, not something secondary to mental acts but as their primary source and governing standard. Architectural phenomenology refers to this ambiguous intellectual realm and to the process whereby architects became aware of its ambiguity, testing, contesting, celebrating, and exploiting it for the purpose of defending the belief that architectural practice embodied a unique mode of intellectuality that could not be separated from aesthetic experience.

Architectural phenomenologists endeavored to systematically analyze the intellectual content of architecture—the intentions in architecture, to use Norberg-Schulz's terminology—in terms of visual and experiential codes. The form of their analytical work ranged from elaborate photo essays to graphic and building designs, as well as more conventional texts, making it clear that architectural ideas circulated as much through words as images. This revelation about the nature of discourse gave intellectual weight to key themes of postmodernism, such as the new attentiveness to image-like, two-dimensional building surfaces and decorations. As a result of their relentless search for an experiential source of intellectuality, architectural phenomenologists tested the accepted limits of what was deemed purely conceptual work. During the postwar era, that limit was synonymous with architectural history, which figured as the model for scholarship, intellectual work, and, most importantly, detachment from aesthetic production. Postmodernism's wider turn toward history was understood to be an intellectualization of the discipline. In that context, architectural phenomenology held the line against architectural historians, offering the prospect that architects might employ their unique experiential and aesthetic means to investigate the intellectual content of history. By raising the prospect of other ways to produce history, architectural phenomenologists effectively called into question the accepted conventions of architectural historiography, such as the reliance on secondary written documents to establish facts such as dates of construction, lines of patronage, and costs. For architectural phenomenologists, these were irrelevant secondary details that distracted historians from their main task of ascertaining the historic significance of buildings. Instead, they raised the possibility that a building's historic significance—or its meaning, to use their preferred term—might be more accurately ascertained through the direct physical experience of the building itself. Their collective probing of the methods and purposes of architectural history raised its intellectual stakes. Their experientialist historiography was a key factor in the development of a distinctly new theoretical kind of history by architects and for architects. Architectural phenomenology played a central role in setting into motion what we now call theory—not only intellectually, through the expansion and rearticulation of architecture's modes of scholarship, but also socially, by staking out a new position for architect-historians within the academy as the custodians of architecture's peculiarly ambiguous mode of intellectuality.

Architectural phenomenology's insistence on this ambiguity, conceived as the unity of theory and practice, pitted it against the very idea of an autonomous architectural theory that it helped spawn. By the mid-1980s, this put architectural phenomenologists in the paradoxical position of having to theorize their own demotion of theory. For the younger generation of postmodern thinkers eager to take up the position of architect-historians, the ambiguity of experientialist historiography began to appear as an intellectual liability rather than an asset. The eclipse of architectural phenomenology was as spectacular and swift as its rise. It became synonymous with an anti-intellectual affirmation of the primacy of practice over theory. When a student show at the Architectural Association in London was criticized under the title "All Phenomenology and No Substance," it was not necessary to read to the end of the review to know that the critic considered it all "superficiality and subjectivism,"[1] without any theoretical grounding. Detractors of architectural phenomenology portrayed its hypostatization of sensory experience as an essentialist, ahistorical, antitheoretical, irrational, and subjective flight from all scholarly conventions and discourse. Significantly, practicing architects felt as compelled as architecthistorians to defend architectural phenomenology—a testament to its lasting influence in the profession even after it became intellectually suspect. Oswald Mathias Ungers (1926–2007), chairman of the Department of Architecture at Cornell University during the critical years between 1969 and 1975, came forward with "I Am Trying to Save the Phenomenology of Architecture,"[2] defending the idea that architects could grasp the historical significance of places, and express it architecturally, by experiencing their primordial form. His was a defense of the idea of genius loci as the experiential origin of meaning in architecture, an idea that had been chiseled by Norberg-Schulz into a foundation stone of architectural phenomenology. At stake in these debates over the intellectual worth of architectural phenomenology were two of the most important themes in postmodernism: history and theory. Indeed, architectural phenomenology emerged in recognition that these two ideas were inextricably (if ambiguously) bound, and that a renewed understanding of history within architecture required a reformulation of the discipline's paradigms of intellectuality.

It is hard for students of architecture today to grasp why the mere mention of architectural phenomenology elicits such polarizing responses from their teachers. Some enthusiastically embrace it (usually design faculty), commonly using it to signify, more or less restrictively, the ideas of paying close attention to the role that sensory experience plays in our understanding of architecture, and of designing so as to reinforce recognizable patterns of experiencing buildings. Others emphatically reject it (typically history and theory faculty) as a soft type of history and theory at best, and at worst as a dangerous form of detheorized history and dehistoricized theory, which takes the critical bite out of intellectual work in order to operatively legitimate architecture's status quo. Students entering the academy encounter architectural phenomenology as a dividing line between theory and design, and therefore also as the element that enables the distinction between those two divisions of architecture. But that line has a history. It comes laden with associations to particular people, practices, places, schools, building projects, publications, and conferences. The trouble is that, despite the divisive role of architectural phenomenology, or perhaps because of it, we lack an unprejudiced account of its history and of its role in shaping the intellectual developments we have come to know as postmodernism. That architectural phenomenology has carried on without a proper description of itself is somewhat ironic, especially since, as its name suggests, it appropriated so much from phenomenological philosophy, which, after all, Edmund Husserl initiated as a method for the unprejudiced description of phenomena as they appeared in experience.

One prejudice standing in the way of a history capable of assessing the role of architectural phenomenology within postmodernism is the notion that intellectual changes happen abruptly. Intellectually speaking, postmodernism did not occur in architecture all at once. Rather, it happened in phases that were marked by the coalescing of disparate ideas and practices into coherent and identifiable patterns of thinking and doing. These phases are sufficiently different from one another to warrant different names and to be studied in detail and in relative independence. Architectural phenomenology was an early phase in the intellectual development of postmodernism. It was important not only for setting the stage for later structuralist and poststructuralist phases of postmodernism but also for radically expanding what was deemed legitimate intellectual work in architecture. It was the testing ground where new intellectual positions, like that of the architect-historian, staked their claim to be a form of architectural practice by retaining various modes of aesthetic production, from graphic design to photography, and by simultaneously detaching themselves from professional building design and construction. It was also the testing ground for new theoretical questions regarding the authenticity of the human experience of architecture and place and the stability of history as a grounding source of design. Significantly, these questions were turned into their negative form during the later deconstructivist phase of postmodernism, but remained its defining themes. By the mid to late 1980s, architect-historians were examining how unfamiliar and uncanny the experience of architecture and place could also be, as proof of the inauthenticity of all claims to experiential authenticity.[3] They attacked the idea of history as the foundation for design as well, emphasizing the unsettling discontinuities and distortions inherent in historical master narratives.

Following such poststructuralist contributions, it is important to emphasize not just the lines of conceptual continuity but also the manner in which discontinuities and ruptures structured the transformation from the early to later phases of postmodernism. One cannot assume that architectural phenomenology always bore an overt similarity to what we know as (late) postmodern theory. The very history that concerns us would escape us if we were to selectively seek to match the dividing lines within contemporary architectural discourse with the past, or to selectively fish out ideas from the postwar period, on the basis that they bear an outward resemblance to those we are familiar with, and to artificially cast them as the roots of a long arc to the present. Perhaps Robert Venturi (b. 1925), whose *Complexity and Contradiction in Architecture* (1966) is widely held to be the intellectual inauguration of a new postmodern thinking, has been the greatest beneficiary of this trend to edit history in the likeness of the present. Yet that approach can never account for the fact that sometimes ideas can also have their roots in their apparent opposites. Quite apart from Venturi, the thought that a building is a complex and contradictory object was also revealed in the need, felt by so many of his contemporaries, to constantly and obsessively affirm its stable identity—the first response to change is very often denial. Certainly in the case of postmodernism, the double disavowal of the possibility of a unified architectural object and a unified self was preceded by an intellectual probing of its opposite condition: of architecture as the stable setting of authentic human experience, one firm and basic enough to help people orient themselves in their new postmodern surroundings, grounding their sense of self, their identity, in particular places. By being careful not to impose the present condition onto the past we begin to notice just how different postmodernism was at the outset from what it later became.

The most obvious discontinuity between the early and late phases of postmodernism is generational. The change in approaches and responses to the questions concerning the status of history and theory in architecture corresponds to a replacement of the players according to the inevitable logic of human aging. Architectural phenomenology was the product of a generation born during the interwar period and reaching maturity in the postwar era, at a time when French existentialism stood as the emblem of intellectual sophistication in the West. Jean-Paul Sartre (1905–1980) was particularly relevant to the new generation both in his insistence on political commitment and in his demand that people should reject bad faith, stop leading lives according to the false conventions of prewar society, and opt instead for the pursuit of an authentic existence. Sartre contributed to the youth subculture of the 1950s by encouraging individuals to express themselves through their actions, to take responsibility for those actions, and to have a strong sense of political commitment. His late postwar writings, which emphasized the importance of communal projects as the path to achieve personal authenticity, resonated with architects more than his earlier works, which were more narrowly concerned with individualistic morality. More important for our purposes, Sartre demonstrated the vitality of phenomenology when in Germany it "seemed to have become a matter of past record, to be left to the historians of philosophy."[4]

Although popular with the young generation, Sartre's brand of existentialism suffered in American academia for being too Marxist and too staunchly hostile to religion in a country where most philosophers, although not overtly religious, "were not far removed from the spiritual traditions of their families and communities, and . . . were averse to a philosophy that trampled too indelicately on remaining religious sensibilities."[5] In American architectural circles, Sartre's phenomenological sources, which seemed less politically charged, became far more influential than existentialism *tout court*. Paradoxically, religion served as the Trojan horse in which phenomenology entered American architectural discourse. During the dark period of McCarthyism, Catholic schools served as safe havens from Communist suspicion, where the young were given the latitude to study Sartre, Maurice Merleau-Ponty (1908–1961), and other phenomenologists.[6] It was those young Catholics who first brought an interest in phenomenology to architecture. Princeton University's graduate architecture program, then led by Jean Labatut, a progressive Catholic, was a favorite destination for Catholic feeder schools. By the late 1950s, Princeton became the first academic hotbed of architectural phenomenology and soon thereafter a major center of postmodern architecture. Charles Moore's early adoption of Gaston Bachelard (1884–1962) in his Princeton dissertation cannot be separated from the fact that some of his fellow PhD students at Princeton were Jesuit priests familiar with phenomenology. Catholic themes are also a palpable undercurrent in Christian Norberg-Schulz, whose turn to Martin Heidegger's (1889–1976) more spiritual late work cannot be divorced from his conversion to Catholicism. It is worth recalling that Heidegger's early education prepared him for priesthood in the Catholic Church, and that although he left the novitiate at age 21 because of ill health, he continued to identify himself as a Catholic philosopher until 1919, when he rejected Catholicism as a system but still expressed high appreciation for the religious outlook of the Catholic Middle Ages.[7] With Kenneth Frampton, Catholicism does not figure intellectually, but it does so socially, inasmuch as he discovered the works of the Catholic phenomenologist Paul Ricoeur (1913–2005) through his friend Dalibor Vesely (b. 1934), who in turn studied phenomenology in Prague with Jan Patočka (1907–1977), a Catholic student of Heidegger. Religion played a central role in the architectural reception of phenomenology, although it remained muted under the more secular language of philosophy. Thus, the obsession of architectural phenomenologists with the body and the flesh as sites of borderline spiritualist and mystic experiences was not a lack of intellectual capacity on the part of architects reading philosophy, but rather a function of the particular historical conditions under which this discourse emerged.[8] The intellectual history of architecture seldom ventures into these spiritual contexts. But for architectural phenomenology, the boundary where architectural discourse is silenced is the key to its comprehension.

The second generation of postmodern architect-historians, trained in the wake of 1968, matured in an academic environment with different intellectual references. French thought remained important for them, but they were attracted to younger Parisian thinkers, including Jacques Derrida (1930–2004), Gilles Deleuze (1925–1995), Roland Barthes (1915–1980), and others. Many of these thinkers, reacting to the sway of Sartre, sought to undermine him by establishing their own direct interpretations of Marxism and of German phenomenology. Barthes's first book, *Writing Degree Zero* (1953), contains an open acknowledgment of indebtedness to Sartre when he stated his goal as imparting a more correctly Marxist dimension to the existentialist notion of commitment. Derrida's introduction to his translation of Husserl's *The Origin of Geometry* (1962) made it impossible for late postmodern architect-historians to speak of deconstruction without having to acknowledge phenomenology and by extension architectural phenomenology.[9] Of the second generation of postmodern architect-historians, Mark Wigley (b. 1956) carried out the most sustained and self-reflective analysis of deconstruction from the perspective of architecture,[10] and he was also one of the harshest critics of architectural phenomenology.[11] Mark Jarzombek (b. 1954), Hilde Heynen (b. 1959), and K. Michael Hays (b. 1952) are also among those who made noteworthy contributions to situating late postmodern thinking in opposition to architectural phenomenology, but inevitably in relation to it.[12] This younger generation reproached architectural phenomenology for mishandling the postmodernist themes of history and theory and for essentializing both into a specious notion of universal human experience. Operating from a Foucauldian intellectual frame of reference, they sought to rectify this shortfall by historicizing the concepts of history and theory within the larger evolution of architectural discourse, showing architectural phenomenology's claims to universality to be contingent on unexamined Western Enlightenment ideals, and proving its depiction of experience as a natural human condition to be highly artificial. They also viewed architectural phenomenology as operating in political bad faith, insofar as it purported to stand for place-based architectural practices found in marginal regions of the world but actually allowed non-Western architects entry only if they spoke its Western language of universal experience. Significantly, charges about politics flew in both directions. The older generation of architectural phenomenologists often presented poststructuralists as being without political commitment and as having turned the postmodernist notion of pluralism into a toothless relativity where every idea was given equal value. This mutual reception (or rejection) across generations helped forge the sense of an overblown gulf between the early and the late phases of postmodernist architectural thought. There were noteworthy attempts at reconciliation, such as the work of Michael Benedikt,[13] but because they did not account for how social relations distort intellectual history, they could not explain why they fell on deaf ears.

The moment of greatest tension between these two generations of postmodern thinkers was the late 1980s, when both were active with equal force and capacities. That is the time when postmodernism, intellectually speaking, is thought to have irrupted in architectural discourse—basically at the time when postmodernism as an aesthetic style expired. In the absence of a social history, the deconstructive phase of postmodernism appeared to have arrived magically, motivated by some internal discursive logic beyond the reach of any human agent. Architectural phenomenology's discursive ramifications are daunting in scope. It exists both inside and outside the academy, somewhere between publications, academic genealogies, built projects, discursive practices, and personal friendships. To fully grasp what gives intellectual coherence to architectural phenomenology, I have attempted to develop a historiographical method capable of relating the history of ideas to aesthetic, personal, sociogenerational, cultural, and political history. Chapter 1 describes that polygraphic historiography.

By foregrounding the social and generational struggles, my aim is first to reclaim a space for individual agency in the history of postmodern architecture's intellectual development. But my focus on individual contributions should not be misunderstood as a new hagiography or master narrative of postmodernism. Rather, I am interested in the discursive heat created by the frictions between protagonists and how it changed the state of what was considered legitimate intellectual work in architecture. My second aim is to expand the chronology of the intellectual history of postmodern architecture back to the postwar period when it began to cohere into a recognizably new way of approaching the questions of history and theory.

Architectural phenomenology articulated itself around these two key concepts of history and theory, which distinguished it from the many previous attempts to argue for the primacy of direct bodily experience in the understanding of architecture. Needless to say, architectural phenomenology drew freely on those preceding examples, especially on the discourse on empathy that flourished in the Germanic world between the 1870s and the early 1900s. Broadly conceived as a reaction to the Kantian metaphysical conception of aesthetics and beauty, the theory of empathy held that architecture was best understood not through abstract mental analytic categories but through direct experiences of the building, during which one would project oneself fully onto it, especially one's feelings and emotions, as a way of fully grasping its intentional content. Philosopher Robert Vischer (1847–1933) first coined empathy as *Einfühlung* (literally "in-feeling") in his 1873 dissertation *Über das optische Formgefühl* ("On the optical sense of form"). He defined the empathic experiential process according to a logic of similarity whereby the sense of, say, a building's beauty was a function of a harmonious correlation between the object's form and the bodily or sensory structure of the perceiving subject. For instance, gently arching lines would be more pleasing than zigzags because they would provoke soft, congenial movements in one's muscles and nerves. Vischer's empathy, although anchored in aesthetic philosophy, has been shown to be part of a wider scientific discourse on kinaesthesia, which construed the muscles as a sixth sense, able to perceive dimensions of architecture that could not be traced directly to the known sense organs.[14] As developed by philosophers like Theodor Lipps (1851–1914) at the turn of the century, empathy theory literally embodied the possibility of a radically different type of aesthetic appreciation, other than the purely visual paradigm underpinning earlier architectural history. By the end of the nineteenth century, the concept of empathy had been widely adopted in Germanic architectural circles by architects like Adolf Göller (1846–1902), Henry van de Velde (1863–1957), Hermann Obrist (1862–1927), and August Endell (1871–1925) and art historians like August Schmarsow (1853–1936), Heinrich Wölfflin (1864–1945), and his students Paul Frankl (1879–1962) and Sigfried Giedion (1888–1968). Their work advanced the idea that beneath the outward appearance of architectural styles there were deeper, more vital and abstract experiential contents to architecture, namely, form and space, two concepts that defined the intellectual history of modern architecture.[15]

Wölfflin was a particularly important reference for architectural phenomenology because he made the aesthetization of questions of form and space into the basis for his historiography. Wölfflin's famous double lantern lectures introduced the idea of image comparisons as a method for training students how to empathize with the form and space of buildings by presenting them with extreme opposites. These image comparisons had an ambiguous status as both aesthetic exercises and intellectual claims about the way the spirit of an age found expression in architecture. Wölfflin used these image comparisons as arguments explaining the transformation of style through history. Giedion adopted the method of image comparison from his mentor and taught it to his students, including Norberg-Schulz, as more than a mere formal analysis—as a way to think *through* the simultaneous perception of multiple photographs to gain access to a deeper and more modern experience of architecture and its history. This Wölfflinian lineage reveals the degree to which postmodernism absorbed the modernist interest in experience, using it to shift its emphasis from notions of form and space to the question of history. For architectural phenomenologists, Wölfflin represented proof that modernism was not so much a break with history but rather a new understanding of history that had yet to find full expression. The desire to fulfill that promise made architectural phenomenologists like Norberg-Schulz discuss postmodernism's experiential historiography as a return to the true *Roots of Modern Architecture* (1998).

The postmodernist attempt to incorporate and indeed rewrite modernist themes must not overshadow the immense differences between Giedion's interwar generation of modernists and Norberg-Schulz's postmodern cohorts. The divergence can be seen most clearly in their different readings of phenomenology, with the former emphasizing the connection between experience, form, and space, and the latter underscoring the triumvirate of experience, history, and theory. In step with their younger colleagues, some of the most respected modernist historians, like Giulio Carlo Argan (1909–1992), began looking to phenomenology for a way to adapt the old concepts of form and space to the new intellectual culture of the postwar years. In *Walter Gropius e la Bauhaus* (1951), Argan expounded on this formalist reading of phenomenology:

> The rationality that Gropius develops in art's formal processes is akin to the dialectic of phenomenological and existential philosophy (especially that of Husserl), with which it is in fact connected: It is substantially to deduct from the pure logical structure of thought the formal determinations, of immediate validity, independently of any *Weltanschauung*.[16]

Among the old generation of modernist architects, two figures began to seriously rethink the question of architectural experience away from ideas of form and space and toward notions of history: Ernesto Nathan Rogers (1909–1969) in Italy and Jean Labatut in the United States. Rogers was considered "the hero-figure of European architecture in the late Forties and early Fifties."[17] He was a partner in the renowned BBPR firm, the editor of *Casabella Continuità*, Italy's premier architectural journal, and an active member of CIAM. Labatut, although now completely forgotten, was recognized in his time as one of the most influential teachers in the United States and a radical modern architect in his own right. Rogers and Labatut were key transitional figures and early catalysts of what would later become architectural phenomenology in the United States and Europe.

During the postwar years, the role of history in modern architectural design became a hotly debated topic in the West. But the issue emerged under very different circumstances on each side of the Atlantic. In Europe, architects were concerned with rebuilding cities that had been leveled during the war. In the United States, the European debates served to reignite a more academic debate concerning the enduring value of Beaux-Arts pedagogy (which was still vibrant, but very much under the siege of ex-Bauhaus teachers) as a model for integrating historical references in design. Responding to their very different local contexts, Rogers and Labatut nonetheless advanced related antiformalist critiques of postwar modern architecture, which charged it with having degenerated into a stale and repetitive style based on the obsolete aesthetics of the 1920s. The way to incorporate the lessons of modernism was not to copy its outer forms but to reach empathically into its inner core and salvage its modern experiential content. Rogers's and Labatut's daring intellectual move was to argue that even nonmodern historic buildings could contain a modern experiential content. Against the convention of traditional architectural history that buildings belong to the age when they were built, they made the startling assertion that architecture belonged to the moment when it was experienced. Every building was potentially modern and of the present, so long as it was experienced in a modern way. Architectural phenomenology's turn toward history was from the start an attempt to rethink its basic conventions and to replace them with the notion that a certain kind of experience, at once of the moment and timeless, was what was really at work driving architectural history.

Socially, Rogers was responsible for some of the earliest contacts between architects and phenomenologists. He named Enzo Paci (1911–1976), Italy's foremost phenomenologist, to the editorial board of *Casabella* and was heavily influenced by Paci's notion of the lifeworld. In terms of the intellectual history of architectural phenomenology, Rogers's concept of tradition was arguably his most important contribution. In his editorials between 1953 and 1964, Rogers laid out his definition of tradition as a phenomenological lifeworld, the reality onto which humans are thrown and which they also constitute through their mental acts. The lifeworld referred to that which preexisted each of us and was the compounded result of accumulating interpretations of historical presents. Anything anyone could do and know emerged out of a confrontation with that preexisting lifeworld. For Rogers this meant that the lifeworld could be understood to be the physical environment produced by a culture's activity over time, a built fabric that contained all of that culture's experiences and therefore all of its history. Rogers defined tradition as the material sum total of a culture's preexisting cultural experiences and as a process that was constantly changing according to the new experiences added by human activity. To be a socially responsible architect meant creating new forms out of existing traditions, to add new experiences harmonious with existing ones. For this, architects had to empathically feel the compounded cultural experiences allegedly locked within the built environment onto which they would add: "Tradition is this perpetual flow and to be modern means to feel oneself consciously a part, an active part, of this process. Those who do not feel in this way are not fully responsible 'modern' artists and might simply be defined 'contemporary,' which means that it belongs to our age only in the chronological sense, without having sensed and expressed its deepest content."[18] With the concept of tradition, Rogers introduced one of the major ideas of architectural phenomenology, that is, the belief that history, the kind of history that matters in architecture, was contained within buildings as a cumulative collective experience and could therefore only be accessed experientially. It was a transposition of the old idea that art contains the intentions of the artist into a collective and historical plane. His notion of tradition undermined the modernist emphasis on form. If modernism was to be the permanent revolution it promised to be, then it demanded the constant, physical revision of obsolete formal elements. Modernism, for Rogers, was the experience of the revolution of history in the present, as the continuous transformation of tradition. Modern architecture could achieve its promise of liberation from the past only by internalizing it, by resynthesizing its present forms within an existing tradition. In his view, to adjudicate modernism only to the architecture originating after the 1920s, as Reyner Banham (1922–1988) and other historians had done, was to negate its liberating potential by reducing it into forms.[19]

In "The Phenomenology of European Architecture,"[20] Rogers anticipated much postmodern theory by arguing that the central question for postwar European architecture was how to integrate history. He considered modernism's break with tradition not as its ontological trait but rather as the result of a premature economic success that had encouraged technological development over research into production and life. This tendency threatened the very existence of modernism. In the absence of history, modernism had degenerated into a formalism disconnected from social and cultural needs. Rogers argued that the only socially ethical way forward for modernism was to refound itself in tradition, to return to its historical roots, as a way to participate in the general advancement of culture.

Rogers cultivated exchanges among the circle of young architects and phenomenologists that formed around *Casabella*, including architects Giancarlo de Carlo (1919–2005), Vittorio Gregotti (b. 1927), Guido Canella (b. 1931), Aldo Rossi (1931–1997), Ezio Bonfanti (1938–1973), Gae Aulenti (b. 1927), and Joseph Rykwert (b. 1926), who worked as a junior architect in the BBPR studio during the early 1950s, as well as some of Paci's younger philosophy students like Salvatore Veca (b. 1943). Under Rogers, a small but influential group of young European architects was forged who explored phenomenology as an intellectual framework for rethinking modernism. Each of them absorbed Rogers's notion of tradition and developed in their own way. Most of them, however, especially Gregotti and Rossi, dropped phenomenology in favor of the more clearly Marxist teachings of the Frankfurt School—the notable exception being Rykwert.[21] I have examined the work of Rogers elsewhere[22] but chose to exclude him from this book because he was not very influential in the United States.

Whereas architectural phenomenology in continental Europe petered out after Rogers, it took root and was developed in the United States thanks to the work of Labatut, the focus of the second chapter. Trained in the prestigious Parisian atelier of Victor Laloux (1850–1937), Labatut emigrated to the United States in 1927, where he transformed the stale Beaux-Arts pedagogy of the American academy into a vibrant new antiformalist approach to modern architecture that remained grounded in historical precedents. The key to his success was his ability to formulate a third alternative to the modernist dyad of abstraction and figuration, which he called Eucharistic architecture, referring to buildings where one could experience a timeless spiritual content within building materials. Eucharistic architecture incorporated images drawn from popular culture, such as the figure of George Washington or the image of Christ, into otherwise abstract spatial compositions as a means to attract and focus the attention of visitors on the experience of material textures, lighting conditions, and sound atmospheres. Ultimately, his designs were meant to entice visitors to turn their attention inward, toward their body, where they could empathically experience the spirit of architecture, or, in the words of philosopher Jacques Maritain (1882–1973), Labatut's friend and interpreter, "the movement of immobile things."[23] Well before his students Robert Venturi and Charles Moore embraced American kitsch, Labatut made the case that the historical sources of architecture should be expanded beyond the reduced vocabulary of classicism to include roadside commercial advertising billboards and other emblems of popular culture. The key to that expansion was Labatut's four-step process to *learn* to experience existing things in a modern way, *assimilate* the inner experiential lessons, *forget* the outer form of the object, and *create* the same experience within a different form.[24] To carry out this process, Labatut developed a sophisticated design methodology to distort and break up the unity of inherited forms according to camouflage techniques that he learned while serving in World War I, such as contour and object matching. In this way, nonarchitectural figurative objects as well as historic architectural styles could be given new abstract and modern architectural forms. At the end of World War II, Giedion proclaimed modern architecture in crisis because of its inability to satisfy cultural demands for symbolism. He presented Labatut's work as an exemplary way out of the predicament and toward a new monumentality.[25]

It is well known that the 1960s interest of architectural phenomenologists in popular imagery was framed by the rise of mass consumer culture. But the religious sources of that interest are less well understood. Labatut's work responded to a crisis in the Catholic Church that eventually led up to the overwhelming reforms put in place by the Second Vatican Council in 1965. A major issue of concern was the perceived sense that the architecture of historic churches no longer answered the spiritual needs of the faithful. At the same time, the postwar boom in the construction of modern style churches caused alarm in the Vatican because they tended to eliminate all figurative representations in favor of abstract themes. In 1947, Pope Pius XII called on modern architects not to be deceived by the illusion of a higher mysticism in abstraction and asked them to return figurative imagery to churches—to remember that the body, and the literal representation of the body, was a touchstone of Catholic faith in the unity of flesh and spirit.[26] Labatut worked on the theoretical problems of abstraction and figuration in two key projects, the prototype for a steel and glass Church of the Four Evangelists (1951) and the Stuart Country Day School of the Sacred Heart (Princeton, 1963) built of rugged concrete in the brutalist style. These projects stood as Labatut's most complete elucidations of his theoretical position. He wrote little, sporadically, and only in short, pithy texts, but he nonetheless regarded himself as an architect-scholar on account of his designs. His projects were the stakes and instruments of his intellectual position, in keeping with the ambiguous status of intellectuality in postwar architecture.

Even if he did not care much for phenomenology, Labatut established the design methods and codes for the architectural aesthetization of phenomenology. His working out of the fine line between abstraction and figuration renewed the Beaux-Arts emphasis on design based on historical precedents. But he changed the whole conception of what history was understood to be. The historical models that the designer was to search for in the past were no longer formal or spatial. Rather, the architect was to search for human patterns of experience and to think of them as the historical content of buildings worth retrieving. The central role played by Labatut in the development of architectural phenomenology underscores the difference between architectural phenomenology and the philosophy from which it takes its name. Architectural phenomenology drew on a much wider set of intellectual sources than its name suggests, including Labatut's own interpretations of Henri Bergson's (1859–1941) philosophy of life, Maritain's neo-Thomism, and Alexander Wallace Rimington's (1854–1918) color-music theory.

Charles Moore was one of Labatut's most talented students. A mercurial personality who reveled in the play of irony and deadpan humor, he became the poster child of America's freewheeling postmodernism and an extraordinarily influential teacher. His buildings are famous for their ironic juxtapositions of high and low cultural references, simultaneously celebrating kitsch, consumer culture, and classicism. Moore has unjustly been relegated to the status of a superficial, touchy-feely architect who operated from the hip, without a well-developed theory of architecture. But as I argue in chapter 3, Moore's anti-theoretical position was a highly sophisticated theory about the primacy of personal experience and memory in the intellectual understanding and aesthetic interpretation of architectural history, which became central to the development of architectural phenomenology. Unlike Labatut, Moore was a prolific writer. Two key texts mark his theorization of architectural phenomenology. His PhD dissertation, *Water and Architecture* (1957), was the first analysis of Gaston Bachelard's work within American architectural discourse. In it, Moore developed the notion that all architecture originated in archetypal psychological experiences, which he called poetic images. For him, the postmodern recuperation of historical precedents in contemporary architecture entailed a search for those poetic images. But this search could not be conducted in a detached, intellectual way: it was a matter of experiencing buildings directly. The second key text was *Body, Memory, and Architecture* (1977), coauthored with Kent Bloomer, in which he made the case for shedding the modernist definition of architecture in terms of the abstract concepts of space and form in favor of, as the title indicates, concrete bodily experiences and place-bound memories. Here, the more concretely experiential notion of memory replaced the abstraction that is history. There were key intellectual milestones on the path that led from the first to the last texts, but they were buildings, not books: especially the three houses that Moore designed for himself at Orinda (1962), Sea Ranch (1965), and New Haven (1966). In these houses Moore developed and perfected the aedicule, a small temple or house within a house, as the archetypal poetic image of inhabitation. The aedicule figured as the elemental architectural frame for human orientation. Wherever it was built, it served to ground human memories in that particular place. Indeed, Moore built one every time he changed residence. The theorization of architecture as a set of archetypal mnemonic experiences became a leitmotif of postmodernism. The intellectual status of the building itself hangs in the balance of Moore's work. He refused to cede intellectuality over to pure mental acts, considering it essential to situate it in the more ambiguous realm of the experiencing body.

Moore's most influential years as a teacher were spent at Yale, first as chair of the Department of Architecture (1965–67), followed by a term as dean

(1969–70) and as professor (1970–75). At the time, Yale was, along with Northwestern University, the most important center for the study of phenomenology in America, a social circle centered around the figure of John Wild (1902–1972), the most prominent American phenomenologist of the postwar years. The Society for Phenomenology and Existential Philosophy (founded in 1962) was highly visible at Yale.[27] Under Moore, the architecture school welcomed other Yale phenomenologists like Karsten Harries (b. 1937), who devoted much of his later career to teaching philosophy to architects. The 1960s political student activism was felt particularly strongly at Yale. Phenomenology presented the possibility of a social commitment without all the Marxist rhetoric. Wild increased the distance between phenomenology and Marxism by arguing that "the connection between existentialist thought and any definitive political philosophy, as it is now presented to us, is wholly arbitrary and unstable."[28] Clearly responding to the pressures of McCarthyism, Wild presented phenomenology as "ideological armament" against the infiltration of Marxist thought into the United States, and therefore as the philosophical counterpart to the cold war arms race.[29] The search for experience made architectural phenomenologists at Yale appear above the fray of politics and business, engaged in a disinterested pursuit of the essence of architecture. Socially, this helped them claim the higher ground of impartiality vis-à-vis corporate modernist architects, and to gather toward themselves all the power generated by the postwar struggle to humanize modern architecture.

The political ambiguity of phenomenology's career, covering the full spectrum between European Marxism and American McCarthyism, came in part from its central claim to be a search for an unbiased description of human experience, an account free from prejudice and therefore free from politics. Put differently, phenomenology claimed the ground of a prepolitical discourse. In American architecture schools, this ground had already been staked out by the experientialist discourse of art psychology through the writings of art historians like Rudolph Arnheim (1904–2007).[30]

Chapter 4 examines the contribution of Christian Norberg-Schulz, Giedion's brightest and certainly most famous student. Although Norberg-Schulz was based in Oslo, his books were nonetheless incredibly popular in the 1970s in the United States and indeed in much of the world. His obsession with rootedness and authenticity contrasts with his cosmopolitan life and upbringing as an architecture student first at the ETH in Zürich, then at Harvard where he was steeped in Arnheim's gestalt theory of perception. His first books, *Intentions in Architecture* (1965) and *Existence, Space and Architecture* (1971), were heavily influenced by Arnheim. The derivation can be seen as much in the texts as in the images, which Norberg-Schulz set against each other in precise ways in order to describe and illustrate various archetypal experiences of architecture. Arnheim asserted that all thinking involved visual perception (in the form of a mental image) and, conversely, that visual perception was commensurate with intellectual work.[31] Diagrams, according to Arnheim, were the link between the visual and the textual, and he therefore spent much of his time trying to figure out the diagrammatic structure of paintings. His theories served to add legitimacy to the central tenet of architectural phenomenology that practice and theory are inseparable and ambiguously related.

Norberg-Schulz became best known for *Genius Loci: Towards a Phenomenology of Architecture* (1979), in which he defined architecture as the expression of the spirit of the place in which it is built. The book instantly made Norberg-Schulz the main interpreter of Heidegger for architectural audiences. Like other architectural phenomenologists before him, Norberg-Schulz's thesis was that architecture was the expression of human experiences. He differed in that he situated the origin of those experiences in nature. According to his theory, the original structure of human experience was given in the landscape. He equated those original experiences with the genius loci, so that in order to express the history of the place in contemporary designs one should not look at historic buildings but should instead go back to the original source in the topography. Following Arnheim, but also influenced by the work of Kevin Lynch (1918–1984), Norberg-Schulz advanced the notion that visual diagramming was the key to the exegesis of the intellectual content of the landscape. But the experiential visual diagram had to emerge from a direct experience of the landscape (not maps). The sheer scale of the landscape made this difficult, so in a sleight of hand Norberg-Schulz turned to aerial photography as a stand-in for direct experience. The photograph thus acquired a status of truth content that could function only so long as the picture was never acknowledged as such. Norberg-Schulz enticed readers to see through the photographs into the visual patterns they contained, referring to them first as "topological figures," then "genius loci," and finally "aletheic images." The last term made reference to Heidegger's notion of aletheia or self-disclosed truth. But this was an instrumental misreading of Heidegger, who after all mounted one of the most powerful critiques of representation as the dominant intellectual paradigm of modernity.[32]

Quite apart from the clearly essentializing tendencies of his photo(historio)graphy, Norberg-Schulz blazed new trails into architectural historiography, bringing with him the visual habits and ambiguous intellectuality of the architect. His books represented a new theoretical way of doing architectural history that shifted the status of photographs from illustrations to narrative interpretations and demoted the text to mere accompaniment. Although he remained committed to the primacy of practice and considered himself an architect, the fact is that his intellectual work was entirely contained within the format of the printed book. Quite against his own intentions, Norberg-Schulz made great strides in carving out a position for architectural theory as something detached from practice.

As architectural phenomenologists slowly codified the ambiguous realm of architectural intellectuality into graphic design principles and ideas, they also began to expose some of its contradictions. Chapter 5 considers the career of Kenneth Frampton in light of his attempts to resolve some of these tensions. Born with a privileged mind into the English working class, Frampton was educated at the Architectural Association and soon found himself drawn into the world of architectural criticism, graphic design, and publishing. He was technical editor of *Architectural Design* from 1962 to 1965, and after his arrival at Princeton University in 1964 he became a well-known figure in New York architectural circles. He continued his career in publishing as cofounder and editor of *Oppositions* in 1973, with Peter Eisenman (b. 1932) and Mario Gandelsonas (b. 1938). Frampton achieved international recognition in the early 1980s for his theory of critical regionalism, which was mostly received as an architectural aesthetic that celebrated the synthesis of industrial building with local craft. But in reality critical regionalism was also intended to be a new theory for understanding (or rather producing) the history of architecture that led up to it. Critical regionalism proclaimed that modern architecture had ended multiple times, in a series of unresolved crises caused by the inability to give proper architectural expression to key advances in industrial building technology. Modern architecture had, in that sense, ceased to exist (or failed to be born), and all that was left was building. Critical regionalism was meant as a call to redress the asymmetry between building and architecture by rethinking what architecture was. He actually had done this rethinking, before he landed on the term critical regionalism, in a series of seminal essays written roughly during the 1970s, including "Labour, Work and Architecture" (1969), "Industrialization and the Crisis of Architecture" (1973), "On Reading Heidegger" (1974), "Constructivism: The Pursuit of an Elusive Sensibility" (1976), and "The Status of Man and the Status of His Objects: A Reading of The Human Condition" (1978). In these essays he borrowed heavily from Hannah Arendt's (1906–1975) phenomenological analysis of the public sphere to argue that architecture was the elevation of building to an aesthetic, which people could experience as the res publica. The existence of architecture, he thought, was ethically necessary as a common experiential foundation for the individual development of fully human lives, that is, lives capable of experiencing a shared social reality. The trouble was that in the age of industrialization it had become impossible to elevate building above the mere labor of construction. Following Arendt's analysis of surplus labor in a capitalist society, Frampton wondered how one could make the labor of building yield an aesthetic surplus. His answer came toward the end of his career with the theory of tectonics, which basically focused attention on construction joints as the sites where the first signs of aesthetic surplus qua architecture could be detected.

With tectonics, Frampton in a sense came full circle to the beginnings of his career, when, working on graphic designs for *Architectural Design*, he had first explored the question of how *not* to represent a building but to graphically produce an experience that was in excess of the building itself, yet tantamount to it. Frampton's notion of surplus experience, as variously revised into critical regionalism and tectonics, was perhaps the last serious attempt to work out postmodernism's themes of history and theory aesthetically. Ultimately, criticial regionalism was a theory of the crisis of aesthetics as model for intellectuality and, as such, it represented the last vital gasp of architectural phenomenology.

To unpack postmodernism's central notions of history and theory requires understanding its intellectual history. Rogers, Labatut, Moore, Norberg-Schulz, Frampton, Rykwert, Vesely, and others looked to philosophy in general and phenomenology in particular for a coherent intellectual framework to recast historic architectural forms into an experiential content. Architectural phenomenology coalesced into a coherent discourse through the intertwining of the search for authentic experience and the search to reconcile modernism with its own history. It was not a wholesale rejection of modernism. Rather, it was ambivalent. Its denunciations of modernism often coexisted with enthusiastic pleas for architecture to be built according to true modernist principles.

Architectural phenomenologists defended the uniqueness of the architect's individual experience, yet they also resisted the idea that experience was purely individualistic. Believing that architects should retain commitments outside the self, architectural phenomenologists pined for a community of shared values and beliefs in which to ground self-expression. They were part of a wide 1960s interest in the intersection of "community" and architecture, ranging from the cries of neighborhood preservation organizations against urban renewal to psychosexual utopias of communal life like Drop City. Frampton's British New Left politics led him to interpret the capitalist opposition to organized labor as an erosion of community. Inspired by the arts and crafts ideology (and socialism) of William Lethaby and William Morris, he envisioned a return to medieval guild societies, with modern architects as master masons at the center. Norberg-Schulz's Catholicism led him to identify modernism's hypostatization of objectivity with the secularization of society, a process he thought led to the collapse of social order and to visual chaos. He called for modernism to return to the "spiritual roots" that he thought were the source of all meaningful and visually ordered architecture. For Moore, who had to publicly repress his homosexuality in order to survive the conservatism of the cold war, the severe minimalist aesthetics of modernism meant the denial of corporeal pleasure and interpersonal contact. To rebuild community, he believed modern architecture had to become erotic, transgressing aesthetic codes to stimulate visitors with intimate sensual experiences. Each of these three architects felt that the dominant forms of postwar modernism excluded the defining experiences of their social community and, by extension, of their generation.

In their search to differentiate themselves from the modernist tradition they were educated into, they faced a new set of problems: the question was less how to create something new, and more how to avoid repeating something old. To renew modernism they felt they had to turn away from modernism's aesthetic conventions. This trait differentiated architectural phenomenologists from many of their contemporaries, most notably the New York Five, who revived the "original" modern style and forms of the historical European avant-gardes. Architectural phenomenologists sought to establish their connection to the origins of modernism not by adhering to its historical style but rather by attempting to experience the world in the same way as the modern masters—that is, originally, authentically, and ahistorically.

Paradoxically, their awareness of modernism's history led them to search for an ahistorical constant underpinning all modern architectural expression. Working independently of one another, they all arrived at the conclusion that sensory experience was this timeless constant—a supposition that surprisingly ran counter to phenomenology's insistence on the historicality of experience. For them, all architecture ever built was organized according to an elemental language of basic bodily experiences. To reconnect modern architecture to the rest of architectural history meant understanding the deeper prelinguistic experiential language that, they believed, was the organizational principle of every building ever built. On the surface, their individual quests to understand architecture in terms of experiential content seem as varied as the aspects of architecture that they each focused on: Labatut was obsessed with how the visual perception of scale and the tactile sensing of texture changed in relation to one's movement; Moore was absorbed by how small interior spaces could feel enormous; Norberg-Schulz was fixated on expressing the relationship of the building to its site in terms of visual patterns; and Frampton was preoccupied with how small tectonic details could visually express the structural logic of an entire building culture. Despite the differences in the aspects of architecture they focused on in their writings, the intellectual operations they performed in those texts shared important commonalities. Architectural phenomenology, the discourse that wove together sensory experience and architectural history, achieved coherence by interlacing three thematic strands.

The first theme, *experience*, entailed the conviction that the senses were not historically determined. That buildings are designed with the human body in mind allowed architects to posit elemental sensory experiences as the transhistorical origin of all architecture. Severed from historic specificity and essentialized, bodily experience became the point of entry for spiritualist and religious interpretations of architecture, which began to turn against modernism's secular objectivity.

The second theme, *history*, involved the modernist belief that historical buildings were expressions of a deeper structuring reality, which was thought to remain constant across time. Architects rejected historicist claims, including that architectural expression is solely determined by its historical context. Instead they explored new forms of historiography meant to identify and understand precisely those aspects of architecture that might not be historically determined.

The third theme, *theory*, emerged as an early instance of interdisciplinarity. To support the thesis that experience was the "essence" of architecture, architects searched for evidence in other disciplines, most notably in phenomenological philosophy. In these early examples of "scholarly" work, before architecture PhD programs were established and the rise of theory in the late 1970s, intellectuality appeared as an ambiguous but unique realm at the intersection of the professional architect's and the historian's practice. The experimental nature of this intellectual realm transformed the tradition of architectural historiography, resulting in important new theories and modes of writing architectural history that incorporated the visual and experiential sensitivity of architectural design.

Woven together, these three strands defined architectural phenomenology and its legacy. The number of architects who participated in shaping architectural phenomenology is clearly greater than four. My intention is not to assign to Labatut, Moore, Norberg-Schulz, and Frampton the status of "founders" of architectural phenomenology. Quite the contrary, I treat their works as formed through their relationships to a wide social web. I use their names as one would invoke the name of a composer to denote a certain genre of music. Each individual is an access point to a broad assemblage of mentors, collaborators, commentators, enemies, and students, who also participated in the broader restructuring of modernism. These individuals were in contact with each other but resisted seeing themselves as a group. Socially, architectural phenomenology was not a self-identified homogeneous block but rather a discontinuous social assemblage. Yet this social disjointedness did not prevent it from achieving coherence as a shared intellectual framework that initiated the intellectual transformation we have come to know as postmodernism.

A Polygraph of Architectural Phenomenology

The nature of architectural phenomenology makes it challenging to historicize. That it presented itself as a new way of doing architectural history requires that one contend with its historiographical conventions without succumbing to them. Yet *after* architectural phenomenology, it is not possible to simply approach it through the traditional historiographical frameworks it undermined and reconfigured. Its very nature and legacy defy that operation. It disappears under the lenses of architectural histories based on personal biography, self-identified groups, individual schools, institutions, geopolitical borders, or architectural styles.

To uncover how architectural phenomenology gained coherence requires a new critical historiography capable of moving between aesthetic interpretations and intellectual and social history. What normally passes as the intellectual history of architecture is seldom more than snapshots that capture an architect's definition of architecture at a particular point in time, which are then presented as "theories" of architecture and collected in edited volumes. Thus, intellectual history appears as an autonomous and transcendent system with a magical capacity to transform itself. Each new "theory" appears to have descended from another pure world of ideas (e.g., the world of philosophy) and caused an epistemological break with how architecture was conceived in the past. But so-called epistemological shifts are the product of changes in the relationships between individual agents, each of whom is motivated by the expectation of being rewarded for effecting change. Individual agency both forms and is formed by the discipline in which it operates. By exposing the different motivations and capacities that led each protagonist to weave together the thematic strands of experience, history, and theory that made up architectural phenomenology, the chapters that follow draw forth the connected web of social, aesthetic, and intellectual dimensions that gave coherence to this discourse, without losing sight of the particular contributions of each person.

My historiographic method, which I describe as polygraphic, differs fundamentally from monographic historiography. The latter has dealt with the question of contemporary architecture in one of two ways: by focusing on individuals or on self-identified groups. When writing the history of architecture, we must be careful not to unwittingly fall into the monographic trap toward which we are gently predisposed by the records, already prepared and packaged monographically for us, by symposium organizers and self-selected groups of architects. That some architects, at one point in time, thought it advantageous to portray themselves as a group, does not necessarily mean that we must take them at their word, or that the monograph is the best way of capturing a chapter in the history of architectural ideas. Selection and self-selection are related social phenomena, but they are not the same thing, and it is important not to unwittingly conflate the two.

The conflation I am arguing against is the kind perpetrated by historians who choose to limit their writing to self-selected groups of architects (e.g., CIAM, GATEPAC, Team X, Archigram). In such cases, the historiographical operation of selection follows the contours of the architects' self-selection. There are some benefits to a historiography that shadows self-selection. One advantage for the historian is the appearance that an objective, self-evident selection has been made. When applied to intellectual history, the historian describes an idea that was explicitly embraced by a group of architects, which shows that idea to have common currency. In the latter half of the twentieth century, countless architectural groups formed to uphold specific ideas. But a library full of books dedicated to each of these groups in isolation would not begin to approximate the transformation of architectural intellectuality that took place during that period.

The historiographical conflation of selection and self-selection clearly has its benefits, but it also has its downsides, especially in regard to intellectual history. A major drawback is that it must remain silent before ideas shared among nonaffiliated individuals and cannot explain what gives intellectual coherence to the larger field of architecture. The monographic selection of self-selected groups skews the portrayal of the intellectual field in favor of the exceptional and the intentional. It also wrongly identifies the particular views of small groups with the entire field. Ideas that might have been commonly shared and debated among architects, yet for one reason or another were not explicitly espoused or renounced by a self-selected group, get relegated to a second plane. Thus, what is central to the field as a whole is rendered as peripheral and is loosely portrayed as context.

Monographic historiography is so deeply engrained in architectural history that it exerts its force in ways that are often hard to see because they have become so conventional that they appear natural. When historians of postwar architecture working within the monographic tradition moved beyond the study of isolated groups, they searched for common causes and assumed common effects. That is the case in recent attempts to describe postwar architectural discourse in terms of institutions, changes in government policies, or the advent of new media technologies such as television. While these analytical frameworks are indeed important, focusing on them in isolation unwittingly perpetuates the sort of positivist historiography initiated in 1864 by Hippolyte Taine (1828–1893), who introduced the ideas of Auguste Comte (1798–1857) to the architectural history curriculum of the École des Beaux-Arts in Paris. Taine attempted to make history of architecture courses more scientific by adopting the positivist methods of sociology. Although Taine did not rule out artistic genius, he thought individual talent played only a minor role in the production of buildings. The architect's expressive range was limited by larger causes such as race, environment, and time. Each of these categories was broken down into smaller classifications. The influence of family, national customs, religion, prevailing intellectual conditions, building traditions, the region's mean temperature, its percentage of sunshine, position above or below sea-level, precise latitude and longitude, all were necessary knowledge for the historian, whose task, Taine explained, was to demonstrate how these infinite causes determined the combined effect: the building.[1] Taine's historiography was appealing because it seems to account for the relationship of the individual architect to the collective.

The positivist emphasis on history as a scientific recounting of the circumstances affecting the architect downplayed, or even repressed, the agency of the architect, the subjective element involved in interpreting those facts. By the early twentieth century, phenomenologists had called into question the strict separation between subject and object presupposed by French positivism. José Ortega y Gasset (1883–1955), a Spanish student of Heidegger, advanced such a critique in 1932 with his famous university lectures on Galileo Galilei (1564–1642). He argued that facts acquire meaning only in relation to life projects. "Reality is not a fact, something given, gifted—rather it is a construction that man makes with the given material."[2] Put simply, our circumstances become our reality only through our interpretations.

The phenomenological critique of positivism is well known by now. But surprisingly, it was not fully assimilated within architectural historiography. For instance, architectural historians continue to impose order on the history of architecture by culling lists of historic buildings simply on the basis of their date of construction. They might, for instance, group together buildings built during the Victorian decades or the postwar decades. At first glance such historiographical groupings appear logical, since buildings can be said to be contemporary when they occur together in time. But on closer scrutiny, the groupings cease to make sense.

Generations

Identifying what is historical on the basis of chronology gives the appearance of historical unity but actually skirts the question of what is the nature of the historical period. To understand historical periods we cannot follow an absolutely regular chronological stream (i.e., year by year, or decade by decade). We must take into account the individual, and indeed the social, experiences of time. Historical time is qualified by ruptures and discontinuities that are chronologically irregular. One cannot decide a priori when postmodern architecture began and ended. The limits must be established from the point of view of those within postmodern architecture. By definition, that will never be one individual, so the historian cannot become the sole spokesperson for the collective.

In order to contextualize individual points of view within a collective framework, historians have modulated their chronological boundaries to coincide with political or cultural events. For example, the history of postwar architecture has been variously organized to fit within the years from the end of World War II to the student revolts of 1968 or to the 1972 oil crisis. Such periodizations allow historians to group together unaffiliated architects on the basis that they were all equal participants in the same society. In order to make such groupings, they must also make fundamental assumptions about how individuals relate to society. For instance, they must assume that all architects experience social events uniquely, with each person's experience being completely different from the next. Ortega y Gasset maintained that this assumption was not entirely true.[3] Although he respected the idea that every individual experiences reality uniquely (i.e., everyone is in his or her personal world), he also noted that not every experience of reality was possible at any time. After Galileo's interpretation of Copernican astrology, the medieval interpretation of the world as the center of the universe was anachronistic. Individual interpretations were circumscribed to worldviews that were historically determined. Since only a certain number of people were alive at any one time, interpretations were also generational.

Ortega y Gasset referred to these generational worldviews as "interindividual" phenomena, which he situated as interpretive hinges between individuals and the larger society in which multiple generations struggled for control.[4] As opposed to sociologists like Georg Simmel (1858–1918) and Max Weber (1864–1920), who described society as the combined effect of interpersonal exchanges, Ortega y Gasset viewed society as preexisting the personal interactions of any single generation. For him, society was there, manifested through customs (or uses)—what is said, believed, and done by people, by anyone, by no one individual specifically. Society was a structure of possible positions and attitudes that were ontologically impersonal, but which people could assume or take up. Individuals were born into societies that imposed a system of customs on them, and each person could freely accept or reject them. But their choices had consequences, since social efficiency required that dissent be repressed and punished.

Ortega y Gasset argued that people's choices in relation to the customs they encountered were inflected by their generational worldview. The same action would have a different historical value and meaning depending on one's generation. That is to say, a person's generation provided the first order of historical structure in his or her interpretation of customs. This elucidation had important implications for historiography: a historian writing about an event would have to take into account the multiplicity of generational perspectives from which that event acquired historical meaning. To account for changes in social customs, or for the transition from one historical era to the next, Ortega y Gasset thought that historians needed to look closer at the struggles between generations. Without a grounding in this generational struggle, macrohistorical changes would appear to happen magically, as if propelled by an impersonal will or spirit.

> In "today," in every "today" coexist, therefore, various articulated generations and the relations that are established between them, according to the condition of their ages, represent a dynamic system, of attractions and repulsions, of coincidence and polemic, which constitute in every instant the reality of historic life. And the idea of generations, converted into a method for historical investigation, consists only in projecting that structure upon the past.[5]

Following Ortega y Gasset's argument, in order to grasp architectural phenomenology, we would have to begin by asking: under what conditions, by whom, and for whom was architecture interpreted as an experience? The selection of the protagonists of this book begins to answer this question, by narrowing the field of study to Moore, Norberg-Schulz and Frampton, members of the same postwar generation whose work was defined by their contacts with architectural discourse in the United States. Labatut stands out as a member of the previous generation, providing access to the background of discourses out of which architectural phenomenology was formed, and which it transformed.

Currency

To begin to account for how generational perspectives inflected the meaning and structure of architectural phenomenology, we must first reconsider the term "contemporary." Rather than a stable period of time (i.e., today, the present), it is an unstable category whose contents are constantly changing in relation to the tensions and power relations between different generations of architects. For a building to appear contemporary to an architect it must respond to what is current and relevant to his or her generation. What is current is what every architect must take as a given: the customs inherited as impositions from previous generations that every architect must count on in order to operate, whether he or she accepts them or rejects them. What is current can be defined as the set of buildings, ideas, practices, social positions (e.g., the master architect, the young architect, the star architect, the critic, the curator, the enthusiast), and institutions that together form the cultural order of the discipline of architecture. What is current is important because it is the system of significance within which architectural works acquire meaning as contemporary.

What constitutes the reality of architecture is nothing more than a palimpsest of interpretations handed down to us, with which we must contend. What we deem to be architectural phenomenology is there as a function of what happened before. The sources of the beliefs, opinions, and forms of practice are found in the past. At the same time, these sources are seldom recognized as sources at all, but rather experienced as norms, pressures, and possibilities that condition current practice and restrict its future.

The generational struggle over the definition of architectural history is waged through interpretations, which are the tools and stakes of the battle. I use the term "interpretation" here in contradistinction to "theory," which in my view is too restrictive to capture the wide range of practices that fell within the realm of intellectuality in architecture since World War II. An interpretation is what makes architecture appear as cultural work. Interpretation can take the form of a written document, a drawing, a picture or a photo essay, a movie, a scaled model, a full-scale building, an exhibition, a class syllabus, a teaching curriculum, and countless other forms. The notion of interpretation attends to the multiple media of architectural intellectuality without giving any one primacy. One could say that there is no mother tongue to architectural communication. Rather, interpretations function as seizures of power, as ways to gain cultural capital and to take up a position within politically charged disciplinary multiplicities.

Positions

For instance, a successful interpretation, like *Intentions in Architecture*, allowed a young architect like Norberg-Schulz to seize the position of architectural historian. Interpretations are both instruments through which architects achieve their positions and also the measure of their investment in those positions. An architect's interpretation, say *Intentions in Architecture*, always intends a particular position, in this case that of architectural historian. To take that position, Norberg-Schulz's book had to display the forms and conventions expected of that position, such as a central thesis, a logical exposition of ideas, footnotes, good-quality photographs, and the imprint of a reputable publisher. The value of that book, as a measure of Norberg-Schulz's investment in the position of architectural historian, depended on its publication and reception. Hence the importance of people involved in interpreting interpretations, for they remade the book a thousand times and gave it cultural value in the process.

To speak of the multiple agents involved in producing cultural works does not take anything away from the work of Norberg-Schulz, it simply puts it in context. In fact, many architectural phenomenologists openly embraced the idea that the production of architecture was a collaboration. Frampton, for instance, particularly valued the work of photographers in shaping the aesthetics of his interpretations.

All this points to the need for a new historiography capable of grasping the instability and mutability of architectural intellectuality, but that does not seek the cause of its changes only in the macrocollective or in the micro-individual. Some historians have taken this step.[6] They have moved beyond the monograph and have begun to experiment with a polygraphic historiography, simultaneously describing the work of multiple architects from contemporaneous generations and mapping their operations through institutional networks.

Polygraphic historiography does not limit itself to architects who formed groups. Rather it studies the struggle between generations, unveiling the systems of significance that framed their respective historical understandings of architecture, and highlighting the resonance and similitude among different architects' responses to the same circumstances. Polygraphic historiography relates the social to the biographical but also provides a better account of the many layers that mediate between these two poles.

One of those layers is the field of architecture itself, the primary interest of architects and architectural historians alike. The field of architecture is not reducible to any one person nor extendable to the whole of society. Polygraphic historiography draws critically on Michel Foucault's (1926–1984) conceptualization of disciplines as an elusive middle layer between the individual and the collective. It also incorporates Theodor Adorno's (1903–1969) analysis of how cultural works function as mediators between social ideology and personal life. It engages and develops both of these intellectual precedents along the lines set forth by Pierre Bourdieu's (1930–2002) notion of the fields of cultural production.[7] He conceived fields as disciplinary microcosms within society, with their own structures, laws, and membership.[8] He defined them as social and intellectual spaces articulated into limited numbers of positions (the orthodox master architect, the heretical young challenger) through the unequal distribution of cultural capital. To take up a particular position, say, the position of architectural historian, one had to have amassed a certain amount of cultural capital by earning the recognition of other historians, architects, critics, students, and the like. Bourdieu likened fields to games, governed by rules that limited the number of positions and possible moves. To be in a field one had to believe it was a game worth playing. For Bourdieu this belief, which he called *illusio,* was what kept fields operating, people playing, and cultural capital flowing.

According to Bourdieu, people were predisposed toward particular fields and illusios through habits acquired in the course of life. The *habitus,* to use Bourdieu's term, was an important mediating layer between the individual and the collective. It functioned as a structuring structure, a lifelong disposition or second nature where society and the individual intersected dynamically.[9] Habitus was therefore doubly historical, combining the evolving histories of the individual and the group. It set limits to one's expectations and explained how behavior could be regular without being the direct product of obedience to regulations. Bourdieu's concept of habitus came close to Ortega y Gasset's notion of generation, although Bourdieu did not study him. Indeed, both the habitus and the generation described an interindividual phenomenon (neither personal nor collective), which both authors defined as the effect and structure of the social and historical struggle between individuals. Yet both concepts had different emphases. Habitus stressed the importance of fields of cultural production, something Ortega y Gasset did not consider in depth. The idea of generation weighed the biological and existential limits of life, something Bourdieu did not sufficiently address in accounting for changes in the cultural order of fields.

The combination of both ideas into what could be called a generational habitus provides the access point into the reality that a polygraphic historiography seeks to uncover: the field of architecture. Polygraphic historiography remains an experiment, the soundness of which can only be gauged by the results. For the moment, it allows the rediscovery of architectural phenomenology as the effect of a collective struggle among a number of contemporary architects to impose their generational habitus.

Through close reading of each individual's writings and architectural designs, a larger constellation of related buildings, texts, and disciplines appears as the context within which they acquired meaning. For instance, Labatut's tactile and inviting treatment of concrete in his Stuart Country Day School of the Sacred Heart (Princeton, New Jersey, 1963) was understood to mean a reaction against the monumental visual patterning of concrete in brutalist works such as Paul Rudolph's Yale Art and Architecture School (New Haven, Connecticut, 1958–64). As a function of his exchanges with philosopher Jacques Maritain, Labatut's tactile concrete was also interpreted in religious terms as providing a spiritual experience of connection to Christ, who stood as a cipher of the ahistorical constant of architecture that architectural phenomenologists were after.

Interdisciplinarity

The formation of architectural phenomenology involved architecture and philosophy coming into relations of mutual exchange and resonance, while maintaining disciplinary autonomy. Interdisciplinarity appears driven by the agency of individuals who were motivated by the structure of challenges and rewards internal to each of their fields. The architect wrote for architecture and the philosopher for philosophy, even when they addressed each other. To explain the simultaneous but autonomous coexistence of these works one cannot rely exclusively on notions of philosophy's influence, or ideas of cause and effect.

Architectural phenomenology was relatively autonomous from philosophy. It operated inside the discipline of architecture, with objectives and aspirations that drew on the long traditions of modernism.

I treat Labatut, Moore, Norberg-Schulz, and Frampton as protagonists of architectural phenomenology in recognition that they played a leading role in an intellectual history that was also shaped by many other actors. The word *protagonist* derives from the ancient Greek words πρωτο (proto), meaning first, and αγωνιστης (agonist), which referred to a combatant in the games, a contender for prizes. The intellectual history of architecture during the so-called postmodern period was a struggle among many agents of one generation competing to be recognized as protagonists, as victors in the struggle over their previous generation. In intellectual terms, to dominate the struggle was to be recognized as being more influential than the rest, as having the authority to define architecture.

In the context of the emerging interest among 1950s architects in architectural history, Labatut, Moore, Norberg-Schulz, and Frampton established their difference by taking up a new position, that of the architect-historian, which enabled them to appropriate all the marks of intellectual distinction associated with the textual instruments and institutions of architectural history.[10] Unlike previous generations of architects-turned-historians, these architect-historians did not renounce their identity as architects in order to appropriate architectural history. Rather, they openly sought to reclaim architectural history for architectural practice, believing that their competence in the intellectual rules of architectural design enabled them to produce better architectural history than art historians. The stubbornness with which these architects insisted that they were "still" architects, regardless of the fact that they were no longer designing or building buildings, slowly began to change the entire cultural order of architecture.

Changes in architecture's cultural order were first felt in the academy. Above all, architectural phenomenology was an escalation in the intellectualization of architecture. Before the establishment of PhD programs in architecture schools, scholarly intellectual work was taught in architectural history courses by art historians, who resisted the encroachment of architects. The confrontation with art history—which played itself out in the corridors of academe—forced an escalation of the scholarly standards of architecture. Labatut led the charge at Princeton University, where in 1949 he founded the first PhD in Architecture program for what he called "architect-scholars," explicitly excluding art historians.

Moore was one of the program's first graduates. The invocation of phenomenology helped architects leverage the academic credibility of philosophy against art historians. It was a response to the hostility of art historians in the form of a new type of discourse by architects and for architects that privileged the authority of architects to speak about architectural history. They resisted the mediation of art history to understand what they felt was their own tradition. They even saw their experientialism as an alternative method for comprehending historic buildings, claiming that architects were best suited to properly understand historic buildings because they inherently understood the expressive intentions of the design. Phenomenology was the touchstone of this discourse: it made it possible to argue that architecture was based on a timeless sensual "language" of immediate experiences that architects could intuit across the spans of time.

The success of architect-historians like Norberg-Schulz and Frampton to take over academic posts traditionally occupied by art historians speaks to the power of architectural phenomenology. They reinvented the job description of architectural historian according to their architectural dispositions. As a result, historiography became more architectural—displacing the traditional centrality of the written word in historiography. In their architectural history books, the clarity of the visual argument, conveyed through page layouts, illustrations, and photographs, became as important as the textual claims.

With its emphasis on the direct experience of buildings, architectural phenomenology protected the long-standing modernist belief that the intellectual content of architecture was not expressible in words alone. That is to say, the intellectual content of architecture had to be translatable, for lack of a better word, into an aesthetic form, and vice versa. But how could the writing and understanding of architectural history, which was understood to be a purely intellectual endeavor, be translated into an aesthetic? Architectural phenomenology was a search to find the key to that translation. Labatut, Moore, Norberg-Schulz, and Frampton thought they found that key in sensual experience, which they cast as the ordering logic behind both the intellectual and aesthetic realms. In their hands, architectural history was recast into the experiential content of architecture. The richness of architectural history became an experience to be introduced as the new content of postwar modern architecture, which appeared to them as experientially dull and empty.

Once established in powerful positions of authority within prestigious universities, architect-historians began to challenge the cultural authority traditionally associated with the professional architect. The established disciplinary lines separating producers (architects) and consumers (historians) of architecture became contested, leading to oppositions and antagonisms over the nature of architectural intellectuality that were not immediately resolved. Architect-historians became influential spokespersons for the intellectualization of architecture and custodians of a new architectural cultural order. They not only helped to establish the official understanding of what constitutes intellectual work in architecture, but also played a subtler historical role: as some of the most educated and cosmopolitan products of the modern movement, they were the point men of the momentous intellectual changes that took place in the 1970s. They were among the first to experience and articulate the intellectual dilemmas and aesthetic problems that came to define the period of postmodernism.

Labatut, Moore, Norberg-Schulz, and Frampton exalted direct experience as the historic content of buildings. Their search to recover the fullness and historicity of architectural experience led them to phenomenological philosophy, including the ideas of Gaston Bachelard, Maurice Merleau-Ponty, Martin Heidegger, Paul Ricoeur, and Hannah Arendt, among others, which they translated for architectural audiences. The degree to which their understanding of phenomenology was philosophically correct is not my focus. Rather, I am interested in their recognition of a certain homology between the architectural discourses on experience and history and the treatment of those two concepts within phenomenology. This homology enabled them to superimpose phenomenological notions of experience and history onto an existing architectural discourse in a way that made the philosophy seem like a natural extension, or even a clarification, of long-established architectural ideas. While a presentation of phenomenology is beyond the scope of this study, it is nevertheless important to remark on how the understanding of experience and history evolved within it. The discussion must be limited to those major features judged to be relevant from the standpoint of the development of architectural phenomenology. We must bear in mind that in its more than a century of existence, the phenomenological movement has taken root around the world and developed into numerous branches, including Husserl's transcendental phenomenology, Heidegger's hermeneutic ontology, Sartre's existentialism, Merleau-Ponty's phenomenology of embodiment, Arendt's phenomenology of the public sphere, Ricoeur's eschatological phenomenology, Levinas's phenomenology of alterity, and countless other equally important offshoots. Not all of these branches have been equally relevant to architectural phenomenology. Sartre and Levinas, for instance, did not attract as much interest as Heidegger and Arendt. The reasons for the uneven architectural investment in these branches have as much to do with the details of personal life, such as Vesely recommending that Frampton read Ricoeur, as with the fact that questions about the nature of human experience and history seemed central to the postwar reconstruction efforts, and later to the rise of mass consumer culture, drawing architects unevenly toward those philosophers who had most clearly elucidated those questions. Alas, the fine distinctions drawn by historians of phenomenology between its branches were not heeded within architectural phenomenology. For instance, Gaston Bachelard was a major reference in architectural phenomenology despite the fact that Herbert Spiegelberger excluded him from his definitive historical study, *The Phenomenological Movement,* on the basis that his philosophy of action opposed Husserl's pure phenomenology and its attendant notions of philosophical contemplation.[11] Whether Hannah Arendt's philosophical method can be considered phenomenological is the subject of ongoing debate. While Spiegelberger did not even mention her, Dermot Moran's more recent *Introduction to Phenomenology* has reclaimed a central place for her within the movement.[12]

Architects were less concerned with the internal struggles for legitimacy within the phenomenological movement. As early as 1964, Frampton had adopted Arendt's phenomenology of the public sphere as a touchstone of his own understanding of architectural experience and its historicity. That said, Frampton's rethinking of architectural history in terms of experience was very different from Arendt's pursuits. It would be unfair, and indeed misguided, to judge Frampton's architectural work by the standards of philosophy. To give primacy to philosophy would be to deny the unique disciplinary stakes with which architects had to contend and to miss the rich, changing history of the architectural understanding of intellectuality. Whereas in philosophy intellectuality was traditionally equated with mental acts, in architecture intellectuality was a far more ambiguous realm involving the mind certainly, but also various bodily practices such as drawing, photographing, model-making, graphic design, and building construction. The advent of phenomenology, with its critique of subject-object dualisms and its radical conceptions of embodied knowledge, was for architects like a resonating chamber in which they recognized the intellectual features of architectural practice amplified within the legitimizing space of philosophy. Phenomenology made architects more aware, reflective, and self-confident about the nature of their intellectuality. They also became more experimental, and it is that intellectual experimentation that is the focus of the present study. Looking upon architectural history as the cultural standard of intellectuality in architecture, architectural phenomenologists probed its methods and conventions, experimenting with new forms of historiography that incorporated photography, graphic design, and buildings themselves into alternative ways of constructing, even experiencing, the historic content of architecture. It was the belief in a link between experience and history that brought architects into a relationship of resonance with phenomenology. With its architectural homologies in mind, we can now turn to the particular way in which phenomenologists articulated the connection between experience and history.

Experience and History

The word experience is commonly used to signify a wide range meanings, from the events that have taken place within the knowledge of a community, as in "the American experience," to the skills acquired in the course of working and practicing in a particular field, as in "she has architectural experience," to the fact of being consciously the subject of a state or condition, or of being affected by an event, as in "I experience discomfort sitting on this chair." This latter sense of conscious experience was the initial focus of phenomenology.

Founded by Edmund Husserl (1859–1938) at the dawn of the twentieth century, phenomenology began as an attempt to provide a description of experience free from prejudice. Husserl believed that previous philosophical accounts of experience, such as those offered by rationalism, empiricism, positivism, or sensationalism, had employed extraneous analytical frameworks borrowed from science, religion, and even folk traditions, which distorted a pure consideration of experience as it is given to consciousness. If experience, as the conscious observation of facts or events, was considered a source of knowledge, then a prejudiced account of experience would inevitably lead to distorted notions of epistemology and to inherently flawed philosophical systems. Husserl rejected traditional representational accounts of knowledge as inner mental copies of outside reality, contained within the mind as if in a box, and presented to consciousness for inspection. Instead, he maintained that a proper description of the knowledge gained through experience must account for the fact that it presents itself to consciousness in the process of interacting with the world, and as an engagement with our environment: "Experience is the performance in which for me, the experiencer, experienced being 'is there,' and is there *as what* it is, with the whole content and mode of being that experience itself, by the performance going on its intentionality, attributes to it."[13] Husserl's famous exhortation, "Back to the things themselves,"[14] became the clarion call of phenomenology, defining it as an attempt to describe things, or phenomena, in the manner in which they appear, that is, as they manifest themselves to consciousness through and in experience.

Husserl's great philosophical achievement was what he called the phenomenological reduction (from the Latin *reducere*, to lead back), a method for peeling back all the layers of encrusted philosophical traditions and metaphysical assumptions about the nature of experience and arriving at a description of it free from any presupposition. In his essay "Philosophy as Rigorous Science" (1911), Husserl called these layers of bias the "natural attitude."[15] The term referred to the scientific assumption that everything in the world is either physical or psychic, and hence should be explored merely by the natural sciences, including psychology. The natural attitude was the common assumption made about the nature of existence when relating to matters of fact, processes, practical aspects, values, other persons, social institutions, and cultural creations. The problem with the natural attitude was that it left no room for ideal entities such as meanings or laws as such, which can only be experienced in conscious acts. The natural attitude denied the reality of consciousness and yet was based on assuming the existence of consciousness to give rise to its picture of reality in the first place. This contradiction made it clear that the natural attitude was nonsensical, and that it lacked a radical questioning of its own presuppositions. The phenomenological reduction entailed "bracketing" the natural attitude from the philosophical description of experience, allowing the philosopher to suspend naturalistic claims about existence while investigating the experience itself— like a jury that is asked to focus exclusively on the evidence and to suspend the kinds of associations and inferences made in everyday life. After the bracketing of particular facts and claims about the actual existence of the things experienced, the philosopher directed a glance through reflection at what was left of the experience in all its aspects in order to intuit what he called its eidetic essence. In this sense, the phenomenological reduction signaled an important shift in emphasis from experience to intuition as the apodictic ground of phenomenological work:

> [The scientific investigator of nature] observes and experiments; that is, he ascertains *factual existence* according to experience; *for him experiencing is a grounding act* which can never be substituted by a mere imagining. And this is precisely why science of *matters of fact* and *experimental* science are

equivalent concepts. But for the *geometer* who explores not actualities but "ideal possibilities," not predicatively formed actuality-complexes, but predicatively formed eidictic affair-complexes, *the ultimately grounding act* is not experience but rather *the seeing of essences.*[16]

To intuit something is to apprehend it directly, without recourse to reasoning processes such as deduction or induction. Intuition was, for Husserl, how the a priori structures that gave experiences their meaning appeared immediately to pure consciousness. This focus on intuition was the basis for Husserl's definition of his work as "transcendental" or "pure" phenomenology, in the sense that it concerned itself strictly with the realm of pure consciousness or the transcendental ego.

Husserl's thinking about essences as a priori structures from which all meaning derives owed its indebtedness to Kant, and his search for the apodictic ground of consciousness came very much out of his long engagement with Descartes.[17] But Husserl's refusal to give up the world of immediate experience to sheer abstractions also differentiated him from the rationalist Cartesian tradition. In fact, Husserl was part of a generation of philosophers who first began to move beyond rationalism and metaphysics through renewed accounts of lived experience, including William James (1842–1910), founder of pragmatism, Wilhelm Dilthey (1833–1911), who advanced the philosophy of life, and Henri Bergson (1859–1941), who initiated modern process philosophy. That these philosophical schools shared a belief in the central role of intuition in grasping lived experience has sometimes led to their conflation. "Indeed," writes Moran, "the prevalence of notions of intuition as a kind of spiritual sympathy with the object of knowledge has often led to phenomenology being widely misunderstood as a form of irrational mysticism."[18]

This conflation was exacerbated within architectural discourse. Even the most sophisticated architectural phenomenologists, like the protagonists of this book, tended to draw freely from unrelated philosophical schools in their descriptions of architectural experience. Norberg-Schulz, who was as intellectually rigorous as any architectural phenomenologist, nevertheless conflated Bergson and Heidegger in his first attempts at describing architectural experience. *Intentions in Architecture,* for instance, described the experience of architecture as a phenomenal totality in terms of Heidegger's notion of being-in-the-world, while claiming that the experience could only be properly grasped through Bergson's notion of intuitive cognition.[19] Labatut's own thinking about architectural experiences also involved placing a heavy premium on intuition, which he understood through the lenses of Bergson and his neo-Thomist friend Jacques Maritain.[20] Clearly, if we judge architectural phenomenology by the standards and schools of philosophical discourse, we will be forced to conclude that it was guilty of sloppy talk. But it would be counterproductive to give primacy to philosophy if our purpose is to grasp architectural phenomenology in its own terms. We must accept that architectural phenomenology entered into a relationship of resonance with the ideas of philosophers whose appurtenance to phenomenology is debated, like Bachelard or Arendt, and others, like Bergson or Maritain, who are clearly outside of the phenomenological school. Architectural phenomenology grew with an intellectual heterogeneity that would be anathema to philosophy. But it kept phenomenology as its central reference point. The Husserlian notion of intuition, as variously reconfigured by his followers, was another important common intellectual thread binding together the work of architectural phenomenologists. Intuition served as an apotropaic concept, warding off claims that knowledge of buildings could be gained only through rational methods, and preserving a subjective kernel in the study of architecture, especially during McCarthyism, when architects felt most pressured to construe their discipline as purely objective and scientific. More importantly, the stress placed on intuition also led architectural phenomenologists to question traditional historiography, especially its circumscription to so-called objective facts and documents as the basis for its historical knowledge about buildings. Architectural phenomenologists posited that a more profound or essential historical knowledge of buildings could be intuited in direct experiences. Their belief that experience should be the foundation of architectural history gained intellectual legitimacy as it resonated with phenomenological descriptions of the historicity of experience, especially those put forth by Heidegger.

"Before Heidegger," wrote Spiegelberg, "phenomenologists had attached only limited and secondary importance to the problem of history."[21] In Husserl's programmatic manifesto for phenomenology, "Philosophy as Rigorous Science," there was even a stern critique of historicism as one of the many contemporary forms of relativism. Husserl maintained that mere historical facts could not prove or disprove the validity of any kind of true knowledge. By contrast, history and historiography were some of Heidegger's major interests. During his early years as a Catholic seminarian, he had immersed himself in historical studies of Thomism, and later he turned more directly to the theories of writing history along the lines of Dilthey—the target of Husserl's attacks. Heidegger's

engagement and transformation of Husserl's phenomenology is a subject beyond the scope of the present study.[22] But in order to touch upon his conception
of the relationship between experience and history, it is helpful to bear in mind
that Heidegger disagreed with Husserl's insistence on bracketing all concerns
with actual existence in order to proceed with the phenomenological description of experience. He criticized Husserl for having prioritized the realm of
the theoretical over the lived moment in experience and for fleeing historical
"factical" existence in favor of a transcendental idealism.[23] Husserl's account
of the human experience of the world remained too Cartesian and too intellec-
tualist for Heidegger.[24] After a decade struggling with Husserl's thinking,
Heidegger eventually became convinced that the only way to avoid the pitfalls of
his predecessor's thinking was to drop the use of his terminology altogether.
In *Being and Time* (1927), he abandoned words like "consciousness" and
"intentionality" and replaced them with *Dasein* (being there), which he described as always experiencing a certain mood, caught up in projects within a
world in which it found itself thrown. As can be surmised from the title of the
book, Heidegger provided a phenomenological description of the relation between Dasein (a particular being) and Being itself, and then turned to describe
Dasein and his relation to temporality. Heidegger's ultimate aim was ontological: to investigate "the question of Being"[25] as it appeared in human experience.
Indeed, one of the fundamental insights of the book was that Dasein's experiences of Being were given in time, because Dasein is a mortal being whose
existence is temporally bound, and that therefore the experience of Being
appeared differently to Dasein at different times, depending on many things
ranging from Dasein's mood to the particular cultural assumptions about Being
current during the particular historical period in which Dasein happened to live.
Heidegger's recognition that both experience and the philosophical insights derived from it were historically given flew in the face of traditional metaphysics,
showing the belief that the structure of Being was timeless and self-same to be
based on faulty premises. He showed traditional metaphysical accounts of Being
to be historical sedimentations of everyday assumptions about reality, which
distorted as much as revealed true insights into the nature of Being. Against
teleological notions of historical progress, Heidegger showed that human
experiences and knowledge of Being waxed and waned in different historical
periods, so that it might in fact be more difficult to authentically experience
Being now than in the past. Indeed, he viewed the modern era as a dark time
when the experience of Being had become mostly concealed to Dasein, receding

behind veils of rationalist and scientific prejudice. Heidegger's search to experience Being necessarily involved his own critical confrontation with his historical moment in particular and with modernity in general.[26] His solution was to advance a radical phenomenological interpretation of the experience of Being, called hermeneutic ontology, that took into account the fact that interpretation cannot be a neutral, detached, theoretical contemplation, but rather must consider the involvement of the inquirer in the inquiry. *Being and Time* presented just such an interpretation of how the structures of Being can be revealed only through the temporal structures of human existence. Heidegger's description of human experience, as always already structured by its "historicality,"[27] was a defining turn within phenomenology, which had a long-lasting impact on his students' work, as in Hannah Arendt's phenomenological description of the history of the concept of history,[28] or in Hans-Georg Gadamer's study of the origin of the idea of history as it appeared within German philosophy,[29] and it has remained influential to this day.

Heidegger's critique of modernity, and his attempt to recover an original premodern experience of Being from under the weight of philosophical tradition, was also enormously appealing to architects during the postwar years, as it resonated with their own attempts to get beyond modern architecture by dismantling the concepts for which it stood, such as the Miesian notion of universal abstract space. "After the publication of Martin Heidegger's *Building, Dwelling, Thinking* in 1954," wrote Frampton, "it was natural that the Enlightenment category of *spatium in extenso* or limitless space should come to be challenged in architectural thought by the more archaic notion of *Raum* or place."[30] Norberg-Schulz attempted his own Heideggerian description of the experience of place in *Existence, Space and Architecture* (1971).[31] The word "place" was the subject of much debate in architectural discourse during the 1960s and 1970s,[32] and by the 1980s it had become widely used to denote a postmodernist sensitivity to the historical structuring of the experience of space. Yet within this new sensitivity toward history, architectural phenomenology also absorbed the Heideggerian thrust to dismantle historical traditions as a necessary clearing of the way toward a more authentic experience of history. Thus, architectural phenomenologists deemed it necessary to strike against what they saw as the encrusted tradition of architectural historiography in order to better appreciate the historical experiential content of architecture.

Heidegger's appeal within architecture also had to do with the fact that some of his later writings, especially "Building Dwelling Thinking," made direct reference to architecture. The essay appeared in English in *Poetry, Language, Thought* (1971), a collection of essays in which Heidegger's interest in architecture is shown to be really part of a wider attention to the experience of art. In essays such as "The Origin of the Work of Art,"[33] Heidegger attributed a special ontological character to artworks—a category that included not just visual works, but also poetry. The experience of art was important because he regarded it as one of the rare instances when we come close to allowing ourselves to experience a thing for what it is, attending only to its phenomena in the manner in which they are given to us in experience, without imposing upon it the framework *(das Gestell)* of scientific or technological assumptions.[34] The experience of art gave access to a type of poetic intuition of Being, which got covered up in ordinary experience and forms of speech. Heidegger described artworks as privileged things that worked on us by disclosing the truth of things. The idea that artworks set truth to work was taken into architectural phenomenology to ascribe a new cultural importance to architecture as a form of resistance to technological society. Frampton's notion of critical regionalism as an *arrière-garde* position would not have been possible without also positing that the direct experience of buildings revealed truths about architecture that remained hidden from ordinary theoretical discourse. Directly appropriating Heidegger's language, Norberg-Schulz argued that architecture "set-to-work" the environment in a way that revealed its truth poetically, and that, as such, building should take a central role in overcoming the technological exploitation of the natural environment.[35]

Other phenomenologists have also assigned a paradigmatic role to the experience of art in approaching phenomena without presuppositions, in their modes of givenness, to use Heidegger's technical term. For example, Merleau-Ponty's accounts of the experience of looking at Cézanne's paintings were a touchstone of his phenomenological description of embodiment.[36] However, Merleau-Ponty placed less emphasis on the historicity of experience, which partly explains why he was so influential for a second generation of architectural phenomenologists, including Steven Holl (b. 1947) and others,[37] who were less concerned with questions of historiography, and who for this very reason remain outside the scope of this study. Hans-Georg Gadamer (1900–2002) also gave primacy of place to the experience of art in his philosophy. His work is relevant for our purposes here because he, perhaps more than other students of Heidegger, attempted to relate the experience of art to history in his magnum opus *Truth and Method* (1960). The first half of the book is devoted to "The

Question of Truth as It Emerges in the Experience of Art," in which he describes art as the site of unique truths not accessible through the normal methodology of the sciences. "Is there no knowledge in art?" he asked. "Does not the experience of art contain a claim to truth which is certainly different from that of science, but just as certainly is not inferior to it?"[38] If art could reveal its truth in direct experience, then, according to Gadamer, one had to question the scientific belief that method is the royal road to truth. Without denying science, Gadamer wanted to expand the understanding of truth beyond the objective facts that were yielded by the narrow application of scientific method.

A proper phenomenological account of the sort of truth revealed in experiences of art required, according to Gadamer, a fundamental rethinking of the notion of tradition. For him, tradition was not just a willful prejudice distorting our access to truth. On the contrary, traditional prejudices were required, as platforms from which to launch our understanding of truth. Indeed, Gadamer wanted to rehabilitate tradition as the historical background against which our experiences are formed. "The overcoming of all prejudices," he observed with regard to that basic principle of Enlightenment philosophy, "will itself prove to be a prejudice, and removing it opens the way to an appropriate understanding of the finitude which dominates not only our humanity but also our historical consciousness."[39]

Gadamer introduced the concept of *Bildung,* translated as culture or cultivation, to refer to the process whereby tradition forms experience. The importance of cultivation lay in the development of a maturity of understanding, which came in the form of an almost intuitive cultural awareness—not scientific explanation. He noted that *Bild,* the German root of Bildung, means form, image, and more particularly picture. Art, as a capacity to form images or representations of experience, played a paradigmatic role in his description of Bildung. One's cultural tradition was not something that could be checked at the door before experiencing a work of art. It was not external to the experience but an intrinsic part of the person experiencing and how he or she understood. Whatever truth was revealed in the experience of art appeared in and through one's tradition and its prejudices, so that truth always involved a simultaneous revealing and concealing that was historically contingent. Further complicating matters, experiencing an artwork, say an ancient sculpture, sometimes also involved confronting *another* historical tradition, that of the artwork's original moment of production. The experience of art therefore entailed a sort of confrontation of two traditions, or horizons of understanding. One's own tradition and prejudices provided the basis allowing us to begin trying to relate to what is both familiar and strange in the artwork. Gadamer called that mode of relating to artworks hermeneutics, from the Greek verb *hermeneuin,* meaning to interpret: "in its attempt to bring about a meaningful agreement between the two traditions . . . this kind of hermeneutics is still pursuing the task of all preceding hermeneutics, namely to bring about agreement in *content.*"[40] Arising out of the description of the experience of art as paradigmatic of a nonscientific form of comprehension, the second part of *Truth and Method* provided a general theory of hermeneutics as an essential ontological structure of human understanding. This existential view of hermeneutics allowed Gadamer to extend the concept of truth in art to the meaning of the concept of truth in history. Writing history also involved moving in a hermeneutic circle between two traditions, one's own and that in which the historical events took place. At every turn, Gadamer emphasized how interpretation was itself bound by historicality, at once formed by cultural tradition and re-forming it as it went: "Tradition is not simply a permanent precondition; rather, we produce it ourselves inasmuch as we understand, participate in the evolution of tradition, and hence further determine it ourselves."[41]

Architectural phenomenology absorbed critical elements of Gadamer's thinking. Significantly, Frampton's definition of critical regionalism as a synthesis of universal rational industrial construction processes and local building cultures owed much to Gadamer's description of reason as operating in and through tradition. In line with Gadamer's notion of Bildung, Frampton defined architecture as not just building, but also as cultural "edification."[42] He also described architectural schools as "cultural regions" within which that edification took place: "it is precisely the self-cultivation of this region," he wrote, "which will enable it to resist without falling either into reactionary hermeticism on the one hand or into the media juggernaut of universal civilization."[43]

In sum, while modernist architectural discourses about experience, history, and theory were current in the postwar lead-up to postmodernism, the exposure to phenomenology set architectural phenomenologists to work accounting for one in terms of the other. Their efforts made postmodernism's retrieval of history appear to be fundamentally bound up in the search for renewed experiences of architecture. In turn, these new experiences of architecture had to be formed out of the background of an existing tradition of architectural history, which, insofar as it identified objective historiographical methods as the basis of historical truth, impeded the recognition of subjectivity as playing a central role in the interpretation of historic buildings and their truth content. Architectural phenomenologists launched their search for experience from the platform provided by the tradition of architectural historiography, but they remade that tradition, participating in its evolution by attending to the many ways in which subjectivity appeared within the cracks of its encrusted conventions. The choice of photographs, the layout of pages, the leading and misleading use of footnotes, word choices, and other instruments became means for expressing a new attention to subjective experience. Phenomenology remained the central point of reference in architectural theorizing on the relationship between experience and history throughout the 1970s and up until 1987, when the publication of Victor Farias's *Heidegger et le Nazisme* dampened the cultural appeal of phenomenology. Farias's argument that there was a strong connection between Heidegger's philosophy, his antimodernist cultural outlook, and his involvement with Nazism unleashed what became known as the "Heidegger Affair," a series of highly visible debates about his work and its legacy.[44] The affair dealt a final blow to architectural phenomenology, which was already under the pressure of new poststructuralist approaches to the questions of history and theory.

What we now call postmodern architectural theory was in reality a consolidation of processes set in motion between the late 1940s and the early 1970s. The premature historiographical synthesis suggested by the label of postmodern theory has come at the price of proper accounting. A lot of the richness of what the postwar generation actually accomplished intellectually has been swept under the rug of labels like deconstruction.

Hesitant to completely let go of the ideals of the modern movement, architectural phenomenolgists brought forth the intellectual changes we know as postmodernism almost reluctantly, oscillating between protest and accommodation. They revived premodern symbols such as the medieval master-mason, or peasant aesthetics "rooted" in traditional buildings, in hopes of returning to what they believed were the more authentic experiential roots of modernism. Their indecisiveness and inability to completely break with modernism produced unintended results after deconstruction, when we witnessed a neomodernist return to formalism and a turn away from the postmodernist concepts of history and theory. In the new neomodernist context, Frampton's figure of the master-mason became the model for architects interested in controlling construction costs through rapid prototyping and in eliminating the skilled craftsmen that Frampton cared so much about. Norberg-Schulz's "spirit of place" was less a path to preserving "rooted building" than an expeditious aesthetic enabling multinational corporate architecture firms to compete with local architects. Moore's exaltation of the body as the path to intense communal experience eased the transition to corporate architecture, which catered to the culture of private exuberance and turned a blind eye to public squalor in places like Dubai and Shanghai. Rooted in a reaction to the collusion of secularism, capitalism, and aesthetic austerity, architectural phenomenology nevertheless adapted premodern symbols to modern ends, eased the adjustment to new modes of production, and aided the transformation of modern architectural practice into the bureaucratic administration of the built environment.

Architectural phenomenology was not an intellectual infrastructure that predetermined postmodernism, nor a transcendental idea that guided the work of architects. Rather, architectural phenomenology was the effecting of what Deleuze called a "diagrammatic function" during the postmodern period.[45] That is to say, it played a piloting role in the path toward contemporary theory, accelerating and decelerating the intellectualization of architectural history, and delineating the contours of a new intellectual reality, which was not yet fully formed.

We now inhabit that reality and call it architectural theory, something some take to be totally separate from practice. But to grasp the history of architectural phenomenology requires that we consider a time when intellectual and aesthetic pursuits blended more fluidly into each other. The contours left by the trajectory of architectural phenomenology are those of the struggle over the definition of architectural theory vis-à-vis history and practice, a conflict that was waged intellectually and aesthetically, with words and with images. Architectural phenomenology both enabled and resisted the separation of theory from history and practice. That double role helps explain why the history of architectural phenomenology is also that of the role that anti-intellectualism played in the intellectualization of architecture.

Eucharistic Architecture
Jean Labatut and the Search for Pure Sensation

In 1973, the University of Virginia awarded the prestigious Thomas Jefferson Memorial Foundation Medal to Jean Labatut for his lifetime contribution to the advancement of architecture.[1] Previous recipients included Ludwig Mies van der Rohe (1966), Alvar Aalto (1967), Marcel Breuer (1968), John Ely Burchard (1969), Kenzo Tange (1970), Jose Luis Sert (1971), and Lewis Mumford (1972). Labatut's name has fallen into obscurity. But to his contemporaries, he was known as one of the most influential teachers of the mid-twentieth century in America. The Jefferson Medal recognized Labatut as a "teacher of teachers." Indeed, his old Princeton student, J. Norwood Bosserman (MFA, 1952), presided over the awards ceremony as dean of the University of Virginia's School of Architecture, while eight of his other pupils sat as heads of prominent architecture schools. Labatut's circle of students included some of the greatest postmodern American architects, from Robert Venturi to Charles Moore. He taught them to despise the rarified abstraction of corporate modernism and to be interested in developing a more popular architecture based on the creative reading of everyday objects (such as the great American road, folk art, commercial signage, or historic architecture), on the frank visual expression of mundane construction materials, and on the organization of spaces around people's ordinary gestures and movements. Labatut understood the architect to be a visual artist who, in order to be effective, should learn not just the academic rules of composition but also the commercial and popular techniques of visual communication. But the architect's promiscuity with crass commercialism was justified only, advised Labatut, to elevate it to a high spiritual art. He taught students that buildings were the organization of attention. Good buildings engaged people, sustained their intellectual and spiritual curiosity, and communicated meaningful experiences to them. Through his students, Labatut's teachings helped shape postmodern architecture and promoted the view that the best way to understand this new architecture was to experience it. Labatut's success as a teacher rested on the clarity of his

message: before architects could create modern buildings, they had to first be able to experience buildings
in a modern way. His pedagogy aimed to define
this modern experience as a bodily communion with
architecture, which was immediately meaningful and
did not require intellectual reflection. Architectural
phenomenology was formed against the background
of Labatut's teachings. Indeed, the emergence and
career of architectural phenomenology cannot be
properly understood without bringing Labatut from
under the shadow of the generation that followed his.

Camouflage

Labatut liked to say that his architectural education
began during World War I when, as a nineteen-year-
old, he served in the French Army Corps of Engineers
and worked on the project to camouflage the Grand
Canal of Versailles, preventing German planes from
using it to orient themselves toward Paris.[2] Such projects were supervised by the French army's Service de
camouflage. Established in 1915, and the first of its
kind in military history, the service enlisted visual artists to paint disruptive
patterns on artillery units and sniper suits, to model listening posts in the shape
of animal carcasses, to paint miles of canvas to look like roads and suspended
above ground to conceal troop movements, and to modify landmark buildings to
avert air strikes.[3] Through the artists of the Service de camouflage, Labatut was
exposed to some of the most advanced contemporary visual art theory. He
quickly learned the practical application of cubist notions about the visual
dissolution of mass through contour and object matching.[4] This was a defining
experience for Labatut. It turned his attention to buildings as material to be shaped
by the visual artist, persuaded him that the visual arts were not simply meant to
delight but also to be socially useful, and forged his sense of an indissoluble bond
between advanced technology, progressive society, and avant-garde art.

As a first lesson in architecture, learning to make buildings disappear
was not without irony. Labatut liked to teach camouflage to his students as a way
to illustrate his view that architects should learn about visual principles from

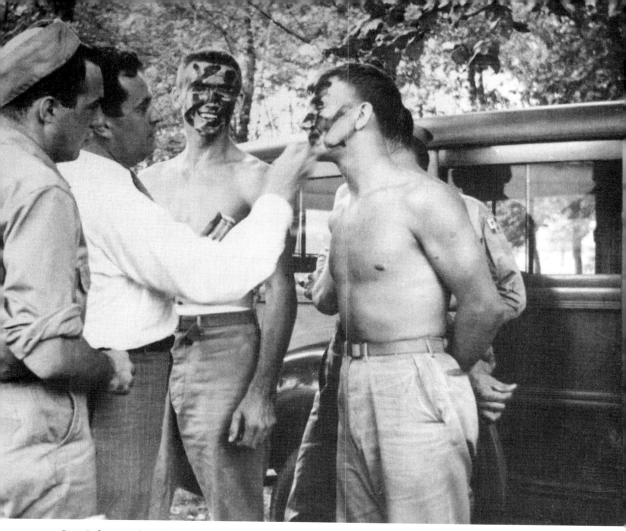

Jean Labatut paints disruptive patterns on students' faces during his camouflage class at Princeton University, ca. 1943. Courtesy of Princeton University Library, Jean Labatut Papers, Manuscripts Division, Department of Rare Books and Special Collections.

existing buildings before venturing to design. To effectively camouflage a build-ing required studying it with precision from various angles and at different times of the day. He had to examine what made the structure visually stand out from its context; everything from the pattern of the shadows it cast, to the uniqueness of its material and color palettes, the distinctiveness of its shape and scale, and the configuration of roads leading to it was critical information for the art of camouflage. In addition, it was necessary to keep in mind the viewer from whom the building was to be concealed. The *camoufleur* had to understand the cultural, technical, and physiological factors that influenced visual reception. Pilots tended to look for long, straight lines because these were easier to distinguish at great speeds from high altitudes. Disguising a structure from a pilot was not the same as disguising it from a pedestrian. Since his first sustained study of buildings, Labatut approached architecture as part and parcel of a broader visual medium, the built environment, which he saw as constantly being reshaped for specific types of viewers according to techniques and principles developed outside of architecture—in painting, commercial graphic design, military surveillance, or transportation engineering.

The disposition Labatut forged during the war for basing design on the intended viewer's reception served him well during his formal education at the École des Beaux-Arts. There, students were taught that design was the synthesis of technical and aesthetic constraints into a logical *parti,* or unifying design orientation, that should be visually graspable. Convention had it that a beautiful drawing of the building's plan was the most eloquent representation of the parti. But in reality, the parti was meant to be experienced visually by the visitor as he or she moved through a sequence of rooms, which varied in scale and ornamentation, thus revealing little by little and without signage, a sense of the building's layout, organization, and meaning.

Labatut joined the Beaux-Arts in 1919, the same year that Walter Gropius (1883–1969) founded the Bauhaus. The Bauhaus curriculum was a direct affront to the Beaux-Arts studio-based and drawing-oriented pedagogy. Gropius organized the school around workshops where art and architecture students became directly involved in contemporary manufacturing methods. By hiring some of the most prominent contemporary visual artists, Gropius gave the Bauhaus the cutting edge aura of bringing together advanced technology and anticipatory aesthetics. This association led to the gradual conflation of Bauhaus-inspired architecture with cubism, the avant-garde par excellence. By the time Sigfried Giedion compared Gropius's Bauhaus buildings in Dessau (1925–26) to Picasso's *L'Arlésienne* in his 1941 *Space, Time, and Architecture,* the pairing seemed almost inevitable.

But not to Labatut, who believed cubism was a French affair and was taught that the Beaux-Arts had in fact initiated the dismantling of the architectural object by questioning historical conventions through aesthetic and technological experimentation. This was the legacy of Henri Labrouste, Joseph-Louis Duc, Félix-Jacques Duban, and Léon Vaudoyer, the Beaux-Arts architects who led the romantic critique of neoclassical architecture in Paris beginning in the 1840s. Labatut saw this tradition continued in the figure of his mentor Victor Laloux, a professor at the Beaux-Arts, whose Gare D'Orsay (1897) was widely admired as a functionalist leap forward and served as an important precedent for McKim, Mead & White's Pennsylvania Station (New York, 1902–10).

But the Beaux-Arts self-fashioning as the standard bearer of modern architecture also faced tough challenges from within France. Much of this jockeying occurred in the lead-up to the 1925 Exposition Internationale des Arts Décoratifs et Industriels Modernes, which was originally announced in 1907 and scheduled for 1915. The government-sponsored event aimed to spur the development of a style moderne that could restore France's primacy in the luxury goods market. Before Gropius had even thought of the Bauhaus, the French were already indexing the modernism of their architecture through instrumental associations to cubism. André Mare (1885–1932), a decorator, first attempted to bring the visual possibilities offered by cubism to architecture with his *Maison cubiste* at the Salon d'Automne of 1912. The installation project unfolded behind a façade designed by sculptor Raymond Duchamp-Villon (1876–1918), which disrupted classical forms with cubist angularity. Inside, the rather bourgeois salon and bedroom were hung with cubist paintings by Roger de La Fresnaye (1885–1925), Fernand Léger (1881–1955), Jean Metzinger (1883–1956), Albert Gleizes (1881–1953), and Raymond's younger brother Marcel Duchamp (1887–1968). The exhibition caused a stir that reached as far as the Chamber of Deputies, immediately raising the interest of collectors and art critics in the possibility of a cubist architecture. During the war, Mare served in the Service de camouflage, where he helped disseminate the visual principles of cubism to young French recruits like Labatut as well as to Italian and British counterparts.[5]

Most of the artists involved in the *Maison cubiste* were members of the Puteaux group, which splintered from the larger cubist movement to pursue a methodology rooted in subjective experience as the basis for dissolving the representational unity of objects. The group was initiated by the Duchamp brothers and included the Parisian architects Auguste and Gustave Perret (1874–1954 and 1876–1952, respectively), who had distinguished themselves for the daring use of concrete construction and glass.[6] As a former *camoufleur*, Labatut was drawn to the thinking of the Puteaux group, and he came under the influence of Auguste Perret. Labatut addressed Perret as his mâitre in his correspondence. In 1951, he mounted successful campaigns to have the AIA grant Perret its 1952 Gold Medal and to bestow on him Princeton's Doctorate Honoris Causa.[7]

The Puteaux group explored the aesthetic implications of advances in philosophy. Through the influence of painter Albert Gleizes, the group became especially interested in Henri Bergson's lectures at the prestigious Collège de France, in which he expounded his "process philosophy." Bergson's view that from the perspective of experience the world was constantly changing, or

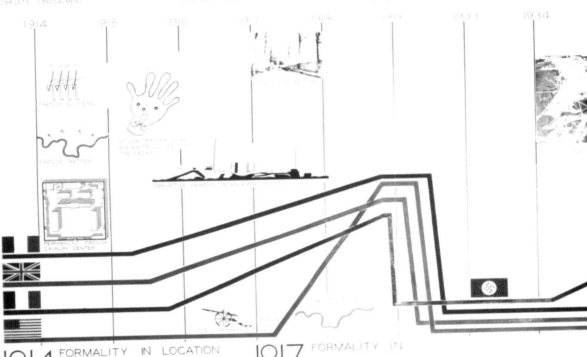

Jean Labatut's timeline, made in 1943, of the evolution of camouflage techniques, comparing advances in France, the United Kingdom, Italy, and the United States from World War I to

...NDMARK INTO THE ENVIRONMENT.

● THE USE OF CAMOUFLAGE MAY BE TRACED TO THE FIG-LEAF IN THE GARDEN OF EDEN. OUR STONE AGE ANCESTORS DOUBT-LESS TOOK ADVANTAGE OF NA-TURAL CONCEALMENT AS THEY LAY IN WAIT FOR A NEXT DOOR NEIGHBOR. IN THE FOURTH CENTURY B.C. THE THEBANS USED CAVALRY TO STIR UP A DUST CLOUD COMPLETELY SCREENING THE ADVANC-ING TROOPS IN THEIR ATTACK ON THE NUMERICALLY SUPERIOR SPARTAN ENEMIES AND DEFEATED THEM WITH LITTLE LOSS. GENGHIS KHAN SWEPT THROUGH ASIA, AIDED

BY THE ABILITY OF HIS HORSE-MEN TO REMAIN CONCEALED BEHIND NATURAL COVER, UNTIL THE MOMENT OF ATTACK. AND BY THE USE OF LEAVES AND TWIGS IN THEIR CAPS TO DISTORT THEIR SILHOUETTES AGAINST THE SKYLINE. ● ALTHOUGH COMPARATIVELY NEW TO MANKIND, IT IS ONE OF NATURE'S OLDEST TRICKS. ABBOT THAYER, AN AMERICAN ARTIST, AFTER AN EXTENSIVE STUDY OF WILDLIFE AT THE END OF THE LAST CENTURY NOTED WHAT WE NOW KNOW AS "COUNTERSHADING"—ANIMALS

BIRDS & INSECTS COLORED DARK ON TOP WITH GRADATION ON THE SIDES GRADUALLY TURN-ING INTO WHITE OR NEAR WHITE ON THE BOTTOM. THIS HAS THE EFFECT OF SUBDUING SHADOWS AND ABSORBING DIRECT LIGHT, CONSEQUENTLY MAK-ING THE FORM LOSE ITS SHAPE, WHICH WOULD OTHERWISE BE CLEARLY DEFINED BY THE SHADES AND SHADOWS. NATURE HAS ALSO CREATED INSECTS TO RESEMBLE NATURAL FORMS, AS IS SHOWN IN THE PHOTOGRAPHS OF THE LOCUST AND PRAYING

MANTIS. IN THE LARGER ANI-MALS THE ZEBRA IS PERHAPS THE MOST FAMOUS EXAMPLE OF NATURE'S CAMOUFLAGE. ● AT THE BEGINNING OF WORLD WAR I MILITARY LEADERS HAD MUCH OF THE FALSE & UNTHINK-ING BRAVERY WHICH IN 1775 LED GENERAL BRADDOCK TO ADVANCE WITH HIS RED-COATED TROOPS ALONG THE BANKS OF THE MONONGAHELA RIVER AGAINST FRENCH AND INDIANS WHO WERE SKILLED IN THE WAYS OF FIGHT-ING IN THE WOODS. THIS WAS ONE OF MANY MILITARY TRA-

DITIONS THAT WERE AS OLD AS SOLDIERY. GEOMETRIC FORMALITY IN THE LOCATION OF MEN, MATERIALS AND BUILDINGS, IMPRESSIVE BUT IM-PRACTICAL, WHICH WAS TO COST AMERICA SO MUCH AT PEARL HARBOR CAN BE TRACED BACK TO THE ROMAN MILI-TARY CAMP. THIS TRADITION MUST GO THE WAY OF THE RED-COATED BRITISH SOLDIER OF 1775.   ROMAN CAMP 41 B.C.

| 1935 | 1936 | 1937 | 1938 | 1939 | 1940 | 1941 | 1942 |

1941 FORMALITY IN LOCA-TION OF MATERIALS AND BUILDINGS

● IN 1934 HITLER BEGAN TO RE-ARM & CAMOUFLAGE WAS AWAKENED. BUT THE ALLIES WERE NOT TO BE BOTHERED DURING THE MANY YEARS OF PEACE. NEW SCIENTIFIC DISCOVE-RIES, NEW MATERIALS, & NEW TECHNIQUES OF WAR DEMANDED THE ATTENTION OF THE CAMOU-FLEUR. THE AERIAL CAMERA FORCED CAMOUFLAGE INTO A TRULY THREE DIMENSIONAL TECH-NIQUE. PLUS STEREOSCOPIC PHOTO-

GRAPHY, PANCHROMATIC, INFRA-RED & COLOR FILM. BUT THERE WERE ALSO NEW ANSWERS—BLACKOUTS, SMOKEOUT, INFRA-RED REFLECTIVE PAINTS, & DECOYS. ● IN 1939 ENGLAND & FRANCE HAD MUCH TO LEARN, & IN JUNE 1940 AMERICA BEGAN HER NEW WORK IN CAMOUFLAGE. HOWEVER, DECEMBER 7, 1941, FOUND US WITH MANY PLANS FOR CAMOU-FLAGE BUT NONE IN PRACTICE. THE GEOMETRY OF PLANES,

BUILDINGS & SHIPS AT PEARL HARBOR SHOWED WE HAD NOT LEARNED THE LESSONS OF 1914 & 1917. THE SITUATION WAS NO BETTER IN THE PHILIP-PINES. SIX OF NINE B-17S WERE DESTROYED IN THE FIRST ATTACK. CORREGIDOR LOOKED MORE LIKE A LARGE SUMMER RESORT THAN THE GIBRALTAR OF THE PACIFIC IT WAS SUPPOSED TO BE. WE WERE STILL CAMP-ING WITH CAESAR IN 41 B.C.

● THE BIG LESSON LEARNED SINCE PEARL HARBOR IS THAT CAMOUFLAGE MUST NO LONGER BE AN AFTERTHOUGHT. IT MUST BE A MAJOR PART OF THE ORIGINAL DESIGN & IS THE RESPONSIBILITY OF THE DESIGNER. IT MUST GO HAND IN HAND WITH THE CON-SIDERATION OF SITE, FUNCTION AND IMPORTANCE OF THE IN-STALLATION, WHETHER MILI-TARY OR NOT. FORMAL GEO-

METRY IN PLACEMENT OF MEN, MATERIALS AND BUILDINGS HAS GONE THE WAY OF THE WHITE GLOVE OF THE OFFICER OF SAINT CYR AND THE HANGARS AT HICKAM FIELD, HONOLULU. IN CONCLUSION IT MUST BE REMEM-BERED THAT CAMOUFLAGE IS NOT A MAGICIAN'S BAG OF TRICKS, BUT A COMBINATION OF ART AND SCIENCE, PLUS A GREAT DEAL OF COMMON HORSE SENSE ON THE PART OF EVERYBODY.

PEARL HARBOR, BOMBED DECEMBER 7, 1941

CORREGIDOR, PHILIPPINE ISLANDS, BOMBED DECEMBER 8, 1941

World War II. Courtesy of Princeton University Library, Jean Labatut Papers, Manuscripts Division, Department of Rare Books and Special Collections.

"becoming," implied that its spatial essence could not be captured with pictorial methods of representation based on a static viewer, such as perspective. To represent this Bergsonian "creative space," the Puteaux group developed a representational method that emphasized the movement of the viewer, and they broke up the object represented by rotating and translating its surfaces in drawings.[8] The lost unity of the object was regained and amplified at the subjective level. The visual experience of the moving viewer was cast as a synthetic continuum that held the object's fragments together. Labatut thought that this cubist idea of movement as both a splintering of the object and a unifying of subjective experience was homologous with the École's emphasis on circulation as the organizing principle of a parti. Movement became a structuring concept in Labatut's notion of modern architecture, which allowed him to reconcile the opposition between the Beaux-Arts and the Puteaux group that defined his formative years.

Beaux-Arts Modernism

But the synthesis that Labatut longed for seemed impossible in Paris, mostly because of the antagonism that prevailed in the social relationships between Beaux-Arts and modern architecture circles. The same was not true in the United States, where the association of the Beaux-Arts with modern styles was much stronger. Beaux-Arts-trained architects were redefining what it meant to be modern with new office skyscrapers, civic buildings, and train terminals. A strong social network linked these modern American architects with their Parisian Beaux-Arts mentors and colleagues. Laloux's atelier attracted twice as many Américains as the second most popular atelier of Jean-Louis Pascal.[9] Through the expatriate community in Paris, Labatut learned of Paul Philippe Cret (1876–1945), a French architect who, after studying with Pascal, emigrated to Philadelphia in 1903 to teach at the University of Pennsylvania, eventually becoming very influential in America. By the early 1920s, Cret had already established a reputation as a proponent of modern classicism with designs such as the Indianapolis Public Library (1913–17) and the Detroit Museum of Art (1923–27). The idea of rooting modern architecture in the abstract spatial principles of classicism was furthered by Louis I. Kahn (1901–1974), Cret's most prominent student.

Convinced that the future of modern architecture was across the ocean, Labatut tried to find work there, his objective facilitated by the trend, during the 1920s, of French architects as world leaders in the export of their services.[10]

Labatut joined the firm of Jean-Claude-Nicolas Forestier (1861–1930), a founding member of the Société Française des Architectes-Urbanistes (SFU), which was established in 1911 to lobby for state support, at home and abroad, for large urban design projects in the world's rapidly expanding cities. The SFU was committed to improving urban health and social conditions. Its strong engineering foundation led it to advocate for the need to rethink the aesthetics of cities in light of technological innovations, especially the automobile. Labatut immediately recognized the connection between the Beaux-Arts idea of movement as the organizing principle of a building and the SFU's advocacy of traffic flow as the structuring law of urban environments. For the SFU's members, cities were objects to be metamorphosed to accommodate new modes of visual perception. The urban environment needed to adjust to faster cars—with wider streets, better night illumination, and new types of visual signage. Significantly, Forestier looked to America as a model for these urban transformations.[11] Labatut put these theories into practice as Forestier's on-site deputy carrying out the plans for Havana and Lisbon. After Labatut established his own practice, he remained committed to the idea of movement as a structuring aesthetic principle. His 1932 urban design for Paris won him the praise of French officials for the "the solution suggested for the traffic problem and because its arrangement permitted the association of the Paris of yesterday with the demands of future circulation."[12]

Despite the excitement of working on the periphery, Labatut's ambition to shape contemporary architecture drove him to seek to establish himself in America, where Beaux-Arts teaching was yielding its most promising and modern expressions. His break came in 1927 through the Beaux-Arts social academic network. Alexander P. Morgan and Gordon McCormick, two American expatriates in Paris and recent Princeton graduates, recommended him to Sherley Morgan, then director of Princeton's School of Architecture, for the position of resident critic left open by Professor Frederic D'Amato's death.[13]

Labatut sailed for New York in the winter of 1927 and immediately began teaching a design studio based on the idea of movement. To make students think abstractly, he asked them to design the circulation of water in a hydroelectric dam. Water intrigued Labatut enormously. Because it didn't hold a particular shape, it seemed to him like the most modern of objects. His interest increased when he discovered, while aboard transatlantic liners, the new challenges the medium presented to the visual artist and camoufleur. In 1928, he crossed the Atlantic five times, spending six weeks at sea with a drafting board in the trunk.[14] Unlike other modern architects, who were mostly interested in the streamlined shapes of the ships' railings and prows, Labatut's disposition inclined him to consider how these shapes could be fragmented to become more like water.

The work of ship camoufleurs was still available to him, as many of the thousands of American, British, and French ships camouflaged during World War I retained their paint patterns well into the 1920s. The art of concealing ships emerged in response to Germany's 1917 order to unleash its U-boats indiscriminately against Allied military and civilian ships. It was at first thought to be impossible to mask a large boat in the open seas, where the color of water and sky were constantly changing. But shape was not all that mattered at sea.

To sink a ship in the years before radar, a U-boat gunner also had to visually estimate its speed and direction with quick peeks through a periscope and to aim his torpedoes slightly ahead of the target.[15] Norman Wilkinson (1878–1971), a marine painter and lieutenant in the British Royal Navy, devised dazzle painting, a technique to paint ships with large colorful and erratic patterns that would make it difficult to grasp in which direction the ship was moving. The gunner's confusion gave the target just enough time to slip out of harm's way and evade the slow-moving submarines. As with the French Service de camouflage, the Dazzle Section of the British Admiralty employed artists conversant with cubism, such as Edward Wadsworth, who played a significant role in developing vorticism (a British combination of cubism and futurism), and served as a dock officer in charge of supervising painting. Journalists regularly referred to dazzle-painted ships as "floating cubist paintings" when describing the spectacle of dozens of these colorful ships crisscrossing in the harbors.[16] Dazzle painting became the object of a popular fascination that broadened its influence beyond the military, most notably to women's fashion.[17] Through Labatut, it entered architectural education, eventually leading to the work of his students (especially Charles Moore) on experimental "supergraphics" meant to expand, contract, or otherwise distort the visual perception of architectural space.

Labatut traveled between Europe and America aboard the USS Leviathan, *which was dazzle camouflaged according to the designs of Frederic Waugh. Here the ship sails in New York harbor on July 8, 1918. Courtesy of the U.S. Naval Historical Foundation.*

Moving Experience

Movement was the symbol of early twentieth-century modernity. The futurists premised their avant-gardism on it, and Le Corbusier expressed it as a flowing promenade of ramps through his Villa Savoye (Poissy, 1928–31). Traveling aboard the *Leviathan*, the largest ocean liner in the world and one of the first American ships to be dazzle-camouflaged according to the designs of Frederic Waugh, Labatut dreamed about the possibility of architecture without stable shape whose sole purpose would be to manipulate the visual experience of movement.[18] This was a radical and original departure from what he had learned in school. The Beaux-Arts premised the organization of room sequences upon the presumed certainty of a normative visual experience common to every visitor. But camouflage had taught him that the principles governing visual experience changed according to the viewer's movement. The SFU had used this notion to argue for changing the visual aspect of cities so that they could serve visual regimes other than the pedestrian's. The crux of Labatut's contribution was to reverse this logic: instead of adapting buildings and cities to accommodate new types of movement, Labatut posited that architecture should itself distort normal visual experiences. For Labatut, architecture should not look like a car, it should perform experientially like a car, capable of transporting visitors into extraordinary ways of sensing and rediscovering their ordinary surroundings. This conceptual leap was simply a return to what he believed to be the source of modern architecture: to the Bergsonian ideals of the Puteaux group to produce "creative spaces," not just buildings.

From Princeton, Labatut quickly reached out to the Beaux-Arts social network in search of collaborations in professional commissions. As he had hoped, the group was actively engaged developing a modern architectural language out of the principles of the Beaux-Arts. Through Cret he was introduced to the faction supporting a modern classicism based on the Beaux-Arts conception of architecture as an evolution of building types. Labatut met Kahn in 1928, with whom he remained friendly for life and later invited to teach at Princeton. He also met George Howe (1886–1955), who had studied with Laloux between 1908 and 1912 and had attempted to modernize Beaux-Arts aesthetics. Howe had strained to theorize his early romantic country estates for Wall Street elites as a functionalist architecture, where functionalism was understood as an "imaginative interpretation of use" that stressed psychological and historical associations.[19] By the time Labatut arrived on the scene, Howe was making a move away from Beaux-Arts aesthetics with his Philadelphia Savings Fund Society tower (1929–33, in collaboration with William Lescaze), which was celebrated as the first international style skyscraper in America.[20] Yet another alumnus of Laloux's atelier, William Van Allen (1888–1954), embraced the more iconographic style moderne (later known as art deco) in his Chrysler Building (1928–30). In 1929, Raymond Hood (1881–1934), also a Beaux-Arts alumnus and architect of the Chicago Tribune Building (1922), offered Labatut the chance to exhibit his work at the prestigious Architectural League of New York, which he presided over. Unfortunately for Labatut, the Dow Jones Industrial Average dropped 50 percent a month before the show, unleashing the Great Depression. Commissions did not materialize.

Labatut's teaching job sheltered him from economic hardship and gave him access to a separate social network through which he slowly began to secure professional work. Stephen F. Voorhees (1878–1965), Princeton's supervising architect, offered him the commission to design the university's monument to Woodrow Wilson.[21] Voorhees was a prominent New York architect whose firm,

Meeting of the New York World's Fair design team, ca. 1937. Left to right: J. Hartman, J. Labatut, S. Downe, S. Clarke, R. H. Shreve, S. F. Voorhees, unidentified, W. Teegree, R. Kohn, W. Lamb, unidentified. Courtesy of Princeton University Library, Jean Labatut Papers, Manuscripts Division, Department of Rare Books and Special Collections.

Voorhees, Gmelin and Walker, designed countless buildings for utility companies, such as the stepped-back Barclay-Vesey skyscraper (New York, 1923) that graced the cover of the English edition of Le Corbusier's *Towards a New Architecture.* He was also chairman of the Construction Code Authority under Franklin Roosevelt's National Recovery Administration and president of the American Institute of Architects (AIA). When New York began preparations for the 1939 World's Fair, Mayor Fiorello LaGuardia and Robert Moses selected him as design chairman. Voorhees involved representatives of the Beaux-Arts such as Cret, as well as fellow members of the Princeton faculty. Labatut joined his colleague Robert McLaughlin in a team with John C. B. Moore, Arthur C. Holden, and Stamo Papadaki to design the Home Building Center, a 30,700-square-foot structure, with a cost of $200,000, whose purpose was to showcase new home construction products. The challenge of the exhibit was to raise the public's interest in goods that were typically invisible, such as electrical wires or sewage pipes, to convey the financial and health benefits of quality, and to associate the sponsoring manufacturers with excellence.

The Home Building Center gave Labatut the opportunity to expand his interest in experience beyond vision to include the other senses. He learned the cutting edge in exhibition design methods for organizing the attention of visitors

**1939   NEW YORK WORLD'S FAIR
HOME BUILDING CENTER**

ESSAY ON AESTHETIC EXPRESSION
BASED ON NATURAL AND ARTIFICIAL
LIGHT, AND INTEGRATION OF DAY
AND NIGHT ILLUMINATION (A 24
HOUR ARCHITECTURE)

12 NOON
ILLUMINATION.......

TWILIGHT
ILLUMINATION.......

12 MIDNIGHT
ILLUMINATION.......

INTERIOR
ILLUMINATION.......

SOME DEVICES FOR DRAWING ATTENTION

*Periscopic Windows—Snow Man on the Fire—Mystery—A
Fountain Map—Mechanical Signs*

A large model house, its interior open to view, was set in a pit and tilted
so that the inside could be more readily seen. Simple as this appears, it
emphasized the invitation to look, like tilting an open box for inspection.

*FACING PAGE: Exhibition board by Jean Labatut showing the changing appearance of the Home
Building Center under different lighting conditions over a twenty-four-hour cycle at the 1939 New
York World's Fair. Courtesy of Princeton University Library, Jean Labatut Papers, Manuscripts
Division, Department of Rare Books and Special Collections.*

*ABOVE: Commercial exhibition devices for drawing attention used at the Home Building Center,
1939 New York World's Fair. From* Exhibition Techniques: A Summary of Exhibition Practice
(New York: New York Museum of Science and Industry, 1940).

around a space. He learned techniques for managing visual, tactile, and acoustic
stimuli and orchestrating them to attract and sustain the interest of distracted
visitors.[22] The designers found that people paid attention when their normal
spatial references were changed. For instance, a stair with unusual tread heights
made people consciously focus on the floor. The designers also found that
slightly inclining the floor and walls attracted interest but sometimes produced
nausea. To achieve the same effect without the risk of injuries, they built large
models of houses and tilted them so that people could look into them. They
also found that visitors were more likely to read an advertisement or evaluate a
product if they could touch it. So they created signs that could be spun on hinges
and installed materials that invited contact. Finally, they learned that people en-
joyed the thrill of exploring spaces that were typically forbidden or inaccessible.

In response, they designed the Home Building Center with large transparent sections to make visible the array of pipes, electrical wiring, steel beams under floors, and insulation materials that are usually hidden from view. Labatut began encouraging the use of these techniques in his students' projects, and they later became staples of his own buildings.

Labatut recognized that the design principles generated to attract and hold attention had larger applications beyond the fair grounds. This research, he thought, could be the basis for a truly modern architecture based on using movement and artificial lighting to generate extraordinary new visual, tactile, and acoustic experiences. But he faced an important hurdle: these principles were considered to be the province of crude commercialism and unworthy of the academy and high architecture. This marginality was, of course, also what made them avant-gardist. And in the logic of avant-gardism, the challenge was to compel the establishment to recognize the value of what is external to it. In this sense, the Home Building Center was a perfect disaster. It was totally ignored by high culture architecture critics and was seriously studied only by industrial and exhibition designers for purposes of reference manuals.[23]

Labatut's intrepidness led him so far out of the modern architectural mainstream as to make his avant-gardist ambitions seem perfectly irrelevant. The overt association of the Home Building Center with business was incompatible with the mantle of financial disinterestedness that lends the aura of authenticity to all architectural avant-gardes. Labatut's keen awareness of this led him to renounce the economic rewards of professional practice and to accept commissions that would allow him the freedom to experiment and pursue modern architectural expressions in their purest forms.

Hypnotic Movement

His first exemplary act of avant-gardist renunciation happened at the fair, when he accepted the commission that most architects ignored: to design the Lagoon of Nations. The commission was tiny by comparison to any pavilion, and most architects felt there was no architecture to design. Basset Jones, lighting consultant to the fair's Board of Design, had already spent two years working out his designs. Before the commission was open to architects, the fountain had been completely designed by a group of engineers including John G. Lawrence, superintendent in charge of production, Howard Cooper, a hydraulics expert who had worked on the Bonneville Dam, T. F. Bludworth, sound engineer, and Richard

Bird's-eye view of Jean Labatut's Lagoon of Nations at the 1939 New York World's Fair, showing the location of the water jets as well as the drums for the gas and fireworks. Courtesy of Princeton University Library, Jean Labatut Papers, Manuscripts Division, Department of Rare Books and Special Collections.

Engelken in charge of lighting. The only thing left to design was the choreography of water, electric light, fire, and music. Without many takers, Voorhees offered the commission to design the fountain spectacles to Labatut, who accepted it enthusiastically as an opportunity to experiment with what he considered to be the essence of modern architecture: the visual expression of movement.

With this commission, Labatut wanted to make the polemical statement that architecture was not defined by style, materials, or even construction techniques, but rather by its ability to control and modulate the perception of movement. Unfortunately for him, his project was not deemed immediately pertinent to the contemporary debates on modern architecture. At first, architectural critics chose to focus on the fair's role in promoting international style modernism and cementing its association with industry (especially automobile manufacturers). But five years later, Giedion recognized Labatut's fountain spectacles as a key contribution to the experiential search for an "Ephemeral Architecture," capable of retraining the basic human emotional need for communal symbols away from historic buildings and toward new abstract forms:

> These spectacles form one of the rare events where our modern possibilities are consciously applied by architect-artists. They use the structural values of different materials as a medium to intensify the emotional expression, just as the cubists like to introduce sand, fragments of wood, or scraps of paper in their paintings. In this case, the architect made use of different "structural" values: incandescent and mercury light, gas flames, colored by chemicals, fireworks, smoke, water-jets, painted on the night sky and synchronized with music.[24]

Giedion thought Labatut's fountain spectacles should be taken as the starting point for a "new monumentality," which remained abstract while satisfying people's needs for symbolic public structures. He asked that Labatut's work be taken seriously as architecture, and not thought of as an amusement: "those who govern must know that spectacles, which will lead people back to a neglected community life, must be reincorporated into civic centers . . . not haphazard world's fairs."

Despite Giedion's endorsement, Labatut's fountain spectacles were not understood as central to the future development of modernism in America. Among the buildings at the fair, that distinction has gone to Norman Bel Geddes's (1893–1958) General Motors Pavilion.[25] In reality, its Futurama ride was a side show compared to Labatut's spectacles. The son-et-lumière fountain shows at the

Lagoon of Nations, performed every night at dusk, consistently drew the largest crowds. At sunset, all eyes in Flushing Meadows turned to the Lagoon of Nations. "For an hour beforehand," wrote a journalist, "the crowd begins to assemble around the rail, and by the time it is dark, and powerful search lights from nearby buildings form an apron above the lagoon, throngs are standing far back in the Court of Peace and are lining Constitution Mall halfway back to the blue-lit Perisphere."[26] It was a defining moment in Labatut's career. He later recalled, "That World's Fair business was the most stimulating thing"— a unique opportunity to assert his view of modern architecture.[27]

Labatut regarded the Lagoon as an awesome "instrument" for stimulating, concentrating, intensifying, and modulating the experience of movement, or the very essence of modern architecture. The instrument in question was a large basin, 400 feet wide and 800 feet long, at the eastern end of Constitution Mall, the fair's central axis. It comprised 1,400 water nozzles, 11 pumps capable of generating 2,700 horsepower and pumping 100,000 gallons per minute, 133 gas jets connected to chemical pumps to color the flames, 600 underwater lighting drums containing 1,500-watt incandescent lamps (for warm colors) and 400-watt mercury lamps (for cool hues), 300 fireworks mortars, 24 loudspeakers, and 113 men (technicians and workmen). The instrument literally networked together the fair grounds. The control room from which the operation was managed was atop the Romanian Pavilion. Fresh water was sucked out of a spring under Fountain Lake by pumps housed in a glass-enclosed rotunda in the Hall of Nations. By day, the architectural character of the fair was dominated by international style modernism. But every night, when the lights went on at the Lagoon of Nations, Labatut imposed his aesthetics.

For each fountain performance, Labatut began by making a series of twenty to sixty drawings with the main arrangement of the water jets, colored lights, and fireworks for each composition. He visualized them as snapshots in a sequence, much like views of rooms that a visitor might see while walking through a building. Were these to have been turned into a conventional architectural design, Labatut would have drawn a plan in the manner of the Beaux-Arts to string these views together in a promenade, changing the relative scale of

OVERLEAF: The control room for the spectacles of the Lagoon of Nations was perched atop the Romanian Pavilion. Technicians looked down on the Lagoon, managing the sequence of water jets, lights, gas, and fireworks in sync with the music. Photograph by Jean Labatut. Courtesy of Princeton University Library, Jean Labatut Papers, Manuscripts Division, Department of Rare Books and Special Collections.

rooms to modulate the time it would take a person to move through them.[28] The problem was that, unlike the experience of a building, the fountain spectacles required viewers to be fixed. Could the fountain produce the *experience* of movement in static spectators?

Here we must be careful not to draw an analogy with film too hastily. Labatut drew his frames with an awareness that he was working with a medium that was physically and conceptually different from film. At best, the fountain displayed one "frame" every thirty seconds. The mechanical limitations of the water pumps introduced a fatal delay between one configuration of jets and the next, which compromised the visual experience of a moving sequence. More importantly, Labatut, as a student of Bergson, was aware of the notion that the filmic experience of movement could be thought of as falsification of "real" motion.

In *Creative Evolution* (1907), Bergson described the "cinematographic illusion" as the failure of rational science to properly account for movement. When cinema attempts to reconstitute movement by stringing images together according to the mechanical projector's "absolute time" of twenty four frames per second, it is only repeating, with contemporary means, an ancient pitfall of classical philosophy, as encapsulated in Zeno's paradox of motion. Zeno mathematically proved that fast-footed Achilles could not overcome a turtle inching forward just ahead of him because he had to first reach the point where the animal started, by which point it would have already moved ahead. The problem, argued Bergson, was that mathematics could only explain movement as the sum of homogeneous quantities, be they celluloid frames or points in space. To explain the act of movement, it tried to reconstruct what took place between points in space as more and more points. The paradox was that, according to this model, Achilles got stuck in an ever-expanding infinity of midpoints between him and the turtle. To solve the paradox, Bergson wrote, required a fuller description of reality than mathematics could provide. Mathematics dealt only with quantity. It had to reduce movement to discrete homogeneous points in space that it could measure. But movement also had qualities. It could range from graceful to clumsy, or flowing to choppy. Mathematics ignored the succession of qualities because they could not be measured. They had to be experienced in real time by a living

FACING PAGE: Labatut's experiential notation for the spectacle "The World and the Cathedral," showing the relative intensity of gas, fireworks, lights, and water jets over fifteen-minutes' time. Technicians in the control booth read this document like a musical score to manage the effect of each of the spectacles. Courtesy of Princeton University Library, Jean Labatut Papers, Manuscripts Division, Department of Rare Books and Special Collections.

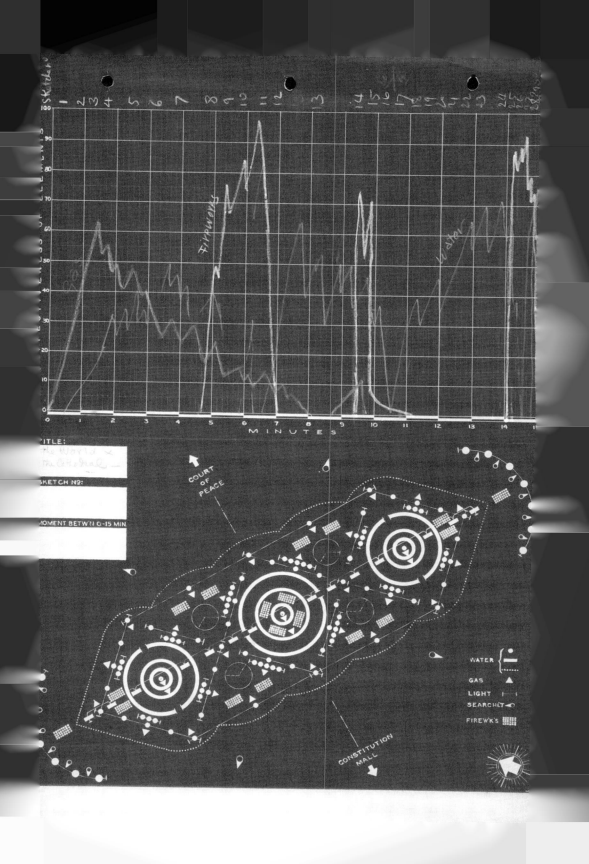

person. Mathematics could not grasp real time. It reduced the heterogeneity of lived time to the homogeneity of space. "Fake" time was a series of discrete measurable instants strung in a line without touching each other—a copy of space. Thus, mathematics brought time back to Zeno's paradox, unable to explain how we move from one instant to the next.[29] In sum, Bergson thought that mathematics missed movement twice, at the level of time and of space. It could not distinguish between the time or "the space traversed and the act by which we traverse it, the successive positions and the synthesis of these positions."[30]

To solve Zeno's paradox, Bergson claimed that philosophy had to stop trying to describe reality with the model of reflective consciousness, which subordinated immeasurable qualities to measurable quantities, and instead philosophers had to attempt to describe it from the standpoint of experience. Zeno's paradox was evidence that space, because it could be thought to contain the multiplicity of points in a movement, was a fake synthesis of particulars. For Bergson, experience was the real synthesis that allowed us to immediately understand or intuit the unity of time and movement as a succession of qualitative changes that melt into and permeate one another while remaining distinct. Bergson explained that science was ill-equipped to describe the "pure heterogeneity" of experience and therefore "cannot deal with time and motion except on condition of first eliminating the essential and qualitative element—of time, duration, and of motion, mobility."[31]

Now it is important to note that music, the nineteenth century's high cultural standard for abstract art, was Bergson's preferred analogy to describe the experience of duration, which was, he explained, like "the notes of a tune, melting, so to speak, into one another."[32] But more importantly for Labatut's purposes, Bergson also used music to describe mobility as a sequence of mental states independent of actual physical movement. Music illustrated how time and movement were uncoupled from causality. Like the interrelation of moments or movements to each other, the relationship between the notes in a composition is qualitative, not quantitative. "The proof is that, if we interrupt the rhythm by dwelling longer than is right on one note of the tune, it is not its exaggerated length, as length, which will warn us of our mistake, but the qualitative change thereby caused in the whole of the musical phrase."[33] Music easily illustrated

FACING PAGE: Labatut's sequence of pastel sketches on black cardboard describing the visual movement of "The World and the Cathedral" fountain spectacle. He used as many as sixty sketches for each spectacle. Courtesy of Princeton University Library, Jean Labatut Papers, Manuscripts Division, Department of Rare Books and Special Collections.

Lagoon of nations   some sketches of "the world & the Cathedral"

the idea that an aesthetic experience is a succession of qualities that are indistinguishable from one another. Yet, in order to experience time or movement as this simultaneous succession, qualities had to vary in spite of being mutually indistinguishable. Bergson held that experienced qualities varied in intensity, unlike abstract quantities which varied in extension. He warned against expressing duration in terms of quantifiable extensity. He was opposed to borrowing the image of space to describe time and movement. He thought it tricked one into the "cinematic illusion" of mistaking qualitative progress, which is given simultaneously when an aesthetic experience varies in intensity, for a succession of discrete units in a line.[34] The "cinematic illusion" falsely interpreted qualitative progress as a change of magnitude and attempted to understand duration through the inadequate model of homogeneous space.

Bergson defended art over nature on the grounds that it allowed humans to experience the full range of qualitative variations, from the highest to the lowest reaches, of aesthetic intensity. Art, he argued, accomplished this by focusing our attention on a single quality. Here Bergson touched on a set of themes that were of utmost interest to contemporary Western artists of the early twentieth century, and that were especially important to Labatut. First, the idea of art as defined by its exploration of a single aesthetic quality was the linchpin of avant-gardist discourse about abstraction. It was the foundation of the impressionist defense of painting as the exploration of the perception of color, and the Puteaux group's definition of architecture as the visual expression of movement. Second, the idea that art was defined by its ability to sustain attention was the foundation for the discursive fashioning of avant-garde art as a healing therapy capable of resynthesizing the "fragmentation" of the object. This second point was at the crux of the arguments for the importance of art over science, and styling over mechanics, that defined the New York World's Fair. Indeed, the logic that cast art primarily in terms of its ability to hold attention served to put it at the service of consumer culture.

The spectator's attention was precisely Labatut's problem at the Lagoon of Nations. The slow transitions between the particular fountain formations made it hard to grasp their succession as a synthetic whole. In a traditional building, the changing qualities of the viewer's mobility provided this unity. But how could the fountain suggest the experience of mobility to a static viewer? Bergson provided the answer: by changing configurations according to a *rhythm*. The measure and pulse of rhythm "suspend the normal flow of our sensations and ideas by causing our attention to swing to and fro between fixed points,"[35] inducing a hypnotic trance that successfully held the audience captive and captivated. Rhythm

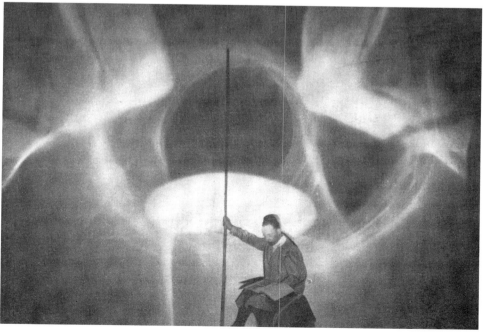

which drew visual artists and musicians from both sides of the Atlantic. Some, like American Thomas Wilfred, continued to perform with their color organs well into the 1940s. Mobile color art furthered the impressionist avant-garde's attempt to liberate color from figuration by associating it with music, which was the high cultural standard for nonrepresentational art. Similarly, Labatut used music to uncouple the experience of mobility from physical movement. This was an important achievement for the field of architecture, which was involved in the seemingly impossible goal of suggesting the experience of movement through immobile constructions.

Labatut's notion of modern architecture linked the question of abstraction to the emerging American discourse on the importance of commercial mass visual culture. Harvey Wiley Corbett (1873–1954), a renowned architect, argued that architects, like industrial designers, should provide aesthetic means for consumers to identify with commodities. Corbett applauded Hood's American Radiator Building, which evoked the glowing cinders of a stove with the nightly glow of its crowning tower.[42] This push toward symbolic literalness had to be negotiated against the premise that modern architecture should strive toward abstraction. American architects felt that the symbolic should not be dispensed with altogether. Apart from commercial pressures, they were also responding to recent changes in the field of art history, where iconography was gaining traction over connoisseurship as a historiographical method, largely through the work of Charles Rufus Morey (1877–1955) and Erwin Panofsky (1892–1968), Labatut's colleagues at Princeton.[43] Labatut's fountain shows satisfied the iconographer's requirement that architecture should tell a story without lapsing into literalness. The musical themes of the shows gave the audience clues for interpreting the narrative function of the jets of water. For instance, critics praised how convincingly the enormous ten-story jet represented the self-assured and commanding "Spirit of George Washington."[44]

In addition to its clever synthesis of the discourses on movement, attention, and abstraction in architecture, the Lagoon of Nations deployed the avant-gardist principle of economic disinterestedness far more efficiently than any other project at the fair. Unlike other attractions, the shows were free. The Fair Corporation touted the Lagoon of Nations as its "biggest gift" to visitors, representing a $1,500,000 investment that cost $1,500 a night to operate.[45] The Lagoon of Nations became the emblem of civic pride free from the commercialism and politics associated with corporate and national pavilions. It was a distinctive space in a fair physically planned in terms of industries, such as housing, agriculture, and transportation. For Labatut, the Lagoon of Nations was the template for a new type of monumental architecture, free from politics and commerce, and geared toward the spiritual enrichment of the people. It was a project "composed at a scale commensurate with an unlimited number of spectators under a ceiling defined by searchlights,"[46] extolled Labatut. "These fountain spectacles were the expression of a wedding of monumental architecture with monumental music, with monumental numbers of spectators attending the ceremony."[47] The Lagoon of Nations was Labatut's answer to the work of Albert Speer (1905–1981) at the Nuremberg Nazi party congress (1933), which was widely published in American architecture journals. As both countries explored the relationship between architecture and mass visual culture, Labatut came down strongly against the univocal dimension of politicized art, searching instead for more apolitical, spiritually uplifting, but still hypnotic architecture.

Labatut's work redrew the outlines of the modern movement in architecture. He was obsessed with making modern architecture into the art of shaping experiences of mobility through sensual means. Like all avant-gardists, he restricted architecture's vocabulary to call attention to it and to sever his aesthetics from the heterogeneity of the larger field. The Lagoon of Nations was an attack on the fair's association of modern architecture with the international style. Its immaterial architecture beat the international style at its own game of abstraction. Labatut's heretical return to the roots of modern architecture in the idea of movement suggested an abstract experience of movement to an immobile audience without recourse to figurative copies of ships, cars, or streamlined trains. Building on the avant-gardist reputation of mobile color art, Labatut cast his architecture as a relentless pursuit of open-ended abstractness, of purity in the aesthetic experience of movement, and of hypnotic deployment of materials—concepts that would become foundational for architectural phenomenology.

The idea of movement as a quality experienced internally, in the depths of the body and mind, without necessarily having to move physically, led Labatut down a profound spiritual path. His interests in camouflage, commercial advertising techniques, and philosophy had informed a modern architecture that could suggest the feeling of movement. But as he reached middle age, his attention turned to the pursuit of architecture that could move the soul. This turn coincided with Labatut's religious awakening and the reaffirmation of his Catholic faith, largely through the intercession of Jacques Maritain, the foremost philosopher of the Catholic church in the decades leading up to the Second Vatican Council (1962–1965).

The Angelic Doctor

Labatut met Maritain at Princeton in 1941, where the philosopher, caught in America since the fall of his native France to the Nazis, was serving as a visiting professor. Labatut was eager to build connections to other departments to assist him in the effort to raise the scholarly standards of the architecture school. He was responding to the founding of the National Architectural Accrediting Board (NAAB) a year earlier, which created a competition among architecture schools to raise the quality of their curricula by developing national standards. This raised the question of what specific type of knowledge architecture schools contributed to the university at large. With the war effort's demands on industry, the pressure was to fashion architectural knowledge as purely scientific, by focusing its ability to advance the industrialization of building technology. The idea had been in circulation since World War I, when it gained legitimacy under the political rubric of "industrial democracy" and the tangible advances made in prefabricated residential construction by firms including Grosvenor Atterbury at Forest Hills (New York, 1912) and Graham, Anderson, Probst & White at Nitro (West Virginia, 1918). But Labatut resisted this reduction of architectural knowledge to cut-and-dried science. Indeed, Princeton's architecture school prided itself in providing a well-rounded education in liberal studies, approaching the profession primarily as an art, and opposing the idea of building construction as an end in itself.[48]

Labatut had a very specific idea that the "art" in architecture was that of manipulating experience, something that, as camouflage demonstrated, was just as critical to the war as any science. He thought Maritain could help him articulate the idea that architecture offered important insights about the nature of movement that were relevant to the university at large. After all, Maritain had achieved international fame with his *Distinguer pour unir, ou les degrés du savoir* (1932; *The Degrees of Knowledge,* 1937), which argued that science is only one among many legitimate ways of knowing reality, including philosophy, art, poetry, and mysticism. Maritain and Labatut began a dialogue that evolved into a lifelong friendship and a profound spiritual bond.

Jacques Maritain (left) and Jean Labatut in conversation at Princeton University, ca. 1941. Courtesy of Princeton University Library, Jean Labatut Papers, Manuscripts Division, Department of Rare Books and Special Collections.

Their common interest in Bergson created the initial affinity and revealed the shared cultural references of their generation of Frenchmen.[49] But contrary to Labatut, Maritain had turned to Bergson not out of love but out of frustration with modernity. For him, the modern experience was driven by "meaningless" rationalism, materialism, and consumerism. Maritain found the modern world so pointless that he signed a suicide pact with his wife Raïssa, only to break it upon attending Bergson's lectures. Bergson's notion of "intuition" suggested a way to gain concrete knowledge of the world as an interconnected whole through sensible experience, in contrast with the abstract knowledge gained from scientific observation.

As Jonathan Crary noted, Bergson's philosophy was part of a wider cultural reaction against what he describes as the "uprooting of perception" from the human body.[50] Crary documents the nineteenth-century emergence of an awareness that perception was not at all "natural" but was rather systematically constructed through technical, artistic, and discursive apparatuses. For instance, vision was decoupled from empirical verisimilitude by chronophotography. The 1878 motion studies of horses by Eadweard Muybridge (1830–1904) were for Crary a "blunt dismantling of the apparent continuities of movement and of time."[51] Crary unambiguously established a common element in the disparate discourses of Bergson's intuitionism, pragmatism, Gestalt theory, and phenomenology: they were all defenses of the unity and primacy of the subject against the atomizing accounts of perception offered by psychophysics, behaviorism, biologism, and reflexology. The awareness that reality was constructed by forces external to the subject prompted these calls to "return to the roots"—to an unmediated experience of reality, or as phenomenologists put it, "back to the things themselves."

The search for an undistorted experience of reality is a well-known recurring theme of nineteenth- and twentieth-century philosophy, architecture, and art. The contribution of theology to these debates is less familiar to architecture scholars, although it set in motion the spiritualization of architectural education. It was precisely through Catholic theology that Maritain developed the notion of "critical realism" that made him famous. In his search for meaningful existence, Maritain was swept up in the Catholic church's response to Cartesian rationalism, the proverbial foundation of modern thought, which it blamed for modern society's scientific detachment from reality and for being the source of its existential pointlessness. Crowned Pope in 1878, Leo XIII issued an edict proclaiming Thomism, a conveniently pre-Cartesian and thus premodern philosophy, the official orthodox system of thought for the Roman Catholic church. Maritain was so transformed by his reading of St. Thomas Aquinas (1225?–1274) that he converted from Protestantism to Catholicism in 1906.

Neo-Thomists sought paternity in this medieval philosophical system in part to counter what they viewed as the modern secularization of the world. They complained that Descartes took the soul out of reality when he founded modern philosophy on the basis of skepticism about the unity of mind and body. At the outset of his career, Maritain caused a scandal by attacking the Cartesian view of reality in *Trois réformateurs* (1925; *Three Reformers: Luther, Descartes, Rousseau*, 1955). Maritain made the startling accusation that Cartesian rationalism was irrational.[52] Descartes ignored external reality and turned to the mind as the ultimate source of authority. For Maritain, this meant that the Cartesian mind, by claiming that thought and reality are nonidentical, and by admitting only that thinking is determined by thought itself, ultimately was a mind that could not (or would not) learn anything from reality. Without a way to go beyond thought to the real, the modern mind could treat the real only as something to dominate and exploit, as it attempted to reshape the natural world according to mathematical formulas. The task of returning existential meaning to the world required, according to Maritain, the philosophical recovery of the unity, or identity, of body and soul upheld in Thomism.

The thesis of Maritain's critical realism was that there exists on the intellectual level a philosophically expressible nexus of thought with reality. He defined this nexus as being. The further the mind strays from this center, the more unreal and irrational it becomes. "Realism," after all, is the claim that our basic concepts are valid for a non-mind-dependent world. How to keep the mind from straying beyond reality? By getting to know being. Maritain defined this act of returning the attention of the mind toward being as the critical dimension of his realism. He was quick to differentiate his notion of critique from that of Kant and later idealists who conceived of criticism as a purely mental a priori capacity of thought to regulate itself and to rein itself back to reason when it went astray. He also strongly separated critical realism from German phenomenology, which he considered as repeating and aggravating the flaws of idealism. He thought that Husserl and Heidegger, like the idealists, stopped their ontological investigations when they arrived at a mental object. But in their case this object was not the idealist's mental product of synthesizing particulars. Instead phenomenologists fabricated a specious (or philosophically naïve) third realm, neither internal nor external to the mind, which they called an essence. "But this object-essence remains for them, like for Kant and for the entire modern tradition, separated from the trans-objective subject or the extra-mental thing."[53]

Maritain was interesting to Labatut because he claimed that there were many nonphilosophical ways of knowing being. Here was a philosopher who thought that philosophy did not have a monopoly on Truth! Since being was not reducible to thought, argued Maritain, one should be able to attain a direct knowledge of it without necessarily using rational thought and inference. In other words, the *intuition* of being preceded rational cognition and was the real origin to which the mind had to be constantly returned through critical realism. "There are diverse ways and paths leading towards the attainment of this intuition . . . What counts is to take the leap, to release, in one authentic intellectual intuition, the sense of being, the sense of the value of the implications that lie in the act of existing."[54] Maritain believed that philosophers exercised critical realism through *conceptual* means. But the mind could also intuit being through *nonconceptual* or "poetic" means such as poetry, mysticism, art, and even architecture. In terms reminiscent of Bergson's "hypnotic" musical analogy, Maritain described the poetic content of art and architecture as a "little shock" that stills the mind and clears it to receive the intuition of being: "Poetry in this sense is clearly not the privilege of poets." One could find poetry everywhere—in a "paste-board model," the "booths of a fair," even in "sign-boards."[55]

Maritain wrote these words in 1943, after many conversations with Labatut. Was he alluding directly to the architect's work? Most probably so. Paste-board models, fair spectacles, and sign-boards were precisely the instruments through which Labatut was working out his modern architecture. Labatut involved Maritain in discussions about the new Bureau of Urban Research, which he founded in 1941 to coordinate research, data, and ethical positions on the built environment across the disciplines of architecture, economics, sociology, engineering, politics, and philosophy.[56] Labatut's interest in managing the experience of mobility in modern society led him to promote ground-breaking research on highways.[57] The work of the bureau became the reference for understanding the impact of sign-boards, night illumination, and scenic vistas on the attention of mobile observers, who were too often dangerously distracted behind the wheel. These studies of what in the thirties was called "ribbon development" became the basis for later research on "strip development," as it came to be known in the sixties. Labatut's work on signage later flourished in his students' work, for instance in Venturi's analysis of the decorated sheds on the Las Vegas Strip and in Moore's supergraphics. Labatut created the bureau to establish architecture's unique contribution to the university at large. Through his dialogues with Maritain, he became increasingly convinced that architecture was a unique way to know reality by intuiting it poetically. Furthermore, architecture, as a sign-board or medium of mass visual communication, could induce critical realism on a national scale.

If sign-boards were discovered as poetic architectural devices at the bureau, Labatut revealed the poetic potential of paste-board models in the camouflage course he taught between 1941 and 1943. As a method, camouflage gave scientific standing to architectural design within the university. In terms of architectural pedagogy, it brought architectural design closer to the visual arts. Camoufleurs worked directly on objects, like sculptors or painters, making adjustments to their designs on the field by trial and error, often without working drawings. To teach camouflage to architecture students, Labatut adapted the design methods of World War I ship camoufleurs. The size of ships, like that of buildings, made full-scale trial-and-error interventions financially prohibitive. So ship camoufleurs built small replicas and placed them in theaters that reproduced the changing environmental and lighting conditions found at sea. They observed the replicas through submarine periscopes and tested their designs for efficacy.[58] Instead of a theater, Labatut used Princeton's Palmer Stadium to test camouflage designs for military facilities. From the topmost tier of seats, the scaled models of air fields, gun emplacements, and factory buildings on the floor of the stadium appeared as they would from an airplane at 80,000 feet.[59]

Labatut's experiments yielded more than just ingenious techniques for concealing buildings. The principal lesson of camouflage and advertising was that aesthetics was a means to an end and not an end in itself. Its fundamental premise was to undermine expectations. As a process aimed at undercutting academic notions of style and design conventions, camouflage was a perfect pedagogical tool for modern architecture, which fed on the ideology of constant innovation. Camouflage allowed Labatut to break the conventions of modernist pedagogy too, by establishing the possibility of paperless architectural design.

Since his early days at Princeton, Labatut had argued that architectural design was not "making pictures on paper."[60] Through his contact with Maritain, he became increasingly interested in paperless design as a method to bring his students back to reality. In 1950, Labatut took this idea to its logical conclusion by founding the Princeton Architectural Laboratory, a large industrial shed where students built full-scale sections of buildings, lifted them and rotated them with special machinery, moved around them, and explored how changing environmental conditions altered their appearance. It was, in essence, an enlarged version of the ship camoufleur's theater.

Poetic Symbolism

When he saw the architectural laboratory, Maritain immediately envisioned its theological potential. He challenged Labatut to design the prototypical Catholic church of the future. Labatut complied with his model Church of the Four

Evangelists. Maritain had just returned to teach at Princeton in 1948, after serving three years as French ambassador to the Vatican during the controversial papacy of Pope Pius XII (1939–58), where he witnessed the enormous internal and external pressure to modernize the church.[61] There were rumblings that the liturgical rites would be brought up to date, and this suggested profound changes in church architecture. Labatut recognized that through Maritain's connections to the Catholic hierarchy, he had a unique opportunity to influence church building across the world.

The church's embrace of modernism in the early postwar era was met by a hesitant profession, which after so many years of preaching abstraction was doubtful it could meet Catholic demands for symbolism. Giedion captured the essence of this anxiety when he reproached modern architects for lacking an architectural imagination capable of satisfying society's need for shared social symbols of monumentality.[62] Modern architects' insistence on abstract forms and their reluctance to accede to iconography reached such a crisis level that Pope Pius XII had to step in to stem the tide of abstractionism. His famous encyclical *Mediator Dei* (1947) warned modernists not to be "deceived by the illusion of a higher mysticism" in abstraction and by artistic claims that nonfigurative spaces brought Christ closer to the people. "Some have gone so far as to want to remove from the churches images of the divine Redeemer suffering on the cross." This was unacceptable. "In order that we may be helped by our senses, also, the Church wishes that images of the saints be displayed in our churches."[63] Figurative symbols, modern or otherwise, were indispensable for elevating worship to the experience of the divine unity of the spiritual and the material. They were the aesthetic equivalent of Maritain's critical realism, whose goal was to guide philosophy back to reality understood as the nexus of body and soul.

The social antagonism underlying the tension between abstraction (advocated by high culture) and symbolism (demanded by popular taste) was quickly detected by the American clergy. Father Hans Anscar Reinhold, pastor of St. Joseph's Church in Washington, a tireless Catholic advocate of modernism

ABOVE: Model by Jean Labatut for the prototypical Church of the Four Evangelists, photographed against Princeton University's Palmer Stadium in the distant background. From the exterior, the large graphics on the glass walls were meant to attract the attention of car drivers like enormous advertisements. Photograph by Jean Labatut, ca. 1951. Courtesy of Princeton University Library, Jean Labatut Papers, Manuscripts Division, Department of Rare Books and Special Collections.

OVERLEAF: Jean Labatut (left) with students at the Architectural Laboratory studying lighting conditions on a large partial model of the Church of the Four Evangelists, ca. 1951. Courtesy of Princeton University Library, Jean Labatut Papers, Manuscripts Division, Department of Rare Books and Special Collections.

and the primary liturgical interpreter of church architecture, boiled down the message of *Mediator Dei:* "To hit the right middle between highbrow, élite, and popular art is the greatest of all problems."[64] *Architectural Forum* ran special features on modern churches as examples of this proverbial middle ground.[65] These debates about the social issues raised by the aesthetics of church building mirrored contemporaneous discussions about the aesthetics of commercial architecture. For instance, the desire of modernist factions like the Independent Group to connect high art and low commercial aesthetics reflected the aspirations of the rising postwar Western middle class.[66]

Labatut thought he had a leg up on the race to find the right mix between abstraction and symbolism. His previous design commissions had made major strides in this direction. In particular, the Lagoon of Nations combined the purest mobile color art with various symbolic narratives, ranging from stories of national pride (the "Spirit of George Washington" show) to religiosity

(the "Garden of Eden" show). For Labatut, the search for a middle ground between high and low culture was at the core of the modernist project to develop a universal language of architecture. He was determined to further this endeavor with his prototypical Church of the Four Evangelists:

> The church, like the fountains, is another example of how the visual arts can contribute to universal language; a universal visual language which permits an enrichment of mind and spirit and leads to better understanding of other peoples in other times, as well as other peoples in our times.[67]

ABOVE: Labatut's suspended study model of the Church of the Four Evangelists under night illumination conditions, ca. 1951. Courtesy of Princeton University Library, Jean Labatut Papers, Manuscripts Division, Department of Rare Books and Special Collections.

OVERLEAF: Self-portrait by Jean Labatut against a full-scale study of André Girard's paintings for the Church of the Four Evangelists, ca. 1951. Labatut placed Girard's linen behind the glass of an existing building to simulate the desired reflectivity. Courtesy of Princeton University Library, Jean Labatut Papers, Manuscripts Division, Department of Rare Books and Special Collections.

FACING PAGE: Labatut's model for the Church of the Four Evangelists, showing how the sun would project shadows through the painted glass enclosure into the interior. Photograph by Jean Labatut, ca. 1951. Courtesy of Princeton University Library, Jean Labatut Papers, Manuscripts Division, Department of Rare Books and Special Collections.

RIGHT: Rudolf Schwarz, design for an ideal "Open Ring" church, 1938. The plan of Labatut's Church of the Four Evangelists was based on Schwarz's precedent. Courtesy of Princeton University Library, Jean Labatut Papers, Manuscripts Division, Department of Rare Books and Special Collections.

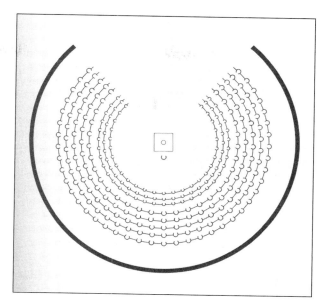

Labatut remained convinced that moving colored light was the best medium for suggesting the (now spiritualized) quality of mobility to the mind of a fixed (or transfixed) viewer. And intuiting inner mobility, or "feeling" the ascent and descent of the soul, was after all the liturgical and devotional mission of the arts, according to Pope Pius XII.[68] Labatut envisioned a church like a movie theater, with the congregation facing a large convex parabolic screen wall towering above the altar, onto which would be projected hypnotic beams of slow-moving lights, perpetually changing in color, hue, and intensity. "The convex parabolic wall will act as an inducement to movement, attraction of interest, and clarity of perception."[69] At the architectural laboratory, Labatut experimented with various methods for projecting colored light onto the screen. He finally settled for using the sun as a moving source of light and placing colored glass on the exterior envelope of the building. By carefully orienting the building toward the moving sun, rays of light would pierce the exterior colored glass and bathe the altar wall in emotive hues.

But the radical abstraction of mobile color art clearly did not satisfy the symbolic requirements of a church. So Labatut called upon André Girard, a French painter best known for his winning poster for the Exposition des Arts Décoratifs, who had developed a niche in painting religious murals for American churches after the success of his wall paintings in the French Pavilion at the 1939 New York World's Fair.[70] Together they came up with a brilliant solution to the tension between abstraction and figurative symbolism. Girard would paint his figurative murals directly on the exterior glass walls, adapting the medieval tradition of stained glass to contemporary technology. Labatut rhapsodized about how the glass mural's "property of transparency, refraction, or reflection and the mobility of light and of the beholder will offer the maximum variety within unity—a church architecture thoroughly alive and in our time."[71] While the exterior would thus satisfy the church's requirement for figuration, the visual effect projected on the interior would remain a composition of moving fields of pure color, which would fulfill the most stringent aesthetic demands of the avant-garde for abstraction. Here, Labatut thought, he had struck the right middle between popular and elite taste.

Labatut employed the lessons learned from his research on the American highway to push the "sign-board" presence of the church on the street. Girard's glass murals would be visible from the outside as well. At night, artificial interior illumination would make the murals glow. "This Church is an example of a truly twenty-four hour architecture," explained Labatut in a furtive allusion to its commercial inspiration. "Illumination by day and by night within and from outside has been considered."[72] After the skyscraper, argued Labatut, churches could no longer compete for height and needed to be conceived for the "mobile horizontal gaze" of the middle-class car driver. The enormous horizontal murals achieved the visual dominance of the built environment once reserved for vertical church spires. At night, artificial lighting in the church's interior served to back-light the glass murals, turning them into illuminated "sign-boards" toward the street.

Much to Labatut's dismay, there was a great deal of opposition among modernist architects to the use of "profane" commercial visual solutions to solve "sacred" architectural programs. Erich Mendelsohn (1887–1953) exemplified this proscription in his famous derision of "grotesque" churches in *Amerika* (1926). He illustrated the degeneration of American sacred architecture with a small church not unlike Labatut's prototype: Moody Church in Detroit, a nineteenth-century, single-story corner store rehabilitated into a church by the addition of two enormous billboards on top of the roof advertising the ministry of Pastor P. W. Philpott. Like Mendelsohn, the conservative elements of the German Catholic church issued a prophylactic "Directives for the Building of a Church" against the introduction of commercial aesthetics, which was circulated internationally: "It is not desirable that the church edifice...be located directly on a street filled with the noise of business and traffic . . . [It is] a mistake also to point out to the public the direction to the church by means of showy sign-boards along the way."[73] These restrictions were absurd to Labatut.

Yet, for all the talk about uniting high and low culture, the dissemination of Labatut's church prototype remained an elitist affair. Despite the design's derivation from commercial sources, no one dared make the comparison. Labatut's strategic association of his work with high abstract art and religion effectively cleansed it of its pedestrian provenance and elevated its cultural status. He was even able to mobilize the symbolic capital of America's elite art institutions when, in 1951, he exhibited the prototype at the Carstairs Gallery, a renowned venue where MoMA, the Smithsonian's Hirshhorn Museum for Modern Art, and other prestigious institutions regularly purchased contemporary art. Another important seal of authentication came from philosophy, penned by Maritain himself: "I would say that we are here in the presence of a great architectural and decorative conception, at once wholly traditional and wholly modern, which blazes new trails and furnishes us with an eminent—and practical—specimen of authentic sacred art."[74] The design's reception within both the New York modern art establishment and the Catholic press illustrates Labatut's skillful weaving together of visual art and philosophical discourses. And so we witness the instrumentality of this early version of "interdisciplinarity," deployed precisely to protect the autonomy of architecture, defined as the artistic freedom of the genius against the scrutiny of "science-biased" university administrators and the mounting pressures of an increasingly administered profession to abolish the figure of the architect-artist.

The Charismatic Body

Apart from the opposition between high and low culture, the conflict between figuration and abstraction also had a history internal to the discipline of art. Abstraction was synonymous with the destruction of the unity of form, the principle that held together figurative art. Given this fundamental difference, a true synthesis of the arts seemed impossible. Yet postwar architects and artists felt this synthesis was necessary to bring unity to a world that had been literally blown apart by war. By the mid- to late 1940s, publications like the popular *Journal of Aesthetics and Art Criticism* indicated an emerging consensus among critics that the right middle between abstraction and figuration was to make art that held together while changing appearance.[75]

Labatut's major contribution to the advancement of this new synthesis was to shift the terms of the debate from an argument about architectural expression to one about individual experience. In his Lagoon of Nations, what united the various configurations of water jets into a composition was the experience of the visitor, in whose mind the visual frames came together into sequences organized with the help of music. His prototypical church further emphasized the centrality of personal experience. The plan of the church showed an area of pews safely separating the figurative exterior glass murals from the abstract interior. The union of the two architectural expressions occurred in the mind of the sitting viewer, who, although stationary, could witness the sunlight transforming the figurative murals into abstract mobile color art, which appeared projected onto the screen above the altar.

Labatut's experiments in abstraction were at the leading edge of 1950s avant-garde art. Similar investigations included those of the Groupe Espace, founded in 1949, which promoted breaking abstract painting out from the canvas and into the urban environment.[76] Their idea was to unify the experience of the built world around the common principle of abstract forms. But Labatut's interest in abstract fields of color brought him closer to painters such as Ad Reinhardt (1913–1967), Yves Klein (1928–1962), Piero Manzoni (1933–1963), and Robert Rauschenberg (1925–2008), who began exploring monochrome compositions in the 1950s. Like Labatut, these painters explored how to concentrate the viewer's attention on subtle gradations of color. Rauschenberg's work is particularly interesting in this sense. His white paintings (1951) were meant to frame ambient fluctuations in light and shadow resulting from the projection of a viewer's fleeting silhouette onto the canvas. Viewers of these paintings became conscious of their viewing. The paintings functioned like mirrors, turning viewers' attention on themselves. As in Labatut's work, these paintings explored the idea that appearances were constantly changing and that what held art together was the viewer's experience.

The focus on individual experience recognized that eschewing figurative conventions did not free abstract art from the viewer's search for meaning. As Hal Foster has noted, the loss of a stable artistic object led postwar critics to reground the meaning of abstract art in the presumed unity of subjective experience (that of the viewer or the artist) or in the materiality of the work.[77] Symptomatically, these were the two categories that Maritain invoked when interpreting the meaning of Labatut's church. What was unique was that Maritain affirmed that these two categories were really one: the church achieved the "total unity" of the spiritual and the material through the "mutual adaptation of the architectural structure to the poetry of light and color."[78]

The idea that churches represent the unity of matter and spirit has a long history in Catholic theology. For instance, in the medieval tradition, Latin-cross churches were interpreted as the literal embodiment of Christ on the cross. This theory of embodiment was revived within modern architecture by modern architect Rudolf Schwarz (1897–1961), a German Catholic. His writings on church architecture were known in American Catholic circles since the 1930s. But in the late 1950s, the claim by Mies van der Rohe (also a Catholic) that Schwarz had been a major influence in his career made Schwarz's writings popular in the wider profession. Indeed, Schwarz was a point of reference for Labatut's work on the church prototype.

While Schwarz was also interested in architecture that made visitors self-conscious, he was more narrowly focused on making church visitors aware of their own bodies. Schwarz theorized the human body as the sanctified "gift" bestowed by God upon Catholic architects. For Schwarz, the body was the highest type of abstract art, for it retained "spiritual" unity as it underwent constant changes in appearance. "The soul," wrote Schwarz, "is wedded to the body far more intimately than was previously supposed."[79] The trouble, he thought, was that modern man thought of his body and his soul as two different things. This was, of course, Descartes' fault. By way of contrast, Schwarz described "premodern man" as someone who worshipped the body as "a work to be continually accomplished between God and the Soul."[80] Like Maritain, Schwartz was convinced that to save modernity, Catholics had to rediscover the body and the soul as two dimensions of the same thing. For Schwarz, this meant designing body-oriented architecture where visitors could experience their body as soulful.

The body, thought Schwarz, was an instrument to know one's soul. Thus, he advocated an architecture that provided a wide range of bodily experiences, from pleasure to pain, and likened the experience of such buildings to "sacred interpretation." This hermeneutics consisted of directing people's attention inward toward their bodies by restricting their positions, delimiting their movements, and organizing their stimulation into precise sequences. Schwarz believed that the body, as incarnated soul, was the real ground for all architecture:

> To build churches out of that reality which we experience and verify every day; to take this our own reality so seriously and to recognize it to be so holy that it may be able to enter in before God. To renew the old teachings concerning sacred work by trying to recognize the body, even as it is real to us today, as creature and revelation, and by trying to render it so; to reinstitute the body in its dignity and to do our work so well that this body may prove to be "sacred body." And beyond all this to guard ourselves against repeating the old words when for us no living content is connected with them.[81]

Labatut theorized that bodily actions and movements were the link between inner intention and outer architectural expression.[82] Labatut's church prototype was conceived, in line with Schwarz's thinking, as an organization of bodily experiences, that is to say, as an apparatus for the faithful to experience the incarnation of their soul in their bodies. This attention to the body was not unique to Catholicism and therefore permitted Catholic beliefs to seep into broader architectural practices. Labatut's students were able to move seamlessly from his teachings on bodily experience to designing buildings for what Alvin Toffler called the "experience economy," with its hedonistic attention to corporeal pleasure.[83] Such transfers inevitably involved repressing the Catholic "soul" (a taboo of secular modernism) and displacing the religious veneration of it onto the body, which was the acceptable reference of architectural humanism.

Transubstantiation

The opportunity to finally translate into built form the architectural ideas developed over a lifetime came to Labatut in 1961, when he was selected by the Catholic Society of the Sacred Heart to design a school in Princeton for 300 girls, including a convent for 30 teaching nuns.[84] The commission came to him through the recommendation of one of his students, who was boarding in the home of Peggy McNeil, one of the three women who spearheaded the effort to found the school.[85] It has been well documented that Labatut's design was informed by his travels to other existing schools in the Sacred Heart system.[86] What is less known is that the overarching architectural concept for the design was shaped by another voyage, this one through France, made in the company of Maritain in 1960. Labatut and Maritain visited French Catholic buildings in search of what they called a "Eucharistic" architecture.

The Eucharist, or Holy Communion, is the Catholic sacrament that commemorates the Last Supper, in which Christ took bread and told his disciples, "This is my body," then took wine and said, "This is my blood." Since the thirteenth century, Catholic theologians have used the term "transubstantiation" to refer to the process by which bread and wine became not a representation, but literally the real presence of Christ. By Eucharistic architecture, Labatut and Maritain meant buildings whose whole substance had been miraculously converted into the body and blood of Christ. They believed that in these buildings the body of Christ was offered for communion through sensual contacts with the body of visitors. Eucharistic architecture, echoing the theories of Schwarz, was

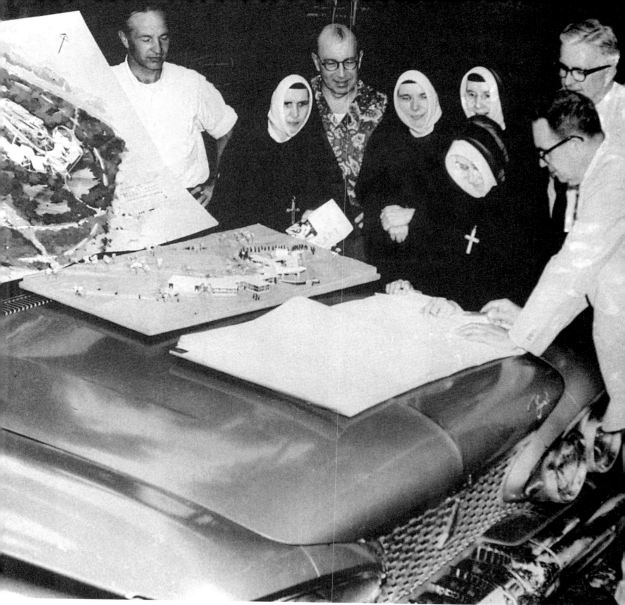

Jean Labatut (right) shows his drawings and model for the Stuart Country Day School of the Sacred Heart to Reverend Mother Agnes M. Barry, Superior Vicar of the Religious Order of the Sacred Heart, the teaching order that established the school. Courtesy of Princeton University Library, Jean Labatut Papers, Manuscripts Division, Department of Rare Books and Special Collections.

meant to turn the visitors' attention toward their bodies, to discover their incarnated soul. Labatut gave a theological turn to his earlier experiments, conducted at the Lagoon of Nations and in the prototypical Church of the Four Evangelists, to induce in immobile viewers the visual experience of inner movement. He defined Eucharistic architecture as a place in which visitors could feel "the movement of immobile things."[87]

For Maritain, the Eucharist was the expression of the real nexus of body and soul on which his philosophy of critical realism was founded. This traditional view of the Eucharist came under attack in the early 1960s. During the lead-up to the Second Vatican Council, a movement emerged among the clergy to revise the church's dogma on transubstantiation. They argued that what occurred in the Eucharist was not a change in the substance of the bread and the wine, but rather a change in their meaning and finality. Therefore, they sought to replace the word transubstantiation with "transignification" or "transfinalization." Maritain was opposed to the suggestion that the bread and the wine were not Christ's real presence. His friend Cardinal Giovanni Battista Montini was of the same view. Their affinities went beyond friendship. When Montini was elected Pope Paul VI (1963–78), he publicly declared himself "a disciple of Maritain"[88] and regularly called on him to weigh in on various ecclesiastical matters. Pope Paul VI oversaw the Second Vatican Council, turning it into an instrument for reforming the Church physically and spiritually. His encyclical *Mysterium Fidei* (1965) acted swiftly to put an end to challenges to the church's dogma on transubstantiation:

> To give an example of what We are talking about, it is not permissible to . . . discuss the mystery of transubstantiation without mentioning what the Council of Trent had to say about the marvelous conversion of the whole substance of the bread into the Body and the whole substance of the wine into the Blood of Christ, as if they involve nothing more than "transignification," or "transfinalization" as they call it; or, finally, to propose and act upon the opinion that Christ Our Lord is no longer present in the consecrated Hosts that remain after the celebration of the sacrifice of the Mass has been completed.[89]

Maritain and Labatut saw their search for a Eucharistic architecture as part and parcel of the wider defense of the church against skeptical arguments that questioned the unity of body and soul. They were answering Pope Paul VI's exhortation to accept the faith even if it contradicted reason and intellect. At the heart of their position were the teachings of St. Thomas Aquinas, who wrote that the mystery of the Eucharist "cannot be apprehended by the senses but only by faith, which rests upon divine authority."[90] This meant that Eucharistic architecture could be recognized only by the faithful. Labatut embraced such sectarianism as an extension of the social restrictions at work in modern architecture, which was supposed to be appreciated only by the initiated avant-gardes.

Labatut and Maritain's special devotion to St. Thomas Aquinas inspired them to conclude that the Dominican convent of Toulouse, where the saint's body had been buried since the fourteenth century, was the best example of Eucharistic architecture.[91] Labatut was deeply moved by the convent's Church of the Jacobins (1230–1385), especially by its famous apse whose vaulting turns on a single central column. Known as "the Jacobins's palm tree," to evoke how the ensemble of crisscrossing Gothic ribs radiates from the common trunk, the column unites the whole composition. As such, it was not difficult for Labatut to liken it to Christ, who Catholics believe united creation and oriented it toward heaven, and who was, after all, flagellated on a column.[92] "The Jacobins's palm tree" stirred Labatut to attempt the expression of Eucharistic architecture with a modern vocabulary. James Harford, chair of the school's founding advisory committee, recalled that Labatut experienced a religious reawakening while designing the building.[93]

Labatut conceived the Stuart Country Day School of the Sacred Heart as more than a series of spaces but rather as an organization of attention, meant to heighten the visitor's awareness of her moving body and through it give her a glimpse of her soul. In plan, the composition radiates from a single free-standing concrete column that splays out at the crown like a palm tree. Placed prominently at the main entrance, it was meant to attract visitors upon arrival, thanks to a series of attention-grabbing devices drawn from Labatut's experience in exhibit design. For instance, he used a flight of stairs to negotiate the upward approach from the front door to the column. This grade-change technique, which he also used in the Home Building Center of the 1939 World's Fair, compelled visitors to look up and discover the circular opening in the ceiling, which seemed to have been cut by the upward thrust of the column's fanning canopy. A cylinder of glass sealed the distance between these two ceilings, bathing the underside of the crown in a reflected circle of light. This spatial composition was meant to engage the visitor's body in an uplifting movement. Labatut wanted to underscore the Eucharistic character of this experience. So he chose to enhance the abstract space with figurative iconography, in accordance with the directives of the Second Vatican Council. The image of Christ's head, heart, and feet were carved into the column's shaft so as to produce the extraordinary effect that one is witnessing the body of the Messiah emerging from the concrete. The circular crown now appeared as the iconic halo radiating outward above his head. The iconography introduced an element of surprise in an otherwise conventional environment, which further attracted attention to the column. Another

FACING PAGE: The Jacobins's Palm Tree in the Church of the Jacobins (Toulouse, France, 1230–1385) served as inspiration for Labatut's Pillar of the Sacred Heart. Courtesy of Mario Pérez Botero, Barcelona.

ABOVE: Jean Labatut, Pillar of the Sacred Heart, showing the bas-relief face of Jesus Christ and his bleeding heart. Photograph by Jean Labatut. Courtesy of Princeton University Library, Jean Labatut Papers, Manuscripts Division, Department of Rare Books and Special Collections.

commercial exhibit technique employed by Labatut to hold the visitor's interest was the use of textured materials that invite the touch. The smooth surface of the column is interrupted by a vertical streak where the pebbly concrete was allowed to seep out of the formwork—with a "fash" method. The sinuous ripples drip down shy of the floor, so that visitors could take pleasure in caressing the column, and as their hands and eyes tracked up the beads they discovered that the source of this emanation was the heart of Christ. In a clear allusion to the Eucharist, the column appeared transubstantiated into the body and the blood of Christ. Labatut called it the Sacred Heart Pillar, a name that remains in usage.

The Sacred Heart Pillar gave visitors the necessary clues for interpreting the building as the embodiment of Christ. The concrete exterior of the school repeated the "fash" technique, suggesting that the entire building was oozing the blood of Christ. Labatut further encouraged this reading by wrapping the

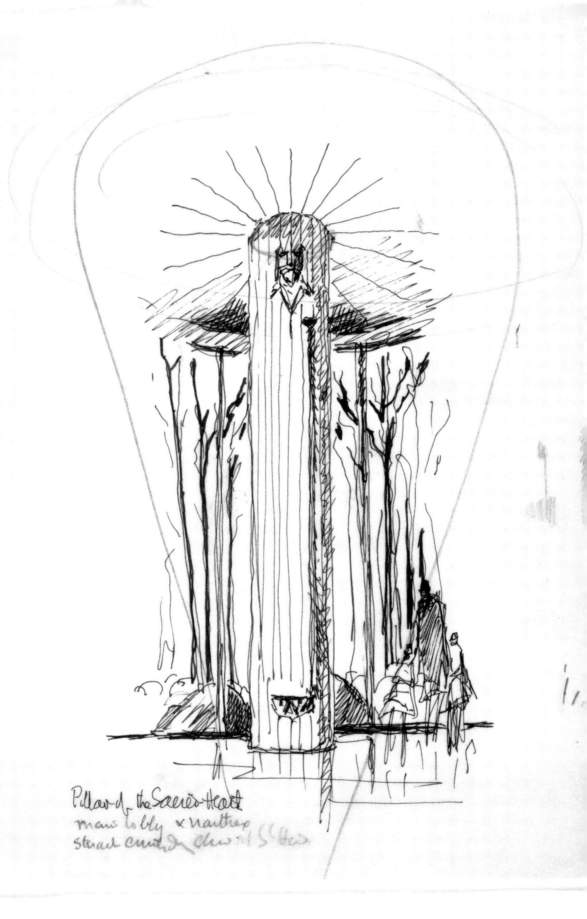

Pillar of the Sacred Heart
main lobby & narthex
steral crucified Chew M 5th Hair

FACING PAGE: Labatut's preliminary sketch for the Pillar of the Sacred Heart, ca. 1962. Photograph by Jean Labatut. Courtesy of Princeton University Library, Jean Labatut Papers, Manuscripts Division, Department of Rare Books and Special Collections.

ABOVE: Exterior detail of the Stuart Country Day School of the Sacred Heart, showing the "fash" technique used to represent the blood of Christ. Photograph by the author.

structure with a crown of copper gutters with projecting scuppers in the shape of thorns. Symbolic devices such as these were carefully orchestrated around the school to organize and focus the attention of visitors: The Sacred Heart Pillar faces a painting of the Virgin Mary executed between panes of glass, with the technique developed by Girard for the prototypical Church of the Four Evangelists; small apertures on the wall next to the Sacred Heart Pillar allowed children to look at the boiler room (the mechanical heart of the building);

ABOVE: Exterior view of a glass-enclosed stairway at Stuart Country Day School of the Sacred Heart, with projecting scuppers in the shape of a crown of thorns. Photograph by Jean Labatut. Courtesy of Princeton University Library, Jean Labatut Papers, Manuscripts Division, Department of Rare Books and Special Collections.

FACING PAGE, TOP: Jean Labatut and Father Prokes, Mater Admirabilis, ca. 1963. The glass painting of the Virgin Mary was executed using the technique developed by André Girard for the Church of the Four Evangelists. The Pillar of the Sacred Heart is seen to the right. Photograph by Jean Labatut. Courtesy of Princeton University Library, Jean Labatut Papers, Manuscripts Division, Department of Rare Books and Special Collections.

FACING PAGE, BOTTOM: Stair in the convent wing, Stuart Country Day School of the Sacred Heart, designed by Jean Labatut. The stair risers were shorter than usual to slow travel up and down the stairs, encouraging the nuns to move self-consciously and preventing them from stepping on their skirts. Photograph by the author.

anthropomorphic tree trunks with "arms" lifted toward heaven as if in rhapsodic oration were placed before the library (named after Maritain's wife Raïssa); the driveway and intermediary walk that surround the school formed the shape of two interlocking hearts, as on the shield of the Society of the Sacred Heart; natural boulders were marked as stations of the cross, made into the altar of the convent's chapel, or brought indoors to give the impression that the building sprang naturally from the ground.

The building was a deployment of poetic events meant to be experienced intimately, preferably through physical contact. These features were strung out along a circulation spine as a series of sensorial surprises meant to heighten visitors' self-awareness by stimulating their bodies. They became the aesthetic signature of architectural phenomenology: grade changes and ramps to modulate the speed of the visitor's walk; changes in the scale of conventional elements (such as shorter tread heights) to force exaggerated bodily movements; emphasis on untreated (authentic) materials; use of texture to invite touch; small niches to hold precious objects; wall apertures framing valued views; dramatic displays of natural and colored light; bold use of large painted graphics and color; and the theatrical display of water (either through fountains, scuppers, or materials that changed in appearance when wet).

The sequential experience of these symbolic devices effectively drew visitors into a reading game that invited them to interpret the building in Eucharistic terms. This was quickly understood by the teaching nuns, who used the building to teach young girls about the Catholic faith. The school sparked a wave of interest among American Catholic educators and intellectuals, many of whom visited it to experience its Eucharistic architecture.[94] Mother Putnam, who taught visual arts at Newton College of the Sacred Heart in Massachusetts, told Labatut:

> Thank you so much for having built a building that does not so much appear "built" as "alive"; as if it grew out of the ground and spread vitally along it. It struck me as real poetry, what Maritain calls "the intercommunication of inner being of things with the inner being of the human self".[95]

Poetic Architecture

As the notion of Eucharistic architecture was translated into the more secularized discourse of the visual arts by ordained or lay teachers, it was labeled "poetic" architecture. Maritain set the conceptual framework for this change in nomenclature. His A. W. Mellon Lectures, delivered at the National Gallery of Art in Washington, D.C., in the spring of 1952, argued that making art entailed a type of Eucharistic experience in which the artist's self was transubstantiated into objects.[96] Art was the objectified artistic subject made available to observers for contemplation. Viewing art was tantamount to witnessing the intercommunication between the inner self of the artist and the inner being of his art. Maritain used the word poetry to refer to the self-determined process of making art, as contrasted with craft, which was subservient to external functional constraints. For Maritain, making poetry meant tapping into the pure and uncorrupted essence of creative freedom—not the conventional sense of versifying. The first poet, he argued, was God, who created the world in the absence of all external conditioning, by transubstantiating his self into worldly objects. Poetry was the manner in which God "assumed flesh" and how "invisible made itself visible."[97] Art made by imperfect humans could never attain the level of creative freedom of God's poetry. But it could strive toward perfection by interpreting the Lord's work. Maritain spoke of the artist as a poet *vates* and described art-making as vaticination or divination that reveals the presence of God as the inner essence of all things. The Latin word *vates* means prophet or diviner and is the root of Vatican—that which pertains to Christ the prophet. The poet vates was for him someone who could prophetically decipher the meaning of God's creation.

At the crux of Maritain's definition of poetry was a theory that equated the act of creating art to that of reading it. He established a charismatic relationship between the genius-reader and the genius-creator. Making art meant interpreting physical reality with the same creative freedom as God who created it. The ability to see in objects more than mere materials, and to recognize the spirit of freedom in them, required a type of "creative innocence" that, Maritain argued, was the hallmark of geniuses.[98] To achieve greatness, artists had to be innocent readers, with the mix of confident belief in the "untouched original purity" of their self and in things as God's creation that comes with naïveté. To make poetry required, first and foremost, knowing oneself to be pure in flesh and spirit. The artist, underscored Maritain, did not know himself in the same way as a philosopher. He did not use reason. The artist achieved knowledge of himself by freely creating art, by translating himself into art objects the way God knows himself in the act of transubstantiation: "In a way similar to that in which divine creation presupposes the knowledge God has of His own essence, poetic creation presupposes, as a primary requirement a grasping, by the poet, of his own subjectivity, in order to create."[99]

Maritain's theory of poetic art secularized the Catholic idea of Eucharistic art into a generalized defense of subjectivity. In this attempt to make his critical realism palatable to art history, Maritain unselfconsciously incorporated some of that discourse's most hackneyed conventions, especially the centrality it ascribed to the genius-creator, a figure of mythical proportions, possessing the gift of an "inner vision" that was the measure of all "essential truth" in art, and the will to pursue it at all costs, breaking through the fog of conventions and thus elevating art to a higher, more honest plane. Maritain portrayed the genius-creator as the harbinger of poetic knowledge about reality (defined as the nexus of objects and soul), which was incompatible with rational thought. As such, he construed the genius-creator as emblematic of critical realism in art.

However, Maritain did not fundamentally rethink the trope of the genius-creator as he incorporated it into his philosophy. Rather, he maintained the conventional concept of the genius-creator, as it was largely molded by the romantic movement. The intellectual history of the idea of the genius-creator, from the eighteenth to the nineteenth centuries, was outlined brilliantly by Isaiah Berlin (1909–1997) on the same podium of the National Gallery of Art, thirteen years after Maritain's lectures.[100] The genius-creator embodied romanticism's three basic doctrines.[101] The first, which Berlin labeled expressionism, held that a fundamental function of human beings was to express their true inner self in whatever they did. If they didn't, it was because they maimed themselves, or were restrained by some outer force, like social conventions. The genius-creator was someone self-confident enough to express his true self without restrictions. The second doctrine was that of belonging, or the notion that the genius-creator was united to his audience by a shared culture, so that what he expressed through his art could be fully understood, in all its intricate nuance, only by a restricted group. Art, therefore, was not only expression but also a special form of intimate communication (or communion, as Maritain would prefer) between genius-creator and reader. The genius-creator's work of art had a unifying social function, for it assembled around itself those who recognized themselves in it. The third doctrine was that true ideals, like those expressed by genius-creators speaking for their culture, are often incompatible with those of other cultures, and cannot be reconciled with them. This notion undermined the Enlightenment belief that the ideals expressed in various disciplines (such as art, architecture, politics, jurisprudence, and physics) were not only compatible but should correspond with one another according to the laws of reason, and that taken together they formed the highest universal ideal of mankind. In romanticism, the genius-creator's culturally "rooted" expressions were opposed to the universalism of the Enlightenment.

Maritain's genius-creator had all the hallmarks of his romantic heritage, including the idea that poetic knowledge was a form of intuition incompatible with Enlightenment reason. When he wrote that the genius-creator expressed universal values he did not mean those of Enlightenment reason. This universalism had a Catholic twist, which was in fact incompatible with reason: When the genius-creator freely expressed his self through objects, he was really expressing his belief in the indivisible nexus of his soul with things. In so doing, his art gathered around it those who believed that they were also unique unions of soul, flesh, and blood, which is the universal belief of Catholics and the basis of their becoming worthy of salvation. Maritain used the romantic archetype of the genius-creator synecdochically to signify an artistic manner of belonging to the faith-based culture of Catholicism.

The romantic notion that culture was superior to enlightened cosmopolitanism rested on the premise that communication between individuals who belonged to the same place and time was more immediate or authentic.[102] In a rooted culture, ideas could be implied that were understood without needing to be explicitly articulated. This notion that cultural norms of artistic production and reception are somehow organically present in so-called rooted societies was largely discredited by sociologist Pierre Bourdieu. His study of how works of art become socially instituted revealed the fallacy of theories, like that of Maritain, which regard art as a form of unmediated creator-to-reader communication between two individuals. Bourdieu emphasized the role of institutions (such as museums, galleries, and academies) in establishing art as something worthy of being created and appreciated. Art is not only a material product, wrote Bourdieu, it is also a symbolic one. Whereas art is materially produced by the artist, its meaning and value are coproduced by others, such as "critics, publishers, gallery directors and the whole set of agents whose combined efforts produce consumers capable of knowing and recognizing the work of art as such."[103] In other words, the relationship between creator and reader is shot through with mediation. Maritain was himself one of those agents of mediation, although had he acknowledged as much in his talks at the National Gallery it would have delegitimized his position as objective observer.

In sum, the Eucharistic or poetic experience sought by visitors to Labatut's Stuart Country Day School of the Sacred Heart was not at all immediate. Its meaning and value were preproduced by Maritain, and indeed by Labatut himself, whose pedagogy imposed a legitimate mode of consumption of architecture. To be sure, his teachings underscored the idea that architectural design was self-expression. However, this cannot be considered his contribution to architectural discourse, as it was already a widely held view. Labatut was the originator of the notion that modern architectural creation began with architectural consumption. Students had to learn to read architecture and become familiar with its rules before they could freely create it. Labatut poured his energy into defining what reading meant and how to properly perform it. He did not want reading to be confused with copying. He thought of reading as re-creating, which was in fact a way to transcend the original and its rules. In the kind of reading he advocated, the original building was "assimilated" by the student. That is to say, the student had to look for the building's similitude to his self. This was similar to Maritain's notion that art functioned as a form of intimate communication between the self of the creator and that of the reader. Reading the building meant searching for the self of the original creator embodied in it while simultaneously looking inward, to one's self, for the basis of comparison. Once this self-to-self connection was established, then the building had to be consciously forgotten. Finally, in an act of poetic vaticination, the student had to re-create the spirit of the building as his own self-expression. Labatut boiled down his pedagogy to four steps: "learn, assimilate, forget, create."[104]

Beneath the apparent simplicity of this four-step sequence hid a complex discursive operation through which Labatut linked the Beaux-Arts to modernism, at a time when the two schools seemed locked in an irreconcilable struggle to control American academia. Labatut lamented that by the postwar period Beaux-Arts schooling had been reduced to copying historic monuments, and modernist education rejected any relation to existing buildings. This split had not always been so pronounced. Until the 1930s, American architects trained at the Beaux-Arts had been developing a modern style organically linked to historical architecture. That promise was in fact what drew Labatut to America, and he always considered that style the authentic roots of modernism. According to Labatut, the development of that style was interrupted by the influence of German immigrants, trained at the Bauhaus, on American academia.

For Labatut, Bauhaus modernism was flawed on two counts: it disregarded the cumulative knowledge expressed in historic buildings, and it negated architecture as self-expression by elevating objectivity over subjectivity. "That neglect of the past," promoted by the German Bauhaus, "was equivalent to throwing the baby away with the bath water."[105] In a heated exchange of public letters, he accused Gropius, then head of Harvard University's Department of Architecture, of removing the architect from modern architecture by relinquishing design to intermediary subcontractors and consultants. The Bauhaus rejection of self-expression, declared Labatut, sent architecture "pointing down toward the drain."[106]

But postwar Beaux-Arts education was no better. It had become co-opted by the "official history" of architecture historians, who likened every new design to a "better" historical building, thereby downgrading the young architect's work to a poor copy and implying that the only possibility for improvement was to copy more faithfully. "Official history," Labatut argued, damaged the architects' originality and reduced them to *pompiers,* who "pumped" from the past without assimilating it. Significantly, Labatut added international style architects, whom he called "neo-moderns," to his list of pompiers, for siphoning modernist forms without assimilating their content. In private, he likened them to excrement that needed to be "cleaned out of the stables" of academia so that "permanent values can shine."[107] Labatut's argument showed that although Beaux-Arts and Bauhaus-modern pedagogies seemed at odds, in reality they were carrying out the same task by different means: the denial of architecture as self-expression.

Labatut proposed a different modernism, one that enshrined self-expression as the central pillar of architectural design. By shifting the emphasis toward the subject, Labatut avoided the historical tangle that, through stress on the object, had ensnared modernism. Historiographically, modernism first defined itself as a movement without a past. But as the third generation of modernists came of age mid-century, this definition was no longer tenable. By focusing on the aesthetics of modernism, neo-moderns had become methodologically indistinguishable from Beaux-Arts architects in their reliance on historical precedents. Labatut recognized that the survival of modernism rested on its ability to reinvent the way it related to its own past. The brilliance of his method was that it simultaneously acknowledged historical precedents and negated their historical specificity. The first step toward self-expression was learning from existing buildings, not about their construction dates or style, but rather about the self that allegedly created them. Reading buildings was simply a form of self-exploration.

At the core of Labatut's pedagogy was what he called "intentional forgetfulness"—erasing from consideration every aspect of the building that made it historical.[108] Bodies, human and architectural, were cleansed of every external reference and made into ciphers for the self. Only basic sensations of warmth, light, movement, and silence were deemed legitimate ways to describe the meaningful relationship between the human body and architecture.

Sensuality became the poetic language of architecture that expressed an idealized, transhistorical self.

In Labatut's pedagogy, the senses served to establish the charismatic relationship between genius-creator and genius-reader. He understood charisma in the strict Catholic sense, as an extraordinary gift (like the gift of healing) bestowed upon chosen Christians by the Holy Spirit for the good of the church. Here again, he was influenced by Maritain, who described the senses as bodily emanations of the soul. The gift of sense perception, wrote Maritain, also "radiates upward into the depths of the Soul."[109] In other words, the soul was not hidden and inaccessible somewhere inside the body. The body *was* the soul. When an architect touched Eucharistic architecture, his soul was literally communing with God. When he touched the built self-expression of another architect, their souls came together. Reverence for the human body as flesh, blood, and soul, and for the architecture body as self-expression, became the condition for architects to belong to one another, not as an indistinct mass, but as a network of intimately connected individual souls—like the church.

The body was holy as an expression of the soul. The body's constantly changing appearance was only a reminder that what mattered was the immortal soul. Ultimately, the soul had to liberate itself from the body. Labatut translated this Catholic belief to poetic architecture. He taught students that to read historic buildings meant to get past their physical presence by intentionally forgetting their particular shape. Labatut could point to his own designs to explain what he meant: his Pillar of the Sacred Heart, for instance, was a reading that intentionally forgot the Gothic style, details, scale, and materiality of the Jacobins's Palm Tree, while keeping its Eucharistic (or poetic) essence. Intentional forgetfulness made Labatut's teaching radically modern. It required students to expunge from their readings of buildings all the physical documentary evidence that made them historic. This sort of reading-to-forget modernized every precedent by severing it from its historical context. Reading meant internalizing and reenacting modernism's apocryphal break with history, which could in itself be considered an act of design—but only if others identified it as such.

Labatut needed an audience capable of recognizing reading-to-forget as an act of designed self-expression, and he constructed it through his pedagogy. He shaped the reading habits of his students so that they would recognize themselves in each other's work and thus feel like they belonged to a social group, which although part of the larger modern movement, had a more restrictive identity centered around the cult of the senses. The core belief of this sensual modernism fathered by Labatut was that reading and creating architecture were aspects of the same process. It is no coincidence that this ideology had its origin in academia. As Bourdieu noted, the educational system is based on the ideology of "re-creation" and "creative reading," which "supplies teachers—*lectores* assigned to commentary on the canonical texts—with a legitimate substitute for the ambition to act as *auctores*."[110] Labatut essentially impressed upon his students the ideology of the architecture professor who struggled to establish creative reading as a way of belonging to modernism as legitimate as the creative authoring of designs.

The Turn to Phenomenology

The pedagogy of creative reading translated the belief in Eucharistic architecture and disseminated it under the rubric of poetic architecture. Its success owed much to the fact that creative reading could be passed off as research, thus satisfying the postwar demand from university administrators that architecture schools become more scientific and less artistic. By putting man at its center, Labatut's emphasis on studying the body seemed to reinforce the doctrine of humanism, then current in architecture. Labatut's senior position in the academy, as professor and director of graduate studies in architecture at Princeton, enabled him to stamp the architectural definition of humanism with his own sensualist ideology of creative reading. He benefited from the fact that, beginning roughly in the late 1930s, humanism had come to signify the attention of modern design to the sensing body, in opposition to strict functionalism. The critic Herbert Read (1893–1868) used "New Humanism" to denote buildings designed to gratify the five senses. "Basic sensory training," wrote Read in 1935, "is the foundation of the new biological or humanistic attitude."[111] While at MIT, Alvar Aalto (1898–1976) answered the institute's demand for research in architecture with his meditations on "The Humanizing of Architecture."[112] Together with William Wurster (1895–1973), then dean of the Architecture Department, they emphasized sensualism as the basis of an indigenous modernism, unlike the international style. Amid the competition between universities to appear at the forefront of humanist pedagogy, the Princeton faculty organized an influential national symposium on architectural education in 1953, in which Labatut promoted his methods before the nation's better-known educators and practitioners.[113]

Since the end of World War II, the definition of humanism had been widely debated in Western culture, especially in regard to its assimilation by the extraordinarily popular philosophy of existentialism. Jean-Paul Sartre's famous lecture "Existentialism Is a Humanism" (1946), a rebuttal against Communist and Catholic attacks, contended that there was nothing but a human universe, which resulted from man's self-transcending projects and was constituted in human subjectivity. Labatut disliked Sartre because he openly rejected Catholicism and because in America he was considered a Communist. However, in France Sartre's philosophy was welcomed by the young postwar generation as a more flexible alternative to the two principal (and uncompromising) schools of thought governing the French intellectual establishment: neo-Thomism (the mouthpiece of Catholicism) and Marxism (which was often at the service of Soviet propaganda).[114] Labatut acted on his beliefs, working unsuccessfully with Eugenio Batista, a former student who became one of Cuba's most prominent modernist architects, to persuade Maritain to debate Sartre in Havana, "under Castro's nose."[115]

But Labatut's effort to dissociate his humanism from that of Sartre failed because of a confluence of social, political, and academic circumstances. Under the institutional pressure to elevate the research standards of architecture, Labatut resolved to broaden his pedagogy of creative reading to include forms of scholarship deemed more legitimate by university administrators. In 1949, he founded the PhD program in architecture, the first within an American school of architecture. It was a degree made specifically for architects to engage in advanced research, reorienting architectural education toward producing "not only an architect of quality but also an architect-scholar."[116] The PhD in architecture elevated the standing of architects within the university. Previously, PhD studies in architecture were possible only in art history departments, and in fact the architecture school was at the time still under the Department of Art and Archaeology. The PhD in architecture began to grant architects autonomy from art historians. Labatut loathed architecture historians and what he called their "official history." He publicly opposed teaching architecture history as a specialized course, insisting instead that it be taught by architects in the design studio as a stimulant to creativity.[117]

The renewed importance of architectural history in the postwar years was for him a measure of how alienated architects had become from their own tradition. In an alienated world, man had to rationally reconstruct the meaning of his relationship to things through historical work. Yet, to win social and institutional independence from art history, Labatut had to develop a new and unique discourse unintelligible to art historians. Labatut's pedagogy was presented as a way to circumvent the alienation of historical work, proposing instead that architects could immediately experience the history contained in buildings. The focus on the body as the primary means for creatively reading the history of buildings relegated any historical accounting to a secondary plane. Thus, the body served to theorize buildings as intrinsically polysemous works beyond the grasp of traditional architectural history, and indeed of all discourse.

Labatut's pedagogy was in the experiential historiography that his PhD students began to develop as well as in the religious topics of research they chose. Between 1950 and 1967 (the year of Labatut's retirement), seven candidates received the PhD in architecture: four did dissertations exploring the theological dimensions of church architecture (heavily influenced by the writings of Schwarz), one dissertation (that of Charles Moore) interpreted the spiritual associations evoked by bodily engagements with water, another theorized the body as the "primitive roots" of building, and one examined the persistence of a building's spirit through architectural (not historic) preservation.[118]

At the outset, the Princeton PhD program attracted students who regarded architecture as a vehicle for their spiritual inquisitiveness. Francis A. Prokes (PhD, 1964), joined the program after having been ordained a Jesuit priest. "Mr. Labatut," wrote Prokes upon applying to the program, "assures me that the Princeton Graduate School will have facilities proper to doctoral research and creative expression for an approach covering: Psychological and Liturgical/ Theological Implications of Architectural Environment."[119] By the time Labatut was nearing retirement, the master's program had also become a popular choice for young Catholics, who sent steady streams of applications from undergraduate programs like Wheeling College, a Jesuit institution in West Virginia.[120]

The unintended consequence of accepting graduate students from Catholic institutions was that they brought with them a knowledge of existentialism and phenomenology. Indeed, as John McCumber has documented, whereas philosophy departments across America avoided "communist" philosophies during McCarthyism, Catholic institutions, because of their anti-communist reputation, became political safe havens where Americans could seriously study existentialism and phenomenology.[121] Catholic students like Father Prokes arrived at Princeton with a basic familiarity with Sartre and Merleau-Ponty as well as with the less political Bachelard. This unique intellectual climate was the foundation for Charles Moore's dissertation, which used Bachelard's notion of "poetic images" for the first time in American architectural discourse, interpreting water *as* architecture, an argument inspired by Labatut's Lagoon of Nations. Labatut's students seamlessly connected his sensualist creative reading, with its emphasis on the incarnation of the self, to the arguments about the embodiment of consciousness offered by phenomenology.

The rising interest in phenomenology among students led Labatut to invite Enrico Peresutti, a partner in the Milanese firm of BBPR (Banfi, Beljoioso, Peresutti, Rogers) with strong intellectual affinities to Enzo Paci, Italy's foremost phenomenologist, and social connections to his circle of philosophers. In Peresutti, Labatut recognized his own attitude toward architectural design as creative reading of historical precedents. "He even assimilated history into his buildings," noted Labatut.[122] While teaching architectural composition at Princeton between 1953 and 1958, Peresutti's firm completed the Velasca Tower (Milan, 1958), which Labatut regarded as an example of design that incorporated precedents through intentional forgetfulness. The high-rise was hailed for its remarkable aesthetics, which vaguely evoked medieval architecture, with long ribs running vertically on the facade and buttressing the overhang of the upper stories.

The circle of PhD students who had formed a clique around Labatut expanded to the master's students with the presence of Peresutti. Some, like Moore, Donlyn Lyndon, and Bill Turnbull, would end up forming professional partnerships or teaming up with student colleagues like Richard C. Peters (who became a lighting consultant). Although the core group around Moore referred to itself as "the family," the wider social circle remained sternly individualistic and reluctant to create a movement in the conventional sense. This anti-institutional ideology would characterize the intellectual and social formation of architectural phenomenology.

Certainly, the anti-institutionalism of architectural phenomenologists had to do with the first stirrings in the late 1950s of the youth movement that would flourish in the late 1960s. But their ardent refusal to recognize themselves as a group was also influenced by Schwarz, who was known in American Catholic artistic circles since the late 1930s as a member of the Quickborn movement.[123] Founded in Franconia, Germany, in 1910 as a Catholic youth movement, the Quickborn movement was regarded as the artistic and intellectual avant-garde that would bring about a new Catholic modernity.[124] Its strength with regard to other competing Catholic modernist groups was its radical requirement that members question every convention of Catholic life in order to free themselves from Cartesianism, "that poisonous compromise which had doomed bourgeois civilization and made Catholics soft."[125] Max Scheler (1874–1928), a social philosopher and interpreter of Husserl who converted to Catholicism in 1920, was among the leaders of the movement and was responsible for structuring the Quickborn questioning of reality within a phenomenological and experiential frame. Romano Guardini (1885–1968), a Catholic priest and philosopher of religion, wrote treatises on aesthetics calling for modern churches to shed historicist motifs, which drew the interest and friendship of modern Catholic architects like Schwarz and Mies van der Rohe (1886–1969).[126] By 1921, the Quickborn movement numbered about 6,000 members in Germany and prided itself in never becoming an organization in the traditional sense.[127] To uphold its avant-gardist self-image in spite of its large constituency, Quickborns rejected conventional means of structuring social groups into institutions. "Its members loathed organizing as being too static, petrified and dead; they wished to be truly dynamic, 'liquid,' and full of life, moving with the times."[128]

Labatut's students read Schwarz's anti-institutionalism according to the frameworks of phenomenology's commitment to the self and American individualism, setting architectural phenomenology into motion as an intellectual formation premised on abolishing every form of structured organization. Architectural phenomenology, while pervasive, never became a self-identified social group. Arguably, this made it all the more powerful in infusing postmodernism with some of the themes absorbed from Labatut, such as the idea that history was something that could be grasped experientially from buildings, and the Catholic belief in bodily experience as a form of spiritual revelation. By grounding expression in subjective experience, Labatut contributed to the dissolution of the architectural object and the liberation from the modernist style that set the stage for postmodernism. Out of the countless students marked by Labatut's pedagogy, the one who most successfully carried the torch of architectural phenomenology was Charles Moore, to whom we now turn.

LSDesign
Charles W. Moore and the Delirious Interior

In December 1979, *Progressive Architecture* **asked** American architects to nominate the most influential architects from among their peers. Charles Moore (1925–1993) made the top ten. He also came in first in terms of number of pages devoted to a single architect by the magazine. His influence was not confined to the profession but extended deep into academia as well. In 1989 the American Collegiate Schools of Architecture, in partnership with the American Institute of Architects, awarded him the Topaz Medallion for Excellence in Architectural Education. The board conferring the award described him as "a brilliant and inspiring force who has transformed the character of architectural education in this country."[1] The remark was not an exaggeration. Moore trained many of the teachers who came to dominate architectural education in the 1980s. The biographies and collections of his essays attest to his intellectual range.[2] Exhibitions of his work have underscored his pivotal influence on the student protests at Yale in the late 1960s.[3] But some of Moore's most significant academic achievements have not received scholarly attention. Partly this is because his defense of fantasy as the poetic source of design has been misinterpreted as the mark of an intellectual lightweight not worthy of serious study. It is also partly because Moore's career involved groping toward goals that were not transparent to him and therefore never overtly stated. Some of his contributions can be appreciated only retroactively in light of their historical unfolding.

Moore was deeply concerned with clarifying the nature of the architect's intellectual work. As a student, he became frustrated by the fact that the standard of architectural scholarship had been established by art historians, who restricted the definition of intellectual work to textual historical analysis. Moore would help legitimize a notion of intellectuality based on different standards of competency, including visual proficiency and the ability to grasp the historical essence of buildings experientially. Moore's interest in experience led him early on to the phenomenology of Gaston Bachelard, whom he interpreted for architectural audiences. Although later in life Moore de-emphasized phenomenology as too theoretical, his work was central to the formation of architectural phenomenology.

Moore's major contribution to architectural discourse has been interpreted by authors like Charles Jencks as turning the attention of architects toward decoration and playful superficiality, instead of the structure of the building.[4] This is not incorrect, but it is only part of the story. Moore's interest in decoration was a function of his fascination with interiors and ultimately with the inner world of human experience. His "superficiality" was rooted in an obsession with achieving profound experiences. To properly situate Moore in the intellectual history of postmodern architecture, we must distinguish between his intellectual work and his architectural aesthetics, even if Moore himself insisted on conflating the two.

Forgetting Modernism

Moore developed his derision of postwar modernism during his student years at Princeton between 1954 and 1957. At 29, and a recent veteran of the Korean War, Moore was more mature than most of his classmates in the School of Architecture. To Jean Labatut, then director of Graduate Studies, it became clear that Moore was unusually talented. Labatut took a special interest in Moore, mentored him, and distinguished him with positions of responsibility. Moore quickly found himself having to take the side of his mentor in the departmental politics that pitted Labatut against Robert McLaughlin, dean of the school, over the pedagogical direction of the program. In competition with other Ivy League universities, McLaughlin sought to increase Princeton's symbolic capital by luring the celebrities of international style modernism to the school. Labatut worked against McLaughlin by attracting renowned architects who "assimilated history" into their buildings, like Enrico Peresutti and Louis Kahn.[5] Moore recalled:

> Dean McLaughlin tried to run a countertrend to people like Labatut and Peresutti. He brought down people from New York to lecture us, like Gordon Bunshaft . . . He was perhaps the most unpleasant creep I ever met. Really awful. All these sharp New Yorkers wheeled in to instruct the young of Princeton . . . When the heroes of the modern movement came, we usually thought they were the prime idiots of all time. I remember Siegfried Giedion announcing (in a thick German accent, suitable only for Harvard) that

the ideal size for a city was seven hundred thousand. And when questioned by us about that presumption—which, apparently, people at Harvard had simply accepted—he announced that Rotterdam was about seven hundred thousand, and Rotterdam was a nice city, and so seven hundred thousand was it. No: the models that were so strong elsewhere in the fifties were just not very strong at Princeton.[6]

The academic schism that Moore experienced at Princeton was part of a wider cultural struggle over the definition of American modern architecture. Even the popular press took sides on the issue, including *Time* magazine and *House Beautiful*, defending the hagiography of a home-grown modernism, from Richardson to Wright via Sullivan, against the intrusion of Gropius and Mies.[7] It is important to recall that these debates took place during the time of McCarthyism. The postwar years saw European modernism come under the attack of politicians such as Congressman George Dondero of Michigan, who made his career as a watchdog against Communism in American education, repeatedly lecturing Congress on the dangers of "transplanted" modernisms.[8]

In that political context, Labatut's pedagogy of assimilating history into modernism was interpreted by Moore and his classmates as way to draw on local American history. At the time, America's university system was experiencing an unprecedented growth that was fueled by anxieties of inadequacy vis-à-vis the Soviet Union. Beginning in the mid 1950s, the Eisenhower administration began increasing federal spending on new university facilities with budgets for education that approached those for the construction of the federal highway system, a trend that continued for much of the 1960s.[9] Labatut's students, especially those graduating from his PhD program, were well positioned to fill the numerous teaching posts being created in new architectural schools across the country. Labatut groomed Moore to become a professor, encouraging him to enroll in the doctoral program upon completion of his MFA. Moore's dissertation, "Water and Architecture" (1958), was an overt homage to his mentor. It explored one of Labatut's lifelong interests: How to use water as a modern architectural material. The dissertation was divided into four parts, as a textual performance of Labatut's four-step pedagogy: to learn, assimilate, forget, and create. In the first part, Moore demonstrated what he had learned about water as a physical medium. In the second part, he established his assimilation of historical examples in which water had been employed architecturally. In the third part, he discussed how the immediate experience of water induced a psychological state of forgetting, in which past and future were "cleansed" to make way for pure self-consciousness. In the fourth part, Moore took the creative leap, designing a series of fountains to "moisten" the experience of a stretch of Arizona's Highway 89 and the "arid" feeling of recently completed modern buildings along New York's Park Avenue: Mies van der Rohe's Seagram Building (1954–57) and Gordon Bunshaft's Lever House (1951–52). Arid architectural experiences, he explained, were those that did not communicate a deeper significance to visitors. With characteristic humor, Moore dug into the masters of the international style for the abstract and anonymous architectural experiences they gave corporate America. To "moisten" Bunshaft's design, he called for bubbles floating from the fountains and into the wind, "because this is Lever House," the soap manufacturer.[10] To communicate the deeper significance of Mies's skyscraper, he envisioned a sculpture of brass rods in the shape of a distillery, "spewing Seagram product out."[11] Moore's dissertation was a slap in the face of Dean McLaughlin. Delighted, Labatut used his power to immediately hire Moore into the faculty. Bitter, McLaughlin began quietly plotting to sack the young teacher.

Despite the humor, Moore was serious in his ambition to change postwar modernism. His dissertation was radical insofar as it invoked historical precedents for design. A few years earlier, Philip Johnson had caused a stir among orthodox modernists for revealing that his Glass House was derived from historical models.[12] Moore went further, claiming that historical buildings could communicate more complex meanings than modern structures. Significantly, he argued that the kinds of meanings available in historic buildings were not themselves historical. Rather, architecture served as a vessel for transhistorical meanings that he believed to be universally accessible through immediate, preverbal experiences. Moore's method for analyzing historic buildings according to archetypal experiences stood in contrast to the iconological studies of historic architecture made current in Princeton's Department of Art and Archaeology by Panofsky. As a historiographical method, iconology opposed the notion that meaning could be transhistorical. Iconologists considered the meaning of historic buildings to be understandable only in reference to the religion, philosophy, literature, science, politics, and social life of the period in which they were built. But Moore was not obliged to follow art historical protocols in his PhD studies. Five years before he completed his dissertation, the architecture school had gained administrative independence from the Department of Art and Archeology. As a result, architects had far more latitude to experiment with historiographical models that incorporated their dispositions toward nonverbal means of expression.

Moore's understanding of architectural meaning owed much to Labatut's Catholic theory of Eucharistic architecture, which encouraged students to forget the actual shape of historic buildings and to focus on their experiential content. The pedagogy of forgetting was particularly appealing for Moore and his generation, as it helped them to both distance themselves from the aesthetics of post-war modernism and establish a deeper connection to the creative source of modernism. But the new generation of modernists faced a new set of problems: the question was less how to create something new and more how to avoid repeating something old. "The past," wrote Moore borrowing from Labatut, "is an example of what not to do in another epoch, on another site, in another climate, for another client."[13] He understood creativity as inextricably bound to historical precedents, which had to be simultaneously assimilated and negated.

Moore appropriated Labatut's theory of Eucharistic architecture, but he secularized it, dropping the theological references and adopting more palatable philosophical ones. In particular, he invoked Bachelard to describe immediate experience as an act of forgetting an object's outer form and grasping its inner content. Moore's invocation of Bachelard is noteworthy in itself, as he was the first to introduce the philosopher to American architectural discourse, nearly a full decade before the French phenomenologist became a household name in architecture schools.[14] To better understand Moore's turn to phenomenology, it is important to recall the social and political circumstances that made it possible.

Phenomenology was not widely studied in America in the 1950s. Moore's turn to Bachelard must therefore be distinguished from that of European artists like Yves Klein, who also cloaked theological discourse (in the case of Klein it was Rosicrucianism) in the mantle of phenomenology.[15] In France, the combined influence of Sartre and Merleau-Ponty made existential phenomenology a dominant philosophical school during the 1950s. But in America, Sartre's Marxism and his open denunciations of McCarthyism as a new fascism made existential phenomenology initially suspect politically.[16] The American International Phenomenological Society lost most of its members and had ceased convening by the early 1950s.[17] When Labatut heard Sartre lecture in Princeton during the spring of 1946, he found the philosopher offensive to Christian faith.[18] The fact that communist subversion was close to unimaginable in American Catholic schools allowed them to operate as safe havens for the study of phenomenology.[19] Significantly, most of the postwar members of the American phenomenological community were Catholics. Reiner Schürmann, a former Dominican teaching at the New School for Social Research, put it best: "continental philosophy came to

America on the backs of priests."[20] Labatut encouraged students from Catholic institutions to study architecture at Princeton. They arrived conversant with phenomenology, introducing it to the school from the bottom up. Peresutti, Labatut's hire, introduced phenomenology from the top down, narrating personal stories to his students about prominent European phenomenologists like Bachelard, Merleau-Ponty, and Paci. Moore was selected to serve as Peresutti's assistant in the architectural composition class and became captivated by his teachings.[21]

Bachelard's *Water and Dreams: An Essay on the Imagination of Matter* appeared to Moore like a philosophical clarification of Labatut's teachings about the need to forget historic architectural forms. Bachelard spoke of the need to "de-objectify objects and deform forms" in order to "see the matter beneath the object."[22] He recognized not just the formlessness of water but also its privileged status as an element capable of dissolving historical forms. Bachelard was speaking not only of how the literal action of weathering on historic buildings slowly dissolves them. He was also describing the effect of water on the imagination: "By grouping images and dissolving substances," he wrote, "water helps the imagination in its task of de-objectifying and assimilating."[23] Moore had stumbled upon the key to unlocking Labatut's teachings: the imagination was, according to Bachelard, the mental power necessary to assimilate and forget historic forms. From this point forward, Moore embarked on a career-long pursuit to establish a place for the imagination in architecture. He helped legitimize fantasy, daydreams, and reverie as sources of creativity and as vehicles for accessing and interpreting historic buildings.

Bachelard argued that one's experience of reality was ruled by one's imagination, which he described as the "pre-reflexive attitudes that govern the very process of reflection."[24] He discussed how, when one experienced an object (say, a historic building), one never experienced it truly objectively. "The realist," argued Bachelard, "chooses *his* reality in reality; the historian chooses *his* history in history."[25] Bachelard's book was an attempt to explain why and how this phenomenon of choosing one's reality took place. He resisted the idea that experience was mere self-projection. He also resisted the notion that the selectiveness of one's experience was a function of one's culture (he called this supposition the "culture complex").[26] Instead he argued that the imagination determined one's choice, by supplying the mind with images according to which one patterned one's reality. These images were therefore the origin of one's "creative eye." But where did these images originate? Bachelard thought that they were not "derived from things seen in the world around us but are nothing but *projections* of a hidden soul."[27] For Bachelard, these images were brief and fleeting unions of subjectivity and objectivity. Neither emulations of the outer world nor mirrors of pure inner consciousness, they had their own specific reality as irruptions of pure immediacy within consciousness. They appeared in the absence of a past, as though motivated by their own inner thrust. Because, according to Bachelard, no causality could explain the onset of these images, he regarded them as the open-ended and primal sources of human creativity.

Bachelard called these images, "poetic images" to refer to the notion of creation that is in the etymological root of *poesis*.[28] The poetic image provided an alternative description of creation to that offered by classical metaphysics. Aristotle believed creation to be governed by the fourfold law of causality. The creation of a Greek temple, for instance, involved a formal cause (e.g., the idea of proportion), a material cause (e.g., the marble), an efficient cause (e.g., the dressing and assembly of stones), and a final cause (e.g., housing the gods).[29] Bachelard critiqued classical philosophy for reducing the creative imagination to a formal cause. He argued that the onset of a poetic image was not caused by rational logic. Rather, a poetic image was a spontaneous "commitment of the soul," which flashed in the conscious imagination, passing "from the original state of reverie to that of execution."[30] Bachelard suggested a bipolar model of the mind's imagining powers: on one pole was a formal imagination associated with rational talent and formal reasoning; on the other pole was a material imagination associated with the soul, inspiration, and openness. Both the formal and the material imagination served the mind to divide, analyze, and interpret the nature of being. But formal and material imagination made divisions according to different laws. Bachelard maintained that the "law of the four elements" classified "various kinds of material imagination by their connections with fire, air, water or earth."[31] Every poetics was informed by both the formal and the material imagination to varying degrees. Therefore, every poetics was also classifiable according to images that "stem directly from matter" either as fire, air, water, or earth.[32]

Bachelard's notion that creation was noncausal had historiographical implications that he did not fail to note. The poetic images of the material imagination were to him both "primitive and eternal. They prevail over season and history."[33] Moore recognized that the idea that architecture originated in poetic images could be turned into an important critique of the "official" historiography of architecture employed by art historians. He was looking for a way to critique art history's monopoly over architectural history in order to establish the academic value of Princeton's fledgling doctoral degree in architecture. The leading art historians of the 1950s, from Henry-Russell Hitchcock (1903–1987) to Nikolaus Pevsner (1902–1983) and Rudolf Wittkower (1901–1971), described creativity in architecture as a series of successive changes in stylistic expression. Philosophically speaking, they described architecture in formal terms and understood creativity as a product of the formal imagination. Informed by his reading of Bachelard, Moore looked upon the historiography of art historians as a failure, insofar as it did not recognize that the material origin of architectural creativity could be detached from formal causes, and that science and technology might not be the only sources of innovation.

In defiance of art history, Moore proposed a new historiography that structured the history of architecture according to the laws of the material imagination. Following Bachelard, he focused his analysis on one of the four elements: water. He thus redefined architectural history with the dispositions of the architect. With shameless disregard for chronology or style, he grouped together buildings according to their poetic origin in various water-born images of life, death, time, calm, movement, purity, and intercourse. For instance, Moore claimed a common creative origin in a poetic image of moving water for a Chinese cottage built in Chian-chou in 817 and Alvar Aalto's Toppila Pulp Mill in Oulu, Finland of 1930. Quoting from a Finnish-born historian specializing in Chinese architecture, he wrote: "The aim was to give expression to something that might be called a poetical or religious dream rather than a historical or philosophic concept, but which nevertheless presented a spiritual reality for the creative imagination.[34]

Moore's historiography implied a research methodology that was equally unconventional. He did not deem it necessary to research building records, census data, letters, manuscripts, and other documents that might help him establish the creative intentions of the architect and their cultural inflection. He believed that buildings spoke for themselves and that he could intuitively feel the poetic images, or creative sources, from which their design emerged. The touchstone of his research methodology was what he called "experiential imme-diacy": the quality that made "an architectural composition affect the conscious-ness of the onlooker"[35] in such a way as to "wipe out" the building's past and future from the person's mind and expose his or her imagination directly to the "original" poetic image.[36]

Moore referred to poetic images as memory-born images. Memory, as he defined it, was simultaneously a way to forget the outward form of a building and to grasp its inner creative source. On the surface, his emphasis on memory seemed to give new importance to architectural history in design, undermining the antihistorical bias of ex-Bauhaus modernists. But Moore's definition of memory implied a view of history that was itself antihistorical: the history that memory was supposed to recall was a transhistorical poetic essence, the truth content of which was impossible to verify through traditional historiographical means, such as cross-checking against related documents.

Moore's concept of memory appears at first to be an attack on postwar modernism for negating historical forms. But the opposite was in fact true: it condemned postwar modernism for being too historical in the traditional sense of being too object-centric and too bound by a historically determined set of (modernist) architectural forms. In other words, Moore accused the postwar modernist establishment of not being modern enough and failing to shed its own reliance on modernist historical forms. His heretical denunciation of modernism left its fundamental structural myths intact: the performative act of "forgetting" history was a prerequisite to modern design, and creativity had a pure poetic origin outside of history and culture.

Moore's attack on the postwar modernist establishment did not go unnoticed at Princeton, especially by McLaughlin. In the context of the bizarre consensual form of social repression spawned by McCarthyism, McLaughlin inflated Moore's intellectual rebelliousness before the university administration, making him appear as an unpredictable and deviant personality. Behind closed doors, Moore's homosexuality was considered a scandal waiting to happen and a liability to the school's image. McLaughlin asked that Moore's contract not be renewed. In a "Strictly Confidential" letter to then Princeton President Robert F. Goheen, J. Douglas Brown, dean of the faculty, endorsed McLaughlin's decision:

> The reasons for not holding Moore were sound, I feel, and are related to personality. Single at 35, Moore did not seem stable or mature in respect to his relationships with students, and while brilliant, was an uncertain quantity personally for the long pull. Bob [McLaughlin] has been anxious to avoid a climate too often associated with art centers. I am inclined to support Bob's judgment.[37]

Moore left Princeton in 1959 and immediately assumed the position of associate professor at the recently founded College of Environmental Design of the University of California, Berkeley. There, he assumed the persona of an outsider rebel to the postwar modernist establishment, which he believed had usurped creative liberty in American architecture in the same way McCarthyism had hijacked free speech. International style modernism was for him analogous to the loss of individuality and over-conformity denounced in books such as David Riesman's *The Lonely Crowd* (1950) and William Whyte's *The Organization Man* (1956). Framed by the larger reaction to the strict social norms of the 1950s United States, Moore's attacks on modernism seemed like architecture's cultural equivalent to political opposition. "It was an easy step to take," recalled one of his students, "condemning Nixon and Agnew one moment, Pevsner and Giedion the next."[38]

Moore encouraged the association of his work with the emancipation of individual experience from the restrictive conventions of postwar modernism. He criticized modernist glass boxes, associating their orthogonality with political orthodoxy. Modernist buildings were now considered "traps," "geometric jungles," "claustrophobic" objects that left visitors "no easy way out."[39] His early architectural designs were studies on how to open up the proverbial modernist box. Significantly, he did not propose to actually dismantle modernist buildings. Instead, he introduced discrete elements within their spaces, such as fountains, to make the visitor's experience more expansive, or as he described it in reference to Bachelard, more immediate and poetic. Moore's turn toward the phenomenological description of immediate experience gained significance at this precise cultural moment, when young Americans were seeking to liberate their culture from official culture, refusing to lead their lives according to the false conventions of society, and seeking authenticity in existence instead.[40]

Immediate Experience

Moore had begun exploring ways of installing new immediate architectural experiences onto existing buildings in his dissertation. His fountain installations at the Lever House and the Seagram Building were meant to give visitors the experience of escaping from the modernist boxes that enclosed them.[41] The water was meant to excite the material imagination with poetic images of oceanic infinitude, providing an experience different from that envisioned by the formal imagination of the original architects. He thought that, in the mind's eye, these images would be layered onto the perception of the physical space, distorting it, making it feel larger than it actually was, and giving visitors the experience of breaking out.

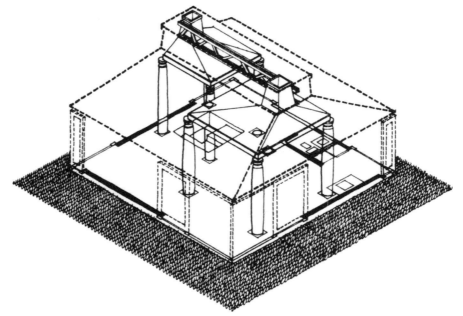

FACING PAGE, TOP: *Exterior view of Charles Moore's house in Orinda, California, 1962. The sliding exterior walls made the single roof appear like a large aedicule and exposed the smaller aedicules within. Photograph by Morley Baer, copyright 2008, the Morley Baer Photography Trust, Santa Fe, N.M. All reproduction rights reserved.*

FACING PAGE, BOTTOM: *Moore's isometric showing the two interior aedicules contained within the larger aedicular roof of his house in Orinda, 1962. Drawing by William Turnbull of MLTW (Moore, Lyndon, Turnbull, Whitaker). Courtesy of the Charles Moore Foundation.*

Moore continued his investigation of water as a stimulant of the material imagination in the house he designed for himself in 1962 in Orinda, a suburb five miles east of Berkeley. The house was one diaphanous rectangular room under a hipped roof. The central feature of the space was a large sunken bath that was filled by a fountain shower spout above. The water was meant to install an expansive experience within the otherwise boxy room and to mentally transport Moore outside of the physical confines of his house. Four wooden columns framed the space around the bath, supporting a small pyramidal ceiling, at the apex of which was a skylight. Moore referred to this combination of columns and ceiling as an aedicule, or miniature house.

The idea to create a miniature house within the house came from Moore's reading of John Summerson's *Heavenly Mansions*, where the British architectural historian described the use of aedicules as miniature temples used for ceremonial purposes in the late baroque and neoclassical villas of the English upper class.[42] But referring to Summerson does little to explain Moore's real design intentions and does not help clarify what became Moore's career-long obsession with aedicules. Moore was less interested in the aedicule as a historical form and more concerned to understand it as a poetic image, or as an immediate experience of the material imagination. The question for him was to de-objectify the aedicule and grasp its poetic source in one of the four earthly elements. But which element was the material source of an aedicule?

The answer was by no means obvious. It took Moore nearly fifteen years to articulate it in his book *Body, Memory, and Architecture* (1977), which he cowrote with Kent Bloomer, a colleague and professor of architecture at Yale. In

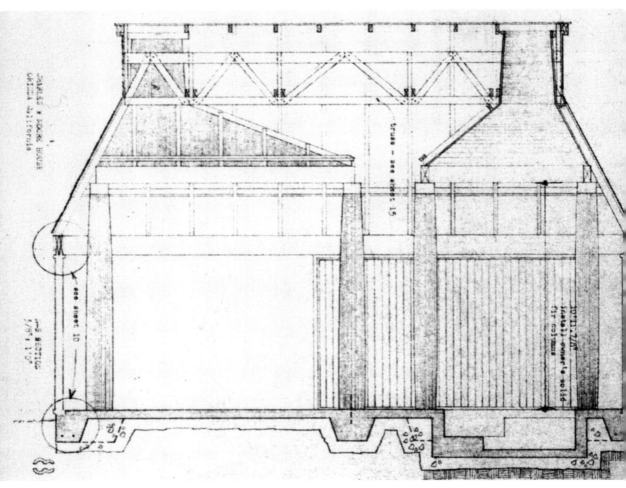

the book, Moore and Bloomer discussed the poetic origin of the aedicule in the material imagination of fire. A miniature house no bigger than a person, the aedicule brought architecture into intimate sensual contact with the body. The aedicule literally rubbed up against the skin, warming it through friction and awakening the dream of "inner fire," which Moore described as the seed of man's fertility and creativity.

Here again, Moore was drawing on Bachelard's notion of the material imagination as the source of creativity. In *The Psychoanalysis of Fire*, Bachelard tried to prove that modern scientific explanations of how humans came to invent fire-making were defective. He claimed that ideas about primitive humans empirically observing ignition in nature and then trying to copy it were flawed. There was nothing in nature that resembled the rubbing together of two dry pieces of wood. On the other hand, there were many "archetypal" human

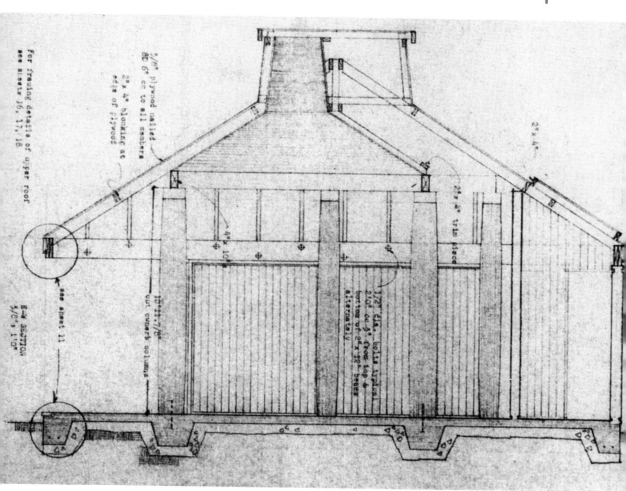

Transverse and longitudinal sections of Moore's home in Orinda (drawn by the architect), showing the bathtub integrated into the floor slab, the four-post aedicule above it, and the skylight further up, ca. 1961. Courtesy of the University of Texas Alexander Archive and the Charles Moore Foundation.

experiences relating warmth to rubbing, such as sexual intercourse. Hence, psychoanalysis was a more adequate method for explaining the invention of fire than historical reconstruction. It sufficed to analyze the poetic images occurring during reveries of fire.

Bachelard thought it was fantasies of sex involving bodies heating up in the course of vigorous rubbing that originally led humans to rub twigs together to make fire. For Bachelard, this was confirmed by similar Jungian archetypes of intercourse in various fire-creation myths. The point was that invention did not involve a causal string of events carefully arranged in time–history that could be turned into a predictive model for the shape of things to come. The truly new resulted, according to Bachelard, from people reaching "inside," getting to know themselves, and then projecting their interiority "outside." As he put it: "The method of rubbing then appears as the *natural* method. Once again it is natural because man accedes to it *through his own nature*. In actual fact, fire was detected within ourselves before it was snatched from the gods."[43]

Moore's association of the aedicule with poetic images of fire was already evident in his house in Orinda. In formal terms, the aedicule replaced the hearth as the traditional symbolic center and most intimate interior of the American single-family home. We can now better understand Moore's decision to place the aedicule over the bath and under a skylight. He was trying to unite all the basic elements of the material imagination in one place: air above in the skylight, fire in the aedicule, water in the bath, and earth in the supporting ground plane of the floor. With this grouping of architectural elements, Moore sought to create a powerful immediate experience of poetic images. Within an intimate and finite interior setting, he tried to install the opposite experience of infinitude. He was persuaded that the aedicule scaled down the cosmic scale and made it graspable to humans, making sensual experience swell to universal proportions. He believed that by creating a protective layer to shut off reality and meditate, he could stand, if only for a moment, in an enveloping miniature universe, outside of earthly culture and time. By severing him from exterior concerns, the aedicule helped to purify his experience. The aedicule's intimate interior was conceived as a device for training the senses to achieve controlled introspection and self-discovery. The aedicule was meant to assist the architect-historian to experience his creative self.

Otherworldly Enclosure

Labatut's theory of Eucharistic architecture had introduced Moore to the idea that haptic experience, now understood as intimate physical contact, was necessary for the visitor to enter into a charismatic relationship with the creative source of the building. Moore replaced Labatut's belief that architecture's creative source was God with a more secular notion that it was a poetic image. In

FACING PAGE: Interior of Moore's home in Orinda, showing the four-post aedicule above the bathtub, ca. 1962. To the left is Moore's bed. Photograph by Morley Baer, copyright 2008 by the Morley Baer Photography Trust, Santa Fe, N.M. All reproduction rights reserved.

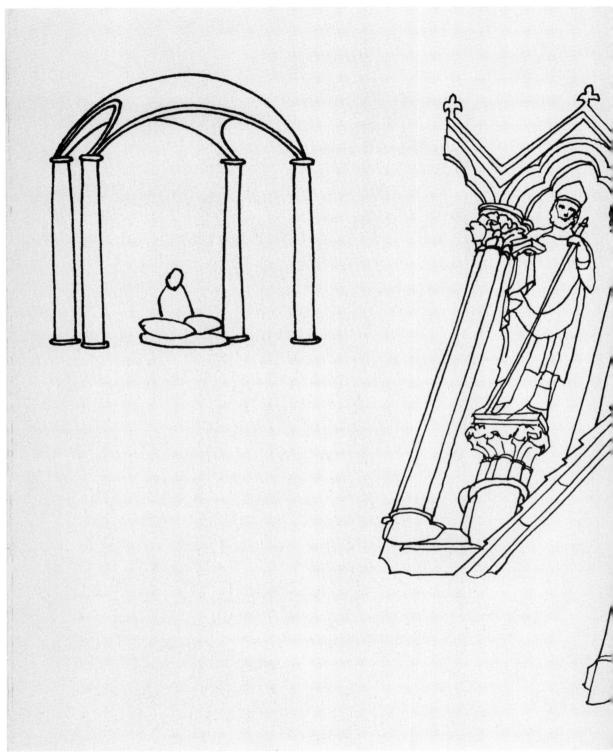

Moore's drawing of a man "renewing virility" under an aedicule, compared to William Hersey's drawing of medieval saints in aedicules. Courtesy of Kent Bloomer.

his design for the Stuart Country Day School of the Sacred Heart (Princeton, 1963), Labatut had used the single free-standing column, the Pillar of the Sacred Heart, as the touchstone of Eucharistic architecture, an element with human proportions where visitors could experience God transubstantiating into earthly matter. Moore's aedicula multiplied the column by four, placing the visitor at the center. The shift was subtle but important. The center and source of creativity was now the human self, not God.

Nevertheless, it is important to note that Moore retained a deep spiritualist rhetoric when speaking about aedicules. For instance, he laced sexuality with religiosity effortlessly by printing two sketches side by side, one of a man in an aedicule described as "renewing virility," and the other of "medieval saints" who had "found similar aedicular homes."[44] For all its humanism, Moore's obsession with the aedicule was not free from mysticism. The aedicule drew its inspiration from medieval forms of architectural confinement. Enclosure was foundational to the Western monastic tradition, which considered internment as a prerequisite for the spiritual life.[45] In medieval European convents, the rooms reserved for mystical experiences were occupied according to highly ritualized practices of meditation and prayer meant to induce the transcendence of the corporeal self and the experience of the "elsewhere" or "otherworldly." In the context of the 1960s countercultural experiments with drug-induced out-of-body experiences, Moore started to associate the aedicule with the liberation of experience from all physical forms, not just architectural, but also human. The aedicule was a form of physical confinement that, like the monastic cell, was meant to induce the contemplation of divine mystery beyond introspection and the transcendence of the body's physical limitations. The aedicule was a means to "stiffen a boundary just beyond the body itself" and create a "body-centered sense of space and place." [46] Moore argued for the need to make intimate architecture that could install the experience of the infinite cosmos within the bounds of the human body.

References to the monastic tradition gave a New Age spiritualist overtone to Moore's claims about the ability of aedicules to concentrate cosmic experiences. It is important to recall, however, that whether or not contemporary audiences believed Moore's claims, they nevertheless would have understood them as part of the larger subculture that, during the late 1960s and 1970s, subscribed to pseudoscientific ideas linking confinement to increased virility, energy, and general health. The most celebrated among these was the infamous orgone accumulator, designed by Wilhelm Reich (1897–1957), an Austrian-American psychiatrist and advocate in the 1930s sexual-politics movement.

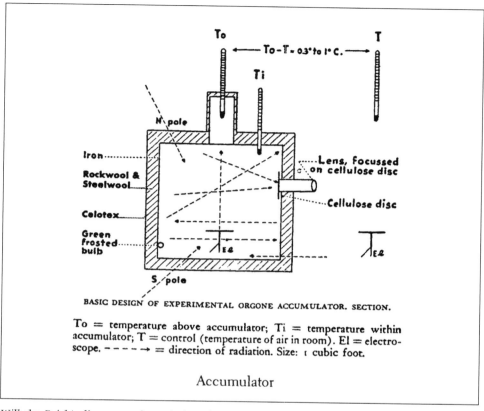

BASIC DESIGN OF EXPERIMENTAL ORGONE ACCUMULATOR. SECTION.

To = temperature above accumulator; Ti = temperature within accumulator; T = control (temperature of air in room). El = electroscope. – – – – → = direction of radiation. Size: 1 cubic foot.

Accumulator

Wilhelm Reich's diagrammatic vertical section of an orgone accumulator, known popularly as an orgone box. Reich's patients sat inside the box for long periods of time, hoping to receive healing orgone energy from the cosmos. From Wilhelm Reich, American Odyssey: Letters and Journals, 1940-1947, *ed. Mary Boyd Higgins (New York: Farrar, Straus, and Giroux, 1999), n.p. (Figure 1).*

Resembling an enclosed phone booth and made of alternating layers of ferrous metals and insulators with a high dielectric constant, the orgone accumulator was said to collect "orgone energy" from the atmosphere and transmit it to orgone-deprived patients, whom Reich would treat for illnesses such as cancer by placing them inside the cabinet. Reich believed orgone to be the primordial cosmic energy responsible for everything from the weather to human emotion and the orgasm, from which it derived its name.[47] In 1954, the U.S. Food and Drug Administration successfully sued Reich for making fraudulent claims about the health benefits of the orgone accumulator. Despite, or perhaps because of the fact that their sale and distribution were banned, "orgone boxes" achieved cult status in the constellation of illicit trance-inducing substances and objects of the flourishing 1960s American counterculture.

Cartoon by Kent Bloomer of a child represented as an aesthetic genius who can immediately experience the essence of his environment. Courtesy of Kent Bloomer.

The aedicule became a cipher for an architecturally-induced pure inward experience of the creative self. Whereas in scholastic mysticism, purity of experience was associated with the otherworldly, Moore associated it with childlike innocence. It is no accident that, as Moore grew older and more self-assured, his drawing style became more infantilizing and naive and his architectural references more fantastic. Infantilization happened also at the intellectual level through a dumbing-down of philosophy. In *Body, Memory, and Architecture,* for instance, complex philosophical arguments were boiled down to one-sentence captions under Bloomer's cartoons. The theory of the innocent self as the source of creativity was represented with the cartoon of a baby. The infant was portrayed as an aesthetic genius who, without intellectual effort, had assimilated the form of his rattle and the sun, forgotten them, and experienced their poetic image as a totally new creation deep inside his pure self.

Bloomer's infant presented the ideal of the modernist architect, who possessed the gift of a unique and innocent vision, entirely outside of this allegedly sham world. Moore conceived of architectural education as the shepherding of young adults in the arduous path of returning to those original images, supposedly contained in their self. The textbook illustration thus returned to its medieval function, when it was used in teaching the preliminary stages of the mystical way. These images were to be abandoned at the highest level of contemplation, when the pupil embraced both vision and mystical union with the otherworldly. This hoped-for moment is illustrated in a fourteenth-century manuscript about the life of the Rhenish Dominican mystic Henry Suso (ca. 1295–1366), who pulls his cloak open to reveal his soul embracing infinite wisdom—an image with uncanny formal and functional resemblance to Bloomer's cartoon.

The medieval Catholic mystic Henry Suso embraces eternal wisdom. From fourteenth-century manuscript, Bibliothèque nationale et universitaire de Strasbourg, MS 2929, fol. 8v.

Moore's fixation with small, restraining interiors was driven by a personal search for experiential profundity against what he saw as the superficiality of contemporary architectural culture. The aedicule gave expression to the fantasy that the modern architect's creativity originated in the absence of a past, outside of history— in the innocent and unsullied self. The aedicule was a means for self-purification, a crutch to help the architect in the mystical path toward achieving the universal, timeless self associated with modernist creativity.

Supergraphics

While teaching at Berkeley, Moore regained contact with his Princeton classmates Donlyn Lyndon (b. 1936) and William Turnbull (1935–1997). Together with Richard Whitaker (b. 1929), they founded the firm MLTW as a moonlighting operation, while each of them held full-time jobs elsewhere. Their first major commission was the

Sea Ranch Condominium (1965), located about one hundred miles north of San Francisco on a steeply sloping site perched above a rocky bluff on the Pacific ocean. The design clustered together nine residences on a 24-foot module around a courtyard, with a common parking lot at the top of the hill. What attracted the attention of critics at the time was principally the compact siting and massing of the complex, the use of shed roofs, and the cladding of the exterior walls with rough vertical wood siding left to weather.[48] These expressive choices were in the tradition of the Bay region style, which had been popularized by architects William Wurster (1895–1973) and Joseph Esherick (1914–1998), who cofounded University of California Berkeley's College of Environmental Design in 1959. The American architectural historian and critic Lewis Mumford coined the term Bay region style in 1947 to describe their attempt to replace the narrow orthodoxy of the international style with a more inclusive modernism capable of assimilating the vernacular aesthetics of local building traditions.[49] Opposing the modernist establishment seemed congruent with the education Moore

had received at Princeton. "I started out thinking of myself as a 'Bay Region architect,'" he recalled.[50]

The design of the Sea Ranch Condominium was a collaborative effort that included exceptional emerging talents outside of MLTW, such as Lawrence Halprin, who worked as landscape designer on the project. The partners divided up the work among themselves, and Moore gravitated toward the design of the interiors. While the exteriors made reference to local building traditions, Moore's interiors were totally unconventional. He subdivided the large, double-story space of each unit into two aedicules. Here again, Moore used the aedicule to anchor and arouse the material imagination. The principal aedicule covered the fireplace, making the association of the aedicule with the poetic image of fire

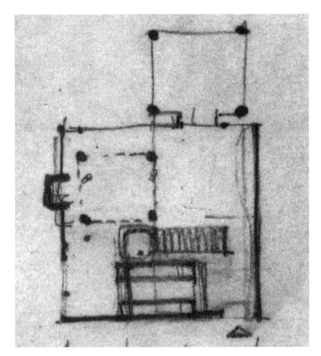

Sketch by Charles Moore for typical Sea Ranch Condominium One, showing the four posts of the aedicula framing the fireplace, with stairs to the sleeping loft, 1964. Courtesy of the Charles Moore Foundation.

more obvious than in his own house in Orinda. Above the aedicule, Moore placed the bedrooms as open loft spaces. The aedicule was meant as the restricted place of reverie, whether awake in front of the fire or in a half-slumber in bed. It was an architectural translation of Bachelard's claim that bodily confinement forced people to experience "concentrated wandering," to feel as though they were "elsewhere."[51]

The clients were not impressed. The directors of the real estate development firm Castle and Cook feared that the units would not sell with such an unconventional loft interior. Moore and his partners eased their clients' anxiety with the argument that the aedicule would be a familiar experience to everyone. It was, they claimed, a small house within a house, like "a child's play space under a card table after you throw a sheet over the top."[52] The aedicule was meant to help inhabitants rediscover the joyful innocence of their inner child. The argument was simple and persuasive enough to turn the clients' opinion around.

Joy was a central concept of Bachelard's philosophy. He associated joy with the immediate experience of the onset of a poetic image in one's consciousness. Bachelard regarded poetic images as "inner visions," in which inner consciousness and outer world came together. As such, they constituted, in the words of philosopher Edward Casey, "the interiorization of the world."[53] For Moore, the aedicule came to stand in for this interiorization, miniaturization, and privatization of outer reality into intimate personal experiences. The aedicule became for him the emblematic poetic architectural space, in the sense that its function was to induce *poesis,* or creativity, by blending inner and outer world. It was a pedagogical crutch to help inhabitants "assimilate and forget" outer reality and create something new.

The aedicule, as the site of authentic experiences, was also conceived as a step toward a more ambitious redefinition of what made American homes genuine. Architectural historians have failed to note this ambition in the interiors of Sea Ranch. Instead, historians like Leland Roth have indexed the building's "authenticity" as a function of its exterior resemblance to the vernacular farm structures of the Bay region.[54] Roth is emblematic of the trend to treat vernacular buildings as the standard of authenticity, which became common among historians in the 1970s, as vernacular architecture studies gained momentum in the United States in the wake of pioneering studies such as Reyner Banham's *Los Angeles: The Architecture of Four Ecologies* (1971) and Robert Venturi, Denise Scott-Brown, and Steven Izenour's *Learning from Las Vegas* (1977). Moore is also rightly considered to be a pioneer in the study of vernacular architecture, as his 1962 article "Toward Making Places" attests.[55] But to focus on vernacular styles is to miss the central point of Moore's theory of authenticity. Moore's esteem of vernacular architecture did not lead him to conclude that new buildings in a vernacular style were more authentic than others. For Moore, what made new buildings authentic was not their shape, but rather the type of experience they offered. In particular, he thought the most authentic buildings were those that immediately induced the experience of familiar poetic images in the visitor's mind. This was a subtle but significant shift in the discourse of architectural authenticity. It moved the locus of authenticity from the object to the subject. The mark of authenticity was the onset of a poetic image in the subject—not the style, materials, or other physical givens of the building.

The shift to the subject did not mean that one could do away with the building entirely. The building remained a means to an experiential end. But Moore's experiential theory of authenticity effectively relieved the modernist pressure to produce finely crafted buildings and to restrict expression to the modernist vocabulary. Moore saw the use of historic architectural styles familiar to visitors as a basic way to encourage them to project their own memories onto the new building, to begin to turn inward and choose *their* reality within reality. Moore was interested in discovering more sophisticated means, besides style, to turn visitors' attention inward toward their immediate experiences of poetic images. For Moore, the highest level of architectural sophistication in organizing the visitor's attention was only achievable in the building's interiors, where the architect was in full control of the environment. This is why during the design of Sea Ranch he gravitated toward interior design. In the interiors, Moore began to mark his differences from the Bay region style, de-emphasizing stylistic form and emphasizing experiential poetic content.

Working with a tight budget as construction neared completion in 1965, Moore decided on modest means to emphasize the importance of the aedicule within the larger spaces of the Sea Ranch units. He designed bold primary-color paint schemes to make the aedicules stand out against the natural wood interiors.[56] Essentially, Moore turned the aedicules into large painted signs to direct visitors toward them. He had learned to paint large abstract graphics while serving in the Korean War, where he designed wayfaring signs for his regiment. At Princeton, he developed that early work into a more sophisticated understanding of the effect of movement on the perception of signs. Labatut's studio courses required students to establish the scale and appearance of their designs as a function of the speed of the observer's movement. Many of Labatut's advisees in the 1940s and 1950s produced theses exploring movement-generated designs. For instance, Frederick C. McNulty (MFA, 1949) did "A study of the effect of modes of travel at various speeds and its effect on architectural scale as preparation to the design of a motor hotel."[57] Moore's own dissertation included visual analyses of how his fountains would be perceived by drivers and was described in the school's exhibition catalogue as a "design of roadside water choreography."[58] Labatut recalled: "All these projects that the students were doing, are strongly related to the sequencing, the experience of creating these sequences."[59] Of all his students, Venturi was the one who most literally (and shamelessly) appropriated Labatut's ideas as the basis for his own teaching and research, publishing them as *Learning from Las Vegas* without a single reference to Labatut.

Sometimes Moore sinned as well by denying Labatut's influence: "I never got as excited about him as Don [Lyndon] and Bill [Turnbull]."[60] But he redeemed himself later in life, recognizing that "in the five years that I had [at Princeton], certainly Labby [Labatut] was the key figure; the subtlety and breadth of his vision made it all work."[61] Labatut, the ex-*camoufleur,* taught his students that the viewer's movement was a perceptual variable that changed the appearance of a building's form, making it seem larger than it really was, or smaller, or even disappear altogether.[62] Camoufleurs used paint to deobjectify buildings and make them vanish in the eyes of enemy observers. Labatut taught paint camouflage to his architecture students as an aesthetic technique equivalent to the mental process of "forgetting" historical architectural precedents. This deobjectification technique, overlaid with phenomenological arguments so that immediate experience

Plate 1. *Charles Moore, proposal for a new fountain in the plaza of Mies van der Rohe's Seagram Building, New York, 1954–57. Courtesy of Princeton University Archives, Department of Rare Books and Special Collections, Princeton University Library.*

Plate 2. *Charles Moore, proposal for a new fountain in the plaza of SOM's Lever House Building, New York, 1951–52. Courtesy of Princeton University Archives, Department of Rare Books and Special Collections, Princeton University Library.*

FACING PAGE: Plate 3. Charles Moore's unit at Sea Ranch Condominiums, showing early experiments in supergraphics. The kitchen is painted in bold geometric fields of red and white against a blue background. Photograph by Morley Baer, copyright 2008 by the Morley Baer Photography Trust, Santa Fe, N.M. All reproduction rights reserved.

ABOVE: Plate 4. Barbara Stauffacher, supergraphics in the locker room of the Sea Ranch Athletic Club, ca. 1965. Photograph by Morley Baer, copyright 2008 by the Morley Baer Photography Trust, Santa Fe, N.M. All reproduction rights reserved.

Plate 5. View up the central aedicula in Charles Moore's house in New Haven, Connecticut. A disco ball hangs from the ceiling, reflecting psychedelic lights. Interiors like this earned Moore's work the label LSDesign.

Plate 6. Charles Moore sits with students in the backyard of his New Haven house. The supergraphic painted on the garden fence used a trompe l'oeil technique to make the number 3 appear when viewed from the interior. Copyright Norman McGrath.

ABOVE: Plate 7. Supergraphic aedicule encloses Moore's bed in his New Haven house, 1966. Copyright Norman McGrath.

FACING PAGE: Plate 8. Supergraphics in the guest room of Moore's house, New Haven, 1966. Copyright Norman McGrath.

Plate 9. Supergraphics in the aedicule above the kitchen of Moore's house, New Haven, 1966. Copyright Norman McGrath.

THE STRUCTURIST

No. 5

1965

Plate 10. Cover of the journal The Structurist, no. 5 (1965).

Plate 11. Kenneth Frampton, Berlin Grafik! 1967. Mixed media on cardboard. Courtesy of Kenneth Frampton.

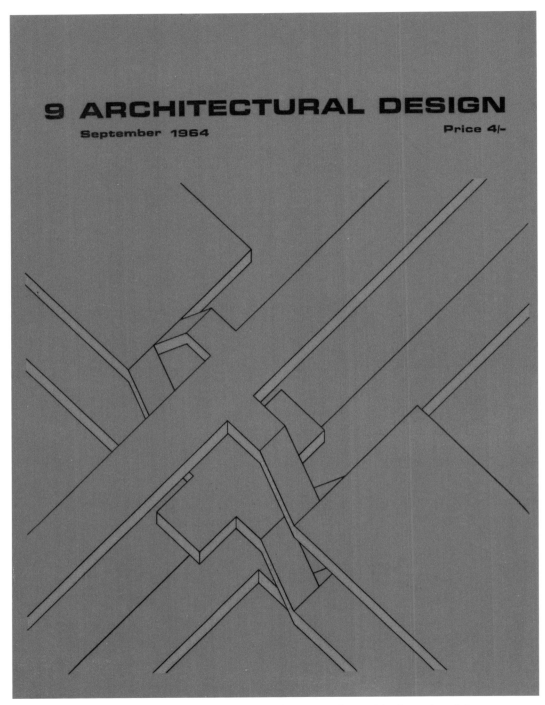

Plate 12. Kenneth Frampton and Anthony Stockbridge, structurist graphic abstraction of the crossover scissors staircase system used in Craven Hills Gardens building. Cover of Architectural Design 34, no. 9 (September 1964).

was a condition of possibility for authentic creativity, were the aesthetic and intellectual sources of Moore's interior painting schemes at Sea Ranch.

At first, critics did not know what to make of "Moore's preoccupation with interior architecture."[63] But two years after the completion of Sea Ranch, Moore's paint scheme design was identified by *Progressive Architecture* as the origin of a new movement in architectural design: supergraphics.[64] By then, Moore had moved from Berkeley to become chairman of the Department of Architecture at Yale University (1965–67), where he would remain for a decade, becoming dean in 1969 and then serving as professor from 1970 until 1975. The move to Yale was, as his partner William Turnbull remembered, a calculated gamble to "roll the dice for the Big Time" and "get your name known by the New York crowd."[65] With Yale as his platform, Moore became one of the most influential professors in America. As biographer David Littlejohn noted, "Once at Yale, Moore was a certified celebrity. Virtually everything he did got into print."[66] The pedagogy that he promoted had a lasting influence on the school as well as on American architectural education in general.

Moore taught Yale students the art of supergraphics as a technique to tap the creativity of the material imagination, instead of the rational mind. While the emphasis on fantasy was attractive to students, Moore's demotion of rationality caused tensions in the MLTW office. Donlyn Lyndon recalled arguing that design decisions had to be rationally justifiable, something Moore disagreed with. "My perception," said Lyndon, "is that Chuck's work *after* we worked together went crazier."[67] Moore surrounded himself at Yale with trusted like-minded colleagues, like Barbara Stauffacher, a rising figure of the supergraphics movement, who had painted the interiors of the Sea Ranch athletic club in 1965.[68] With Moore's blessing, Stauffacher asked students to "destroy" the interiors of the much-maligned Yale Art and Architecture Building with "experience expanding" supergraphics.[69] The act of painting directly on buildings achieved important pedagogical and symbolic objectives: it made students experience architectural design as something immediate by removing the intermediary step of technical drawing. It also linked architectural design to painting, a high cultural paradigm of self-expression. Moore's active demotion of technical drawing was meant to promote intuitive design instead of reasoned analysis. "Students came to mistrust drawing as a biased representation of architecture, incapable of showing how one would really experience a building," recalled one of his students. "It was an anti-intellectual approach to architecture, a nononsense seat of the pants attitude."[70] Moore told students that "the opposite of rational is real" and that reality was perception.[71] Authentic design, as Moore instructed it, required that students first discover their inner feelings and then exteriorize them directly without the mediation of thought. "It was both an act of learning, and a process of deprogramming—erasing the preconceptions."[72] Supergraphics entailed a twofold erasing. It was a technique meant to operate both on the subject, suspending the rational mind, and on the object, under-mining the spatial order of the building from the inside. Supergraphics was an aesthetic performance of the act of forgetting, which Moore held to be the pre-condition for authentic creativity.

Progressive Architecture emphasized that the supergraphics movement was not simply a decorative style but rather a new architectural form of "spatial experimentation." Ada Louise Huxtable (b. 1921), architecture critic for *The New York Times,* labeled Moore an "architecture-destroyer," whose supergraphics exploded the orthogonal orthodoxy of modernism's interiors. Supergraphics, she argued, was "wildly sense awakening."[73] Huxtable hailed Moore's unabashed bright-colored interiors as "a rebellious attempt to expand experience by breaking down the traditions of the Establishment" and an astonishing disclosure of how "experientially repressive" corporate modernist interiors were.[74] Moore was typecast as the enfant terrible of architecture, who pressed forth a "genuinely revelatory expansion of visual and sensuous experi-ence."[75] The "destruction" of the modernist interior was justified in the name of achieving more authentic subjective experience. In an indirect way, super-graphics also helped Moore more openly embrace his own sexuality and liberate himself from the homophobic profession. Journalists such as Rosemary Kent in "Is Decorator a Dirty Word?" did not fail to note the connection of super-graphics with interior design, a traditionally female practice. Using language that recalled Moore's own dissertation (which proclaimed to be "moistening" the aridness of modernism), Kent portrayed him as refreshing the "austere International Style interior" in order to "break down the Monumentality" from the inside out with "bold colors, supergraphics, and unusual juxtapositions of space and furnishings."[76] Supergraphics was not without critics. "At its worst," wrote Huxtable, "the style is superficial, tricky, repetitive, and shallowly orna-mental ."[77] Its expressions were at first tolerable only as long as they were safely contained within the interiors of buildings. But by 1968, supergraphics began appearing on facades across the country. *Progressive Architecture* noted: "You may not be ready, again, for more Supergraphics, much less for learning that they are spreading to the outside."[78]

Nearly ten years after finishing his dissertation, Moore had succeeded in bringing his interest in immediate experience to the center of architectural culture, where it was eagerly received as the liberating promise of a new horizon beyond modernism. Moore de-emphasized the phenomenological sources of his thinking, perhaps intuiting that bookishness was incongruous with his new persona as architectural spokesman of youth counterculture. His interest in immediate experience earned his work the label of "LSDesign," for its capacity to induce "groovy " and "mind-warping experiences."[79] Doug Michels (1944–2003), Moore's Yale student and later cofounder of Ant Farm, who did much of the actual painting for him, described supergraphics best: "These are space trips."[80] Moore's work came to denote illicit experiences, as free from the right-angle "laws" of modernism as acid trips were from the conventions of "square" postwar society.

Creative Experience

The precise techniques Moore used to awaken the senses are best understood in relationship to his built projects, particularly his residence in New Haven. Upon accepting his appointment at Yale, Moore bought a two-story suburban Victorian house and began a renovation project that was substantially complete by 1966. He left the exterior essentially untouched, focusing his intervention exclusively on the interiors. As in his prior residential projects, he populated the house with aedicules. Three of them were large, double-height rectangular voids cut out from the existing floorboards. The two aedicules in the front and back of the house linked the first floor to the basement, while the central aedicule spanned the first and the second floors. The fourth aedicule was a small cabinet-like enclosure for his bed.

Each aedicule was wrapped in thin sheetrock walls from which sections of oversized circles and other geometric supergraphics were cut out (instead of painted on). The intention of the cutouts was to create immediate experiences that, as Moore understood them, involved as much sensual reception as mental projection. The mark of an immediate experience was the conflation of outer and inner worlds. Moore hoped that visitors would project their familiar inner images of circles onto the existing aedicules and complete the cutout figures in their minds.

The aedicules seemed like playful and simple exercises in Gestalt perception. But they were the result of what was then cutting-edge research. Moore's theoretical grasp of supergraphics was informed by a wider academic interest in

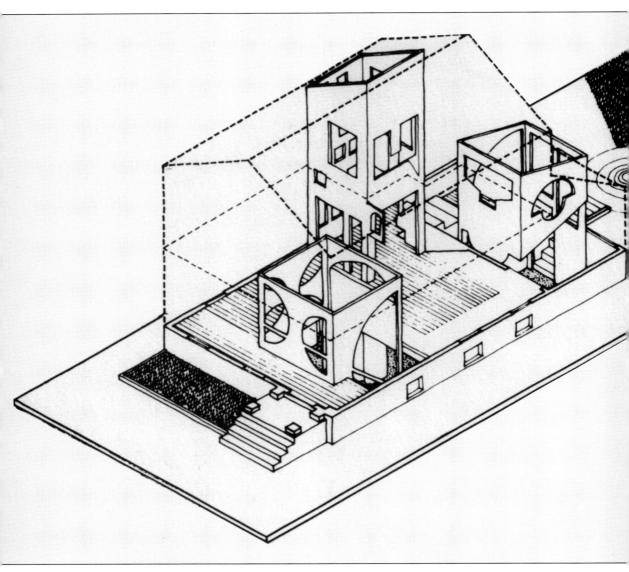

how environments affected human emotion. The epicenter of applied research on the subject was the West Coast. From 1966 to 1968, Moore worked with Bill Turnbull on the design and construction of the new faculty club for the University of California at Santa Barbara. The university was renowned as a pioneering center of sensitivity training and encounter groups (now known as group therapy). Kathleen Plummer, who was a graduate student in architecture at Santa Barbara while the faculty club was being built, recalled how Moore was drawn to the faculty's research on the influence of environments on self-awareness.[81] Moore's interest in immediate experience was informed by ongoing research at

Santa Barbara on preverbal or "direct communication," which involved experimental ways to break down social hierarchy by, for instance, seating students in a circle instead of in rows. Direct communication was seen as a radical new way to "break down 'hang-ups' and old ways of doing things."[82] Likewise, supergraphics were understood as environmental devices to turn people's attention back on themselves, empowering them to discover their inner images and project them, through the power of their imagination, onto the spaces implied by the paint.

Apart from supergraphics, Moore also placed found objects in his interiors to awaken experience. Playing on the label of LSDesign, he hung a disco ball from the ceiling of one of the aedicules in his Yale residence. The overt reference to youth culture encouraged interpretations of the aedicule as a space for experiential discovery. Moore used objects to play with scale, encouraging visitors to experience not just reality but also their inner fantasies of cosmic and minuscule worlds. He filled niches with toys and miniature houses, suggesting a diminutive scale. His use of found objects extended to drawings and graphics. He used a Volkswagen billboard as wallpaper. He copied a baroque drawing for a trompe-l'oeil dome on the ceiling above his bed, creating a virtual aedicule. The walls of this aedicule were painted with white stars like those found in the American flag, but here against a red background. It was a tongue-in-cheek reference to the idea that reverie was an immediate experience of celestial immensity.

The stars on the aedicule were also a clear reference to contemporary pop art, initiated ten years earlier by works like Jasper Johns's *Flag* (1954–55). Indeed, Moore was trying to do to architectural modernism what pop art had done to abstract expressionism. Modernism, like abstract expressionism, seemed self-referential, having eschewed nonmodernist aesthetics in an effort to arrive at the abstract essence of a building. By the mid 1960s, Moore's generation of architects began to question the claim that modernism expressed *the* timeless essence of construction, free from all historically determined symbolic content. In the jet age, modernism's functionalist aesthetics seemed part of a bygone world of transatlantic ships and Model T cars, as Banham noted polemically.[83] Venturi accused modernism of having evolved a new form of self-referentiality centered on the subjective "heroic" visions of macho author-architects.[84] To these young architects, it seemed that modernist architecture, like abstract expressionism, could only achieve meaningfulness through references that pointed back to an author. Modernism seemed to have reduced buildings to large signatures, whose cryptic messages were decodable only by an endogamous circle of initiated connoisseurs. The breakthrough of pop art was that it reintro-duced a symbolic content into art other than the authorial self.

Pop art worked on two levels. Artists incorporated popular imagery to make a basic level of artistic meaning available to general audiences. They also worked on a deeper abstract level, using collage and other techniques, to com-municate more complex art-specific meanings to initiated audiences. As Jasper Johns explained: "Using the American flag took care of a great deal for me because I didn't have to design it . . . so I went on to similar things like the targets . . . things the mind already knows. That gave me room to work on other levels."[85] By the late 1970s, art scholars had come to understand the dual icono-graphical and "infra-iconographical" nature of pop art.[86] Surprisingly, architec-tural scholars to this day insist on stopping their interpretations of postmodernism at the level of its popular imagery. Popular symbolism and classical motifs freed postmodern architects to work on other levels, which a full accounting of the movement must necessarily engage. In Moore's case, it allowed him to pursue his obsession to achieve authentic experiences through architec-ture and to use space to organize visitors' attention inward, so they would become self-conscious of their experiences. Moore's postmodernism was not a displacement of the myth of ontological primacy from the structure to the sur-face of buildings. Rather, it was a transfer of that myth onto the experiencing subject, which resulted in a search for experiential profundity.

Although it was seen as radical in architectural circles, Moore's interest in experiential awareness was already a major theme in the world of contemporary art. Moore drew freely on different artistic movements that were also exploring ways of involving the subject in the creative process, such as countercultural, psychedelic, and comic strip art that tried to alter consciousness, and body or performance art that used reality as creation. But optical or op art spoke most directly to his interest in immediate experience. The Responsive Eye, the 1965 MoMA exhibition curated by William C. Seitz, presented the ability of op art to induce the involuntary participation of viewers in the painting through visual solicitation techniques such as the after-image, consecutive movement, line interference, ambiguous figures, reversible perspective, and the effects of dazzle. Op art techniques were drawn from the breakthroughs of camouflage, Gestalt perception, and psychophysiology. Significantly, the work of op artists like the Hungarian Victor Vasarely (1908–1997) and the Venezuelan Jesús Soto (1923–2005) spilled into architecture. They explored the optical superimposition of elements in three-dimensional space, anticipating the 1963 "discovery" of phenomenal transparency announced by Colin Rowe (1920–1999) and Robert Slutzky (1929–2005) in Yale's journal of architecture *Perspecta*.[87] Moore openly acknowledged his indebtedness to op art in the mural he painted on his backyard fence in New Haven. He also played the circular cutouts in the aedicules against a circular op art painting of the letter "O." Moore's architecture aimed at the total implication of the visitor in the aesthetic process of creating space through the three-dimensional organization of visual and haptic relationships.

Moore's supergraphics work in his Yale house reveals his greater ambitions. He wanted to awaken and expand the visual sense of visitors beyond the perception of physical space and toward the inner experience of imaginary poetic space. Because he believed the inner world of experience to be cosmic in proportions, he looked for ways to create an equivalent outer visual experience of larger-than-life incommensurability. His solution was to blow up the size of the cutouts, making it appear as though the geometric figures were so large they didn't fit into the confines of the interior space and had slipped into spaces beyond. Supergraphics were meant to titillate the imaginary to visualize worlds beyond the real.

The architectural press reported on the house as an otherworldly experience: "The space extending process of this super scale induces one man to infer that the gigantic graphics are part of a world beyond the one he is in."[88] "Supergraphics," wrote the *Progressive Architecture* reporter, gave visitors the "giant vision of an extraterrestrial observer," and "make Superman of us all."[89] But who did "us" refer to? The short answer is architects. The discourse surrounding supergraphics held the architect's experience of architecture to be more authentic than that of other mortals. Indeed it pretended to liberate regular folk by making them experience the world as architects:

> For ages, architects have been looking down onto plans and into models, but the layman seldom shared this private, lofty view. Today, the fragmented super-scale graphics of the Supermannerists make a superarchitect of even the layman.[90]

Despite its populist appearance, supergraphics was elitist with regard to the architect's aesthetic experience. It sought to educate and elevate the average man to the experiential level of an architect more than it sought to learn from popular culture. That is not to deny the influence of popular culture on supergraphics but only to underscore the degree to which supergraphics began as an academic movement. Regardless of how much it tried to appear antiacademic, it could not shed the educational impulse to frame everything as a pedagogical exercise. Supergraphics aimed at teaching the average person outside the classroom how to improve his or her experiential capacities. But it was also aimed squarely at the very structure of learning that was institutionalized in architecture schools. In academia, the experiential elitism of supergraphics served to exclude and delegitimize art historians as a group incapable of feeling the very thing that made buildings truly authentic.

Visual Historiography

By hiring new faculty, and mostly through his own teaching, Moore tried to turn Yale into a center for research into a new type of architecture that could be experienced as existing beyond physical reality, in the realm of the possible (the virtual), which was one of the main characteristics of supergraphics. Moore referred to this virtual dimension of architecture as its poetic image. He also equated the virtual poetic image with a more authentic architectural history of buildings.

One of Moore's greatest frustrations at Yale was his powerlessness, even as chair, to break the hold of art historians like Vincent Scully (b. 1920) on the teaching of architectural history.[91] Moore's famous "image gathering" was a reaction to what he saw as an overtheorized way of teaching and learning architectural history. Image gathering consisted in simply visiting buildings and learning their history through direct experiences. The image gathered was nothing more than the architect's loose recollection of what he deemed personally significant about that building (e.g., the proportions of the space, the quality of the

Charles Moore, Eric Hurner, Dmitri Vedensky, and Dona Guimares inside a classical aedicule in Stafford, England. From Kevin P. Keim, An Architectural Life: Memoirs and Memories of Charles W. Moore *(Boston: Little, Brown, and Company, 1996), 100.*

light, or the shape of a stair). To experience an image, in other words, entailed a great deal of self-projection.

Moore was well-traveled and possessed an extraordinary ability to recall a storehouse of mental images on command. His memory was aided by a collection of over fifty thousand slides, which he maintained religiously. An architectural history class of Moore's consisted of his unscripted commentary on slides of "his favorite eccentric places" [92] from around the world and across time. The purpose of his lectures was to "free the imagination"[93] of students instead of teaching them specific historical information. Even his more academic lectures, after being transcribed, polished, and edited, rarely mentioned the construction date of a pre-twentieth-century building.[94] Moore was not being careless. His history classes were structured according to what he saw as an alternate historiography— for architects by an architect—and based on images, not texts.

He believed his historiography was more modern and authentic than that of art historians because it was more attuned to the way architectural meaning was communicated in the postmodern era. In the mid- to late 1960s, there was a veritable explosion of architectural media communications, with television, trade journals, and little magazines quickly circulating information about architecture around the world.[95] Images were more effective than texts at crossing language divides. Moore wanted to update historiography to also be more visual, and not be simply circumscribed by textual interpretation. Conceived as a form of immediate preverbal visual communication, historiography became a performative, experiential act.

The key distinction between the architect-historian's historiography and that of the art historian was its ultimate purpose. Whereas the art historian aimed to build a corpus of objective knowledge about the past, the architect sought to relegate objectively verifiable facts to a secondary plane. Historiography served the architect-historian as a tool to find his own subjectivity beyond historical research. Its goal was to subdue the objective differences between buildings of different periods and establish a common ground between them, which invariably turned out to be the observer himself. In this sense, the architect-historian's historiography was antihistorical. It invoked history in order to negate it and disguise it as pure self-projection, that is to say, as authentic modern design. The architect-historian's historiography allowed architects to learn, assimilate, and (most importantly) forget the aesthetic pluralism of history. In Moore's own words:

> Like it or not, he [the contemporary architect] is an eclectic. He is faced with problems which have never existed for him before, and it is incumbent on him to understand them and the influences acting on him, to be able to crystallize their meaning for himself and only then to be able to push them to the back of his mind, to practice "creative forgetfulness" so that he is free to create architecture which will be the answer to these problems.[96]

Moore celebrated the idea that his historiography could build historical significance up out of layers of unrelated images of buildings from different periods, calling it his "conceptual triumph that may save the world, if there's any air left in it to breathe."[97] This triumph was really the victory of architect-historians over art historians. His reduction of historiography to a visual phenomenon played into the modern architect's prejudice that everything learned must play itself out in images.

Moore posited his recollections of historic buildings as primordial sources of pure creativity. He presented these recollections as an alternate historiography, which distinguished between historically significant and insignificant buildings on the basis of one's emotional response to them. He deemed this subjective historiography to be more authentic than that of art historians, who restricted historical significance to objective factors such as rarity or stylistic purity. Moore was indeed more inclusive than art historians in what buildings he accepted as historically significant. But the pluralism of his historiography also resulted in the exclusion of historical documents other than the building itself from consideration, negating the traditional historiographical protocols of verification through cross-checking of multiple sources. It reduced the various types of abstract knowledge achievable through the study of historical buildings (e.g., social, technical, and economic) to one: immediate visual experience.

Visual historiography also constituted a lowering of scholarly standards insofar as Moore's attribution of significance could not be verified by third parties. Students had to simply believe that the master's inner vision truly embodied the building's historical significance. His rejection of the methods of art history was based on a life devoted to readings in architectural history and philosophy. But he did not ask the same rigorous intellectual study from his students. Quite the contrary, he promoted an anti-intellectual approach to architecture. His students came to mistrust reading and even drawing as biased representations of the images available only through direct experience.[98] By the early 1980s, the idea that design was the arrangement of images in experiential sequences had taken over the design studios of most major U.S. universities.[99]

Body-Image

Moore retained the modernist idea that architecture should be the outward projection of the hero-architect's inner experiences. Yet he insisted that the architect maintain commitments outside of the self, helping to interpret and develop the historical relationship between communities and their environments. How could the personal fantasies of the architect be a service to communities? Moore advanced the notion that poetic images were not purely personal, but had their origin in a communal fund into which people deposited and withdrew images. Students were confused. "Certainly at Yale," exclaimed one student, "we talk about it [images] a lot."[100] But, complained the frustrated pupil, no one at Yale explained how "his" image could also appear in everyone's mind. Moore explained:

> An attempt is made to add to that fund of images, to enter into some set of transactions that enrich the image bank, call it "educating" I guess. Then some imagery that comes out of the people present develops which is going to mean more to the people than some image laid on them . . . So I press for a catholicity of image collection. In the absence of any clear knowledge of where images ought not to come from, it's legitimate to have them come from anywhere that means anything to anybody.[101]

Moore's explanation was deliberately cryptic and superficial, denying us access to his intellectual sources. The intersubjectivity of experience was a fundamental concept in phenomenology, discussed at length by most phenomenologists from Husserl to Heidegger and Bachelard to Merleau-Ponty. Moore seemed to have absorbed some of these phenomenological descriptions of intersubjectivity in his idea that poetic images resided in communal funds. According to Moore, communal poetic images were created by many people through their repeated experience of a particular place. This was Moore's central argument about the historical significance of Walt Disney World.[102] The question was what attracted people to those particular places and not others. As the title of *Body, Memory, and Architecture* suggested, Moore believed that meaningful, memorable experiences occurred when there was a harmonious relationship between the human body and the "body" of buildings (the core principle of Labatut's theory of Eucharistic architecture). If outward forms had something in common, then their inward spirit must also be analogous. The "body-image," as Moore and Bloomer coined their theory, entailed a problematic conflation of subjectivity and objectivity, whereby whatever idea that surfaced in the architect's mind while looking at a building was immediately understood to be "objectively" *the* generating idea of the building. It did not matter when or who built the building.[103] The meaning of architecture ceased to be situated historically. Instead, the meaning of every building was subjected to the present moment in which it was experienced. This reduction of historical significance to self-projection deceived architectural phenomenologists into believing all particulars were really universals: "Indeed it is impossible to imagine a spatial organization more universal, more valued, and more immediately understandable to everyone than the one provided by the human body."[104]

The theory of the body-image was a modernist denial, or forgetting, of the historical specificity and aesthetic particularity of locations, which was done precisely in the name of history and place. When architectural phenomenologists researched historical buildings as the basis for their designs, the theory of the body-image became their means to freely transform historical styles into something new. In this sense, the body-image allowed them to abide by the strictest code of modernist design: that every building must be a totally new expression. But unlike the modernists of the early twentieth century, architectural phenomenologists of the 1960s were less concerned with creating something new than with avoiding repeating what had already been done. Their reinterpretation of the modernist style was methodologically the same as their handling of any and all historical styles.

As Moore's theory gained support within the academy as a central concept of architectural phenomenology,[105] the term body-image was replaced by others like "embodiment of place" and promoted by architects and phenomenologists commenting on architecture.[106] In the discourse of architectural phenomenology, place and body, objectivity and subjectivity, became inextricably bound in a mythical (and constantly receding) common origin. It became the principal idea around which publications like the *Environmental and Architectural Phenomenology Newsletter* were founded as late as 1990.[107] The success of the theory of embodied place in architecture attests to its ability to allow architects to appear to be engaged with local history while simultaneously continuing to operate under a modernist ahistorical paradigm of creativity.

Anti-Intellectualism

Moore resisted close exegeses of his theories, as if reflection would sully the experiential purity of the poetic image's provenance. He decried the intellectualization of architecture, arguing that semiotics and linguistics missed the arational way in which, he believed, buildings and people "exchanged" meanings sensually. Even a book as patently unscholarly as Charles Jencks's *The Language of Post-Modern Architecture* (1977) was too academic for Moore. Professing faith in the correspondence of body, feeling, and architecture, Moore argued that the history of architecture should be learned through "full corporeal experiences" of buildings, not books.[108]

Moore's antitheory stance must not be confused with the brand of anti-intellectualism that characterized the American middle class at the time. Moore was among the beneficiaries of America's elite university system and among the most highly educated architects of his time (very few architects, even to this day, hold a PhD). In *Body, Memory, and Architecture* he construed his opposition to theory as an extension of what he saw as a long antirationalist tradition in philosophy, from Diderot to Hume, the Earl of Shaftesbury, and Bachelard. He pitted the mind against the body, arguing that thought was a reductive abstraction of the full reality of corporeal experience. The book made clear an unresolved contradiction in Moore's thinking: the introduction of philosophical references created a prerequisite of intellectual competence that was antagonistic to the presumed spontaneity of his sensualist epistemology. This contradiction reveals the degree to which Moore's anti-intellectualism came to be at odds with the rising scholarly standards of 1970s architectural discourse. The success of the Princeton doctoral program prompted other universities, such as MIT, Harvard, and later Columbia to also establish PhD programs in architecture. *Body, Memory, and Architecture* was Moore's response to this new intellectual climate. The book was meant to capture and disseminate his view of architectural pedagogy as a deintellectualized experientialism based on the self-discovery of inner poetic images. And yet, by writing the book, Moore was caught in the contradictory position of having to theorize his own demotion of theory.

With *Body, Memory, and Architecture,* Moore and Bloomer returned reluctantly to phenomenology, presenting Bachelard as a key interpreter of the poetic image as a source of creativity.[109] Their invocation of phenomenology at this point was a means to put a theoretical gloss on their antitheoretical convictions. Once summoned as a legitimizing footnote, the philosophy's substance was quickly discarded. Moore and Bloomer were trying to stay current with the times. By the time they were writing the book, phenomenology had become enormously popular among architects at Yale, partly thanks to Moore, and partly thanks to coincidental historical circumstances. Significantly, John Wild, then America's most prominent phenomenologist, had moved from Northwestern University to Yale in 1963, beginning what phenomenologists commonly referred to as the "Northwestern-Yale axis." Wild was the cofounder with James Edie (1927–1998), of the Society for Phenomenology and Existential Philosophy (SPEP)[110]

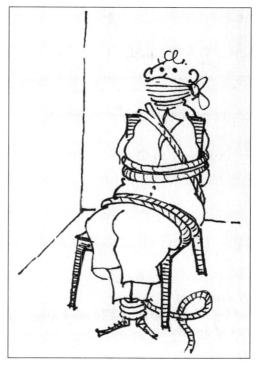

Cartoon by Kent Bloomer illustrating Hegel's philosophical position on human experience. Charles Moore and Bloomer used cartoons like this to interpret the history of philosophy and phenomenology for architectural audiences in Body, Memory, and Architecture *(New Haven, Yale University Press, 1977). Courtesy of Kent Bloomer.*

and of the book series *Northwestern University Studies on Phenomenology and Existential Philosophy,* which made seminal phenomenological texts available in English. The series was aimed at a scholarly yet non-philosophical audience.[111] Phenomenology expanded into psychology, communicology, and economics with sufficient force to warrant the foundation of a separate Society for Phenomenology and the Human Sciences. Phenomenology influenced the work of Yale art students, most notably Richard Serra, who was there from 1961 to 1964. It also influenced architecture students. Under Moore's chairmanship, Karsten Harries, a phenomenologist teaching at Yale since 1961 and a key member of the Yale-Northwestern axis, became active in the architecture school, participating in architecture studio reviews, writing for the school's journal, and eventually writing phenomenological books on architecture.[112]

Other architecture programs followed suit, especially those run by Moore's disciples. At Tulane, for instance, Dean Ron Filson, Moore's former student at Yale, brought phenomenologist Michael Zimmerman into the school's fold.[113] Some phenomenologists even took up permanent teaching positions in architecture schools, such as Robert Mugerauer, a protégé of Moore at the University of Texas, Austin, who later became dean of the Architecture School at the University of Washington. Phenomenologists celebrated their new popularity publicly but worried privately about the zealousness with which architects upheld phenomenology as the only path to "authentic" expression. By 1969, James Edie noted with apprehension that "phenomenology in this country has already been accused of becoming a new form of dogmatism."[114] If phenomenologists felt that the assertions of architectural phenomenologists about the nature of aesthetic experience and visual communication were blunt and doctrinaire, it certainly did not stop them from taking advantage of their newfound status to infiltrate architecture schools.

The ease with which phenomenologists moved into architecture speaks to the ambiguous definition of intellectual work in architectural education during the late 1960s and early 1970s. Prior to that, architectural history had been regarded as the standard of intellectual work. Labatut, Moore, and their circle of architectural phenomenologists had managed to differentiate their methods for studying architecture from those of art historians. Architectural phenomenologists rebelled against the hegemony of the written word over visual expression. They questioned the supposition that writing provided a measure of objective detachment from the visual. Instead, they advocated a performative, subjective, and visual historiography based on loose notions of immediate experience and pre-verbal communication. Unable for the most part to fully expunge art historians from architecture schools, architectural phenomenologists created new, more open-ended seminars on theory, which were seen as the intellectual complement to their studio courses. The content and nature of these theory seminars became a perfect access point for phenomenologists who were brought in to elevate the quality of the classes. Readings in phenomenology, especially Bachelard, were first introduced in these early theory courses. In sum, the ambiguous intellectual realm defined by architectural phenomenologists, while appearing as a rebellion against abstract, text-based intellectual work, also served to accommodate new and more rigorous forms of text-based interpretation, which we now call architectural theory.

Donlyn Lyndon introduced these new theory courses at the University of Oregon when he became head of the Department of Architecture. [115] It was a means to elevate the symbolic status of the school vis-à-vis the top ranking East Coast schools. Jerry Finrow, who joined the architecture faculty in 1968, recalled that Bachelard was the most important intellectual reference shared by the faculty: "We viewed him as working to clarify fundamental experiences of space . . . We thought he was doing what we were doing."[116] Bachelard, continued Finrow, was easier for architects to understand than Heidegger or Husserl, which also made him more teachable. Earl Moursund's "Spatial Composition and Dynamics" class was among the most popular theory courses at Oregon. The class reading list mixed the writings by architect-historians like Moore and Bloomer's *Body, Memory, and Architecture* or Norberg-Schulz's *Existence, Space, and Architecture* with works by phenomenologists like Bachelard's *Poetics of Space.* Moursund referred to architectural composition as the induction of "image-responses" in

Charles Moore in the course of a lesson to architecture students. From Heinrich Klotz, "Charles Moore in Miniatures," in Eugene J. Johnson, ed., Charles Moore: Buildings and Projects, 1949-1986 *(New York: Rizzoli, 1986), 39, Figure 1.*

people. For Moursund, learning to experience poetic images was the prerequisite for a student "to discover, daydream, speculate, imagine, explore," and "find orientation which connects him/her to the world (universe)."[117] As architectural phenomenologists began to take positions of power in the academy and influence pedagogy, they were able to pass off their subjective experientialism as an objective and scholarly study of the living past.

Academe

Charles Moore's rise to prominence within American academia during late 1960s and early 1970s happened during a key moment when architectural education was both expanding and undergoing an important transformation of its goals and purposes. A chief change was the move from a pedagogical system aimed at producing architect-heroes, individual visionaries with an authorial command over architecture, to one aimed at producing socially committed architects, team players who gave architectural expression to the values of the communities they served instead of imposing their own views. Moore was less committed to bringing down the model of the architect-hero than he has been made out to be. But he was extremely important as a transitional figure whose ambivalent views blended protest against the authoritarian visions of modernist architects with accommodation to the modernist ideology that architects possessed a unique inner vision. Moore's extraordinary success as a pedagogue rested on his ability to incorporate these two ideals of the architect into his pedagogy. He did not resolve the contradictions inherent in these two models. Rather, his work is interesting precisely because it reveals those contradictions.

The challenge to the figure of the architect-hero had intradisciplinary triggers, such as the deaths in the postwar period of the first generation of modernist architect-heroes (Wright in 1959, Le Corbusier in 1965, Gropius and Mies both in 1969). Moore's third generation of modernists questioned the legitimacy of the second generation, which included Charles and Ray Eames (1907–1978 and 1912–1988, respectively), Gordon Bunshaft (1909–1990), Eero Saarinen (1910–1961), Paul Rudolph (1918–1997), and others, to inherit the mantle of architect-heroes and the authority over the discipline. This insurrection was strengthened by extradisciplinary factors, especially the widespread climate of protest in Western universities during the late 1960s. Students actively rebelled against various forms of authoritarianism, which they identified with institutions of all sorts (from university administrations to professional associations). Moore crystallized the antiauthoritarian position within architecture. He attacked the modernist masters for restricting architectural expression to a modernist vocabulary. Significantly, he extended his campaign against authority to art historians, whom he condemned for reducing the value of historical architecture to a set of stylistic rules and exceptions. He suspected any attempts to rationalize architecture into an objective system of mindlessly advancing the domination of the creative subject. Moore's distrust of reason as a standard of creative competence led him to oppose theory—above all the theories of history employed by art historians to establish architectural significance. The subordination of traditional historiography led him to the hypostatization of practice as a way to create architectural history, which he understood to be the accumulation of immediate experiences or poetic images, not a textual reconstruction of objective events surrounding the design and construction of buildings. In this way, Moore helped to define a new position for himself within the field of architecture: the architect-historian.

The position of architect-historian emerged as the result of the first serious questioning by modernist architects of what constituted intellectual work in architecture and what dispositions were required for such work. As such, the architect-historian can be said to prefigure the contemporary architectural theorist. The important difference was that Moore believed the dispositions required of the architectural-historian were mainly experiential (visual or haptic), not intellectual. It was an antitheoretical theory that had unfortunate consequences. With the rise of architect-historians within academia, vital segments of architectural education fell into the hands of professors who joyfully and militantly proclaimed their hostility to theory, and who eagerly identified with students who showed the least intellectual promise.[118] The dumbing down of architectural design education in the United States answered the logic of an unfounded opposition between intellect and emotion. The less a student thought out a design, the more chances it had of being fresh, of emerging immediately from the inner self, as a pure expression of the soul. [119] Stupidity was reassessed as the precondition to the expression of an aesthetic essence, which was treasured for its alleged innocence. Intuitive design came to be prized for being unfettered by culture and politics.

But Moore's definition of the architect-historian was Janus-faced. The architect-historian mixed denunciations of authority with accommodation, indeed perpetuation, of the authorial model of the architect. The difference was that the architect-historian did not seek authority over society, only control over the discipline of architecture, and more specifically over the way architects experienced and understood architecture. Moore's figure of the architect-historian gave a new lease on the architectural life of modernist fantasies about aesthetic expression, namely, that it should have a pure origin or that it should be absolutely outside of bourgeois culture.[120] The trope of the architect-hero involved the cultivation of the self as something uncontaminated by history, and thus the source of the authentically new. The modernist theory of tabula rasa extended to the architect's inner self. Freeing the site of historical impurities was matched with an equivalent procedure of self-purification.

Moore helped turn the attention of architects toward history, expanding the range of buildings and types of spaces that they concentrated on and learned from. In particular, he encouraged architects to discover intimate spaces, like aedicules, as secure environments in which to meditate inwardly and rediscover their pure self in the form of a poetic image in the material imagination. In a tangible way, Moore did help free modern architects from the modernist ban on aestheticizing architectural history. But while he helped to overturn the aesthetics of modernism, he also left some of its fundamental intellectual frameworks intact.

Photo[historio]graphy
Christian Norberg-Schultz's Demotion of Textual History

Christian Norberg-Schulz was one of the most influential architecture theorists of the 1960s and 1970s. He was a key interpreter of phenomenology in general and of Martin Heidegger in particular for architectural audiences. His popular definition of architecture as a meaningful expression of the genius loci, or the spirit of place, was animated by a peculiar understanding of historiography, which he developed over the course of his career. In three pivotal texts, *Intentions in Architecture* (1965), *Existence, Space and Architecture* (1971), and *Genius Loci: Towards a Phenomenology of Architecture* (1979), Norberg-Schulz set out to reformulate how architects looked at and conceived of architecture. Specifically, he did not want them to understand modernism as a historic style. Instead, he proposed a return to the roots of modernism by visualizing the self-renewing origin of architecture. This undertaking required both rewriting the history of modern architecture and rethinking how modern architects engaged history.

Acknowledging that architects were "visual thinkers" who worked mostly with images, Norberg-Schulz put forth the polemical idea that architectural history was grasped more truthfully in images than in words. To prove this, he developed a new type of history book in which the pictures were not mere illustrations to the text, but alternate narratives. Through his carefully staged photo-essays, Norberg-Schulz theorized the history of architecture as the recurrence of visual patterns. My claim is that his photo[historio]graphy was fundamentally antihistorical; it attempted to ward off critical reflection by concealing its own historical construction. Norberg-Schulz passed off his photographs as universally valid visions of a timeless natural order that modern architects were invited to return to, in order to escape history.

Norberg-Schulz used photography to depict visual patterns from which he thought all original architecture emerged. During the course of his career, he used different names to refer to these visual patterns: first he called them "topological figures," then "genius loci," and finally *"aletheic* images." The term *aletheic* made reference to Heidegger's description of truthful experience, which Norberg-Schulz construed as synonymous with the visual experience of photographs. His hypostatization of photographs as revealing architectural truths signals a fundamental misunderstanding of Heidegger, whose hermeneutic ontology articulated one of the most powerful twentieth-century critiques of representation as the dominant intellectual paradigm of modernity. My intention in pointing out the instrumental misuse of Heidegger is not to give primacy to philosophy over architectural phenomenology, the discourse that Norberg-Schulz helped shape. Rather, my goal is to understand Norberg-Schulz's brand of architectural phenomenology in its own terms and in the wider historical and intellectual context that made it so influential among architects.

The Historian's Charisma

Norberg-Schulz's visual education began at the Eidgenössische Technische Hochschule (ETH) in Zurich, where he studied architecture between 1945 and 1949. His intellectual aptitude was quickly recognized by his professor, Sigfried Giedion, the noted architectural historian and first secretary general of CIAM, who took a special interest in mentoring the young pupil.[1] At the ETH, Norberg-Schulz encountered Giedion's view of modernity as an age of crisis in which humanity could either satisfy its material needs through science or its emotional needs through art but was unable to meet both demands holistically. Giedion discussed the historical relationship between science and art as two sine curves with "split paths."[2] The points when the two curves crossed represented times of harmony, the "high period" and perfected end of an era, when all human expression was a perfect mixture of both science and art. Giedion's diagram suggested that no matter what the current distance between science and art might be, the two would eventually come together (even if only to diverge again). In other words, he understood architectural history teleologically. Its telos, or final cause, was immanent in its origin as the impending synthesis of science and art.

The young Norberg-Schulz assimilated Giedion's teleological historiography and emulated his habit of expressing it visually. In his personal journal entry of 5 April 1950, Norberg-Schulz diagrammed the conceptual framework derived from Giedion. The horizontal axis represented time, and the vertical axis plotted the distance between scientific thinking and artistic feeling at any one moment. The result was a series of rhombuses strung in a line, each bound by

antikk–middelalder da *it* har en "stor" *tasvellsel* etter
Buschor.) Det er da et spørsmål om den nye *retningen*
for *målsettingen* er der allerede i overgangstiden, på en
måte ubevisst eller uopplevet. En kan i et hvert fall ikke
se bort fra disse overgangene da de har *sitt unmiskjennelige*
særpreg i uttrykkellet som nettopp har de uløste spenningene
som *hoveduttrykk* (også i det innholdsmessige ved
simultaniteten av to *realitetssfærer* – *Bruegel*, etc.)
spenningen i *forholdet* masse rom (*hverken* *rolig* "nebeneinander"
eller *dynamisk* "ineinander".) *spenningen immassen* alene
— da *først* og *fremst* i *flaten*, – i proporsjonene, *spenningen*
i rommet *som ledes* i *hårde baner*. *Intervikets* *kilde*, *hårde*
rivdling, men ofte *lette* og immaterielle *karakter*.
man *kunne* *kanskje* tegne en *slik* figur:

epokens   den ut.   den
stigning   løbende   nyes
               epoke   stigning

— Det *strekverk* betegner de nødvendige
overgangsfenomenene som ikke tilhører *uren* epoke; men som *tjener*
kl *2* *til* *konstansen* i *kvantiteten*. En kan tegne figuren *slik*:

og får to *flater* som *trenger* inn i hverandre: den ene kan

Christian Norberg-Schulz, journal entry, April 5, 1950. The two crisscrossing lines represent the cyclic relationship of science and art, which converge at the end of each historical era. Courtesy of the Norberg-Schulz Archive, The National Museum of Art, Architecture, and Design-The Norwegian Architecture Museum, Oslo.

two moments of synthesis between science and art, which also represented the moments of transition from an old to a new epoch. Norberg-Schulz shaded the sections outside of the rhombuses, noting that "the shaded area signifies the necessary transitory phenomena which could not be connected to any epoch."[3] These spaces outside the rhombuses were "pockets" filled with artistic expressions "without historical direction."[4] The question that immediately followed from such a diagram was where to locate the present. Was modern architecture evidence of the rise or decline of an epoch? "Our period," stated Giedion unequivocally, "is a period of transition," at the closing stages of modernity and the beginning stages of a yet unnamed "new tradition."[5]

Norberg-Schulz learned this theory from Giedion's history class. At the time, architectural theory as we conceive it today was not taught as a separate subject. Giedion complained that too much time was spent training architects on technical matters and not enough on methods of feeling. "Thinking is trained; feeling is left untrained."[6] Giedion poured his energy into teaching students that architecture was a means to "reabsorb" and "humanize" scientific facts into "an equivalent feeling."[7] The idea that aesthetic experience could subsume science and render it meaningful would serve as a foundation for Norberg-Schulz's later thought.

Norberg-Schulz was deeply influenced by Giedion's visual presentation of architectural history. Photographs, many of which Giedion took with a Rolleiflex Twin Lens Camera, were his principal teaching tools. His *Methodengleiche,* as he called it, consisted of projecting two slides on a screen, then comparing and contrasting them in search of visual similarities.[8] For instance, to demonstrate the omnipresence of the space-time worldview, he produced a photomontage of Rockefeller Center in New York City (1927–35) and H. E. Edgerton's strobe-light photograph of a golfer striking a ball. The photomontage visualized his argument that the space-time of urban space could not be grasped from any single location (unlike a baroque perspectival street, which was viewed most favorably from its axial extremities). To see space-time, the historian's eye had to become photographic: "To obtain a feeling for their interrelations the eye must function as in the high-speed photographs of Edgerton."[9]

Giedion's theoretical method was reductive. It pared down the complexities of science and art to visual similarities between photographs. For Giedion, this reduction was a part of being modern. Eliminating "superfluous facts" from history was his way of matching modern architecture's purge of decoration. Giedion promoted *Methodengleiche* as the "modern" way of writing architectural history. "The

457. Rockefeller Center. *Photomontage. Expressions of the new urban scale like Rocke-feller Center are forcefully conceived in space-time and cannot be embraced in a single view. To obtain a feeling for their interrelations the eye must function as in the high-speed photographs of Edgerton.*

It possesses symmetries which are senseless in reference to the aesthetic significance of the whole. It requires comprehension in space and time more closely analogous to what has been achieved in modern scientific research as well as in modern painting.

754

In Edgerton's stroboscopic studies, in which motion can be fixed and analyzed in arrested fractions of 1/100,000 of a second, a whole movement is shown separated into its successive components (*fig.* 458). At Rockefeller Center the human eye must function similarly (*fig.* 457); it has to pick up each individual view singly and relate it to all others, combining them into a time sequence. Only thus are we able to understand the grand play of volumes and surfaces and perceive its many-sided significance.

Rockefeller Center embraces many different activities. Leisure and entertainment, which were the initial motive in projecting the Center, are provided in Radio City, with its music hall, theaters, broadcasting studios, and night clubs; international trade is represented in the foreign buildings, journalism in the headquarters of the Associated Press, which gives its name to one of the buildings, and in the offices of two popular magazines,

Civic center

458. EDGERTON. Speed photograph of golf stroke. *In Edgerton's stroboscopic studies, in which motions can be fixed and analyzed in arrested fractions of 1/100,000 of a second, a whole movement is separated into its successive components, making possible comprehension in both space and time.*

755

Comparison of New York's Rockefeller Center and H. E. Edgerton's golfer striking a ball. From Sigfried Giedion, Space, Time, and Architecture: The Growth of a New Tradition *(Cambridge, Mass.: Harvard University Press, 1962), 754-55.*

historian," he wrote, "must be intimately a part of his own period."[10] In a period of transition, method mattered most. Science and art could only fuse together if their methods were homologous. The significance of modern architecture, Giedion argued, was that its methods exhibited an "unconscious parallelism" to those of science. Healing modernity required making humanity aware that a synthesis was at hand. This responsibility belonged to the architectural historian: "The only service the historian can perform is to point out this situation, to bring it into consciousness."[11] In "the common struggles of the moment," the architectural historian must lead by example.[12] To do this he needed a modern historiography that was recognized as both scientific and artistic. His *Methodengleiche* aspired to that dual classification.

Inspired by Giedion's notion of the historian's healing role, Norberg-Schulz decided to leave a promising architectural practice and become a historian. Pragmatic reasons also influenced his decision. Norberg-Schulz's modernist education was in many ways lagging behind the realities of the discipline. It did not prepare him for the postwar bureaucratization of architectural practice, which saw the rise of architect-specialists. The dispersal and segmentation of creativity among countless anonymous agents undermined the romantic image of the architect as genius-creator, who was supposed single-handedly to author his designs. Unlike professional practice, academia continued to value and reward the work of an individual. Academia offered Norberg-Schulz a position he considered analogous to that of the genius-creator: the architect-historian, a person who authors architecture by redefining how others see it.

Visual Thinking

With his first book, *Intentions in Architecture,* Norberg-Schulz attempted to establish a new theoretical framework for achieving an architectural synthesis of science and art. He suggested that Giedion's notion of space-time was no longer the dominant paradigm for viewing the world. "Since the second world war," he stated, "architecture has obviously entered a new phase."[13] Modern architecture was becoming historical, yet the crisis of modernity it was meant to heal had persisted. Modernism had failed to restore meaning to human existence, and postwar society had become disillusioned with its worldview. "One of the reasons why the public reacts *against* modern architecture is simply that it does not offer any *new visual order* as a substitute for the 'devalued' styles of the past," Norberg-Schulz explained.[14] *Intentions* was meant as a theoretical description of a new visual order for the postwar era. Norberg-Schulz hoped that, armed with his novel paradigm, architects would finally bring modernity, and its existential contradictions, to a meaningful close.

In *Intentions,* Norberg-Schulz aimed to redefine architecture by modeling a new visual experience of buildings. His approach was a development of, not a clean break from, Giedion's historiography. In a masterful translation of Giedion's *Methodengleiche, Intentions* embodied its theoretical method in the arrangement of its sections. The book was divided in two equal parts by a central index, which referred the reader to pages of text in the front of the publication *and* to corresponding images in the back. The experience of reading the book involved constantly moving between image and text, as Norberg-Schulz ingeniously annotated the margins of the text with references to the images from which the textual principles were derived. This system of annotation referred to the same image multiple times and slowly built the reader's understanding of it. Norberg-Schulz arranged the images in groups on the page, with as many as three or four photographs gathered under a single caption that mentioned only their common visual principle (for example, "Definition of the mass through varying treatment of the corner") and obviated historical details such as dates, location, and architect. The images were not simply illustrative; they stimulated meditation. Indeed, the book reversed the traditional primacy of text over image.

The new visual order of *Intentions* aimed to capture the "architectural totality" and unite the divergent paths of science and art.[15] Thus, Norberg-Schulz relentlessly sought what was missing from the modern worldview. To his mind, Giedion's historiography liberated architectural design from copying the forms of the past and history from analytical categories based on style, but it failed to explain how psychological factors influenced the acceptance or rejection of modern architecture.[16] In fact, Giedion explicitly acknowledged Gestalt psychology as the origin of the modern understanding of space and the end of "pseudo-mathematical mechanistic laws," crediting the Austrian psychologist Christian von Ehrenfels for the breakthrough.[17] Norberg-Schulz, paraphrasing his mentor without citing him, also claimed Gestalt psychology and Ehrenfels as the origin of his proposed new visual order.[18]

Norberg-Schulz's claim that a psychological approach was missing from modern methods of architectural analysis intentionally dehistoricized his theory and effaced—however imperfectly—its derivation from Giedion.[19] Norberg-Schulz knew that psychology was a central reference in the modernist understanding of architecture. Architectural psychology asserted that the creative essence of architecture could be understood through direct experience. By contrast, architectural history judged a work's creative content by its departure from past expressions, thereby requiring the mediation of historical documents to establish whether a work was innovative. In terms of historiography, the legacy of this psychological discourse was both positive and negative. The upshot was that

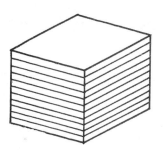 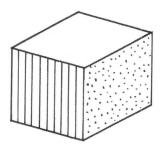 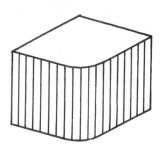

41. The cube as a function of its bounding surfaces.

Borromini: Palazzo di Propaganda Fide in Rome.

Self-contradictory corner treatment in a modern apartment house in Rome.

J. Dientzenhofer: The Castle of Pommersfelden.

42. Definition of the mass through varying treatment of the corner.

Comparison of buildings from various periods. From Christian Norberg-Schulz, Intentions in Architecture *(Cambridge, Mass.: MIT Press, 1965), n.p., Figures 41 and 42.*

architectural psychology exposed the artificial sense of closure assigned by architectural history to past events. To the architectural psychologist, the past was an endlessly unfinished process that resisted synthesis as much as modernity itself. The downside was that architectural psychology produced its own fake sense of closure. It upheld the subject's aesthetic self-expression as wholesome and a cure for the sense of anxiety, self-doubt, and self-deficiency that are concomitant experiences of modernity. *Intentions in Architecture,* like the discourse of architectural psychology it perpetuated, was both a powerful critique and troubling affirmation of modernism.

Through *Intentions,* Norberg-Schulz explicitly articulated that the text in architectural discourse is both literary and visual, and he revealed the historian as a creative agent who redesigns the conventions of architectural aesthetics through an artfully persuasive manipulation of images. In so doing, Norberg-Schulz helped raise the standards of scholarly accountability. His message was unequivocal: "I address myself both to the practicing architect and to the architectural historian."[20] He challenged architects to be more intellectually discerning and defied historians to be more visually literate. Thus, he described the dispositions required to inhabit an emergent position in the field of architecture, that of the architect-historian. Giedion had already begun to delimit the contours of the architect-historian outside of traditional art history. Not surprisingly, this outsider position appealed to architects like Norberg-Schulz who also were trying to distinguish their way of doing history visually from the conventions of art history's historiography.

Intentions was indebted to the work of Rudolf Arnheim, which Norberg-Schulz had encountered during the 1950s while interpreting the research he had conducted as a Smith-Mundt Fulbright scholar at Harvard University in 1952–53. The technocratic slant of Harvard's architecture curriculum dismayed Norberg-Schulz, who was less interested in building construction than in constructing visual perception. Frustrated by Gropius's absence and heavy dependence on assistants to teach his courses, Norberg-Schulz began to study independently in the art history library of the Fogg Museum. He was drawn to the writings of Arnheim, an influential art critic who promoted psychology as a form of aesthetic appreciation that eliminated the scholarly burden of using "past experience for the interpretation of perceptual observations."[21] For Norberg-Schulz, Arnheim's approach happily upheld modernism's opposition to history. Arnheim derided "learned" philological interpretations of art based on "too much" historical research, promoting instead an "untrained eye" open to

the "core of expression that is perceptually self evident."[22] Historians, argued Arnheim, missed the
forest for the trees when they analyzed art as the
sum of disparate figures and elements. Using
Gestalt theories of perception, he claimed that
artistic forms appeared first as immediate "total"
visual experiences. A square, for instance, resulted
not from a mental exercise that joined four equal
lines at right angles. Rather, the mind was
prewired, so to speak, to see squares. Even if the
square were imperfect, an observer would still perceive it as a square. All the mind needed in order
to see a square, argued Arnheim, was five nodes
arranged according to the "structural map" of a

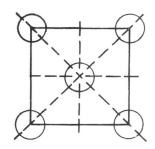

*"Structural skeleton" of a
square drawn by Norberg-Schulz
after Rudolph Arnheim. From
Christian Norberg-Schulz,*
Intentions in Architecture
*(Cambridge, Mass.: MIT Press,
1965), n.p., Figure 7.*

square (four corner nodes "gathered" diagonally toward a fifth central node that
was expressive of their "synthesis").[23]

The idea of unity, expressed in the central node of Arnheim's square diagram, captivated Norberg-Schulz. According to Gestalt psychology, the diagram
was really not a diagram at all, but rather the a priori forming structure common
to everyone's visual experience of squares. Gestalt psychology, as a description of
the unified aesthetic impact of objects, claimed that there existed a mutual
experiential source code for both conception and reception of the square. For
Norberg-Schulz, this code implied that the work of architects and historians
derived from the same starting place. Designing and looking involved the same
forming experience. The veracity of this claim is not the issue here; the important point is that to make this claim appear plausible, Norberg-Schulz developed
a unique discourse that moved seamlessly between images and words.[24] The
stated objective of *Intentions,* to train people how to see buildings, was tantamount to training them how to design.

Topological Historiography

Intentions contended that the design of buildings and their historical interpretation began with the same visual perception. As an experience, visual thinking
was subject to the laws of Gestalt psychology, which held that objects were
perceived first as wholes. Norberg-Schulz used the term "topology" to describe
the geometrical properties of Gestalt diagrams. Topology is the study of those

properties an object retains under deformation—specifically, bending, stretching, and squeezing, but not breaking or tearing. Thus, he used topology to define a common diffuse and amorphous origin for Gestalt diagrams. For a topology to be "expressed" required that it be "concentrated" or "closed."[25] Norberg-Schulz believed that visual experience, being bounded or framed by the visual field, was paradigmatic of wholeness, synthesis, and closure. Norberg-Schulz blamed postwar modernism for lacking visual order, and in a leap of logic, he linked the design of informal visual arrangements to the promotion of a "formless" society of criminals without religion or civic values.[26] Closure was precisely what modernity needed, Norberg-Schulz thought; the challenge was to "translate" the diffuse unity of topologies into closed and organized visual environments.[27] The way out of the crises of the age had to be visual.

In Norberg-Schulz's view, the inability to reconcile modernism and historicism in architecture had forestalled visual unity. The problem was that both modernism and historicism visually expressed only one dimension of the architectural totality. Modernism considered the historical evolution of functional tasks, whereas historicism narrowly focused on the historical development of forms. Both had fallen victim to an idea of history as a succession of facts that had reduced their grasp of the historical totality of architecture.[28] To move beyond modernism and historicism and into their synthesis required a new way of conceiving and receiving the history of architecture; it necessitated the (re)formulation of historiography in psychological terms.

The Gestalt notion that architectural analysis should begin with the whole implied a reversal of the traditional art historical method of connoisseurship, which proceeded in an additive fashion from an analysis of the parts of the building (columns, beams, ornaments), to an examination of the rules governing their assembly, to final conclusions about the style of the whole composition. At least since Sebastiano Serlio's 1537 codification of architecture into five orders, and certainly in modern times from Gottfried Semper (1803–1879) to Le Corbusier, architects had theorized that all architecture derived from the combination of basic elements. Against this tectonic theory, Norberg-Schulz argued that design involved the division of a preexisting amorphous visual whole through "geometrization."[29] His position drew inspiration from Heinrich Wölfflin's Swiss school of art history, which maintained that classical tectonic compositions were only one way of making art. There was a freer, more dynamic, "atectonic" way of design that began with visions of the whole building and then articulated it into parts—a method Wölfflin identified with baroque architecture.[30] Wölfflin claimed that a proper historical analysis of atectonic design also had to begin with the historian's holistic visual experience of the work. Fortunately, psychology made this easy. Forming perception of wholes was natural to human vision. Norberg-Schulz replaced the term "atectonic" with "topological" to describe his historiography. In allegiance to Wölfflin's tradition, he considered topological historiography as a method for analyzing *and* designing architecture.[31]

To gauge the success of Norberg-Schulz's book, we must examine the intellectual context in which it appeared. *Intentions in Architecture* issued a defense of the atectonic school at the time when it faced intense criticism. By the 1960s, the discourse of psychologism on which the atectonic school was founded was clearly in decline. The linchpin of Wölfflin's historiography was the correspondence it proposed between stylistic evolution (say, from classical to baroque) and irreversible developments in the human psyche. But Wölfflin never clarified the foundational rules governing this psychological growth. The whole edifice of the atectonic school appeared in jeopardy when, in the late 1950s, new research suggested that pictures were perceived in a piecemeal way, with their parts determined more by local factors than by their whole configuration.[32] Some young disciples openly broke ranks with Wölfflin, as did Ernst Gombrich, who accused Wölfflin of essentialism and derided his historiographical method as subjective.[33]

Norberg-Schulz picked up where Wölfflin left off, escalating the debate by shifting psychological questions to an epistemological plane. He turned to the Swiss psychologist Jean Piaget, whose interest in epistemology had led his groundbreaking research during the 1910s and 1920s on the development of children's mental capacities. Popular in the mid-1950s, Piaget's thesis of genetic epistemology influenced pediatricians, teachers, and parents, and through Norberg-Schulz, architectural theory. It stated that certain concepts were learnable only when the child's mind had achieved a specific level of maturation. Norberg-Schulz thought Piaget provided scientific proof for atectonic historiography. Invoking Piaget, Norberg-Schulz argued that infants began to understand objects topologically, as vague self-referential totalities that remained constant even as they underwent physical changes. The perception of roundness, for instance, preceded and structured the infant's grasp of the difference between a tennis ball and a potato. These morphing perceptual totalities, he claimed, were the first and highest categories of architecture; together they formed the *summum genus* from which all possible dimensions of architecture were to be differentiated.[34] In topology, Norberg-Schulz found the origin of architectural space. Spurred on by his psychologism, he remained blind to the deceitful logic that equated the child's development with the (adult) architect's creative capacity.[35]

Norberg-Schulz's use of the term topology imparted a scientific varnish to psychological historiography. As a nineteenth-century offshoot of geometry, topology was a legitimate mathematical field of study (a *pure* science, no less), known as analysis situs before the nomenclature was changed in the 1890s by Henri Poincaré.[36] Unwittingly, Norberg-Schulz stumbled on an idea that would fuel the rest of his career: the visual description of topologies could be interpreted as a scientific site analysis, which aimed to reveal topologies as the original site or grounding source of architecture and its history.

Norberg-Schulz recognized that topologies, as the origin of both words and images, were figures beyond representation and therefore beyond history. He reached this conclusion after reading Ludwig Wittgenstein's (1889–1951) *Tractatus Logico-Philosophicus*. Wittgenstein claimed that, in order to convey meaning, a proposition had to be a "picture of reality."[37] The simple signs making up a sentence had to correspond to the basic elements of reality—otherwise, the proposition was nonsensical. For Wittgenstein, the terms of this correspondence were established by a common yet invisible "logical form"; it preceded language, reality, propositions, and even thought. His conclusion that logical form, the origin of logic, could not be represented meant that logic depended on premises it could not examine and hence was helpless to determine its own starting position.[38] Thus, Wittgenstein recognized incertitude as constitutive of truth.

Wittgenstein used seductive visual terms to describe logical empiricism, and Norberg-Schulz astutely took this as license to liken his concept of topology to logical form. Topology was for him the invisible origin of architecture and its history. Had Norberg-Schulz really followed Wittgenstein, he would have concluded that his topological historiography was incapable of determining its topological source. This would have been a very important contribution to architectural history, highlighting the incertitude that underwrites the process of historicizing and marks it with incompleteness. Indeed, the recognition that topology cannot identify its own origin would have emphasized the inability of history to provide the closure the discipline insists on. Instead, Norberg-Schulz succumbed to the pressure to remove uncertainty from the consideration of history, and he deployed remarkable means to carry out this purge. Like most historians, he concealed doubt behind an authorial mask. But unlike most historians, who depend on words to camouflage self-projection within a field of objective facts, Norberg-Schulz employed photographs. He also relied on other types of images, such as diagrams, but he privileged photographs because they more easily concealed the hand of their author, allowing the photos to stand as an objective visual discourse. In what follows, I will examine how Norberg-Schulz theorized photographs as objective truths.

Invisible Images

Topological historiography insisted that the same source code regulated the architect's artistic representation of topologies through designs and the historian's scientific depiction of them through verbal interpretations. Both architects and historians faced a difficulty: the invisibility of the original topology. Arnheim's theory of visual thinking inspired Norberg-Schulz to conceptualize photographic representations as more truthful evidence of the original topology than verbal accounts. For Arnheim, the measure of a theory's conceptual clarity related to its translatability into a visual diagram. Arnheim asserted that all thinking involved visual perception (in the form of a mental image) and, conversely, visual perception shared the character of thought.[39] What is at stake in Norberg-Schulz's work is the relationship between the intellectual scaffolding that supported his theorization of photographs and the visual thinking used to organize his understanding of concepts.

Norberg-Schulz took most of the illustrations for *Intentions* with his Rolleiflex Twin Lens Camera (the same model used by Giedion), which shot large-format, square negatives of 6 by 6 centimeters.[40] Norberg-Schulz ascribed great importance to the square format; indeed, he designed the book to have a square shape. Recall that the square, as described by Arnheim, represented a total Gestalt geometry with four nodes gathered toward a center. The camera's square frame appeared always to create a total visual pattern. Norberg-Schulz hoped that *Intentions* would be expressible, in terms of visual thinking, as a square diagram. The architectural totality would be composed of a strong central idea with four "corner" categories. Alas, Norberg-Schulz failed. He could only "see" three dimensions to the architectural totality—"Task, Form, and Technique."[41] The resulting triangular diagram did not imply balance, since one of the dimensions could be stretched with impunity. A triangle did not indicate a stable gathering center, nor did it contain a point of synthesis like a square.

With *Intentions*, Norberg-Schulz arrived at an impasse. He could not express in words what he could express with pictures. Jean-François Lyotard (1924–1998)

Norberg-Schulz prepares to photograph Ricardo Bofill's Pyramid Monument, La Perthus, Spain, 1978. From Byggekunst 68, no. 6 (1986): 328.

argued that when people face such predicaments they have two possible ways to advance knowledge: "one corresponds to a new move (a new argument) within the established rules; the other, to the invention of new rules, in other words, a change to a new game."[42] Norberg-Schulz chose to change the rules of architectural history. Instead of using images to illustrate the text, his photographs became essays in their own right, narratives independent from verbal exegesis.

For Norberg-Schulz, a work of architecture involved the visualization of an original topology. Architecture, he thought, emerged from the architect's ability to sense the invisible topology and represent it visually. But not all architects could do this. The power to sense the invisible was reserved for genius-creators with an intuitive inner vision. Historians, he argued, required the same special visualizing power as architects if they were to produce authentic architecture. Still, Norberg-Schulz had to provide proof that he *felt* the ahistorical truth content of architecture. For this he used photographs as evidence. His historiography began with the opening of his camera's shutter when he sensed the invisible presence of the original spirit of the place. Photography was his spontaneous capture of that eternal truth.

We know too much about photography to accept it as an objective medium.[43] What did Norberg-Schulz gain by treating photographs as self-evident? He never said a word about the camera that always hung from his neck, the professional photography laboratory in Rome that he trusted with his negatives, or his graphic design work for his books. Norberg-Schulz's treatment of photographs as truths that can be immediately grasped amounted to an unfounded epistemological claim about photographs. His concealment of the history of his photographic production was part of a program to dehistoricize his theory of history. The result was a historiography reliant solely on the historian's subjective opinion as the ultimate and inscrutable source of authority.

The question therefore becomes, what kind of history does topological historiography yield? The short answer, I would argue, is antihistorical history. With its hypostatization of the invisible as the origin of history, *Intentions* was ultimately a manifesto for that which escapes historical representation. Norberg-Schulz introduced a static model whereby architectural history was thought to arise out of topologies, invisible sites with no history, which were supposedly rendered temporal through architecture. With the removal of history from topology, analysis situs became *analysis genius,* a conflation of spirit and site that would in time lead Norberg-Schulz to his theory of genius loci, to which I will return below. My intention here is to reinstate history in Norberg-Schulz's historiography, something that goes against the grain of his work and constitutes my critique of it.

Despite its shortcomings, Norberg-Schulz's obsession with visual thinking helped him evolve his theory of architecture from the triangular construct of "Task, Form, and Technique." He thought the architectural totality was a square, the first visible expression of a topology geometrically described by a center equidistant from four points. So he kept looking for the fourth point in his argument. As he was finishing *Intentions,* he wrote a meditation on a possible fourth architectural category. "But what we are fighting with is to present a diagram that *describes* the architectonic unity. It is clear that the task, form and technique are three sides of that, but what about the place? . . . If the place should come in

OVERLEAF: Christian Norberg-Schulz and Franz Wozak, Marist Catholic Church (top of hill) and Senior Residence (wing on right), Stabekk, Norway, 1958–60. Courtesy of the Norberg-Schulz Archive, The National Museum of Art, Architecture, and Design—The Norwegian Architecture Museum, Oslo.

as a separate main dimension then it should be differentiated . . . For now we can hold on to the Δ even though the □ *can be used in special cases."*[44] By the mid-1960s, the term *place* was gaining wide currency in architectural publications, mostly as a result of Jane Jacobs's groundbreaking *Death and Life of Great American Cities* (1961) and Kevin Lynch's *The Image of the City* (1960). The concept of place does not appear in *Intentions,* but Norberg-Schulz quickly adopted it in his square book of 1971—*Existence, Space and Architecture.*[45]

Catholic Phenomenology

The first evidence of Norberg-Schulz's interest in phenomenology is *Existence, Space and Architecture.* Although the philosophy of phenomenology receives cursory treatment in the book, Norberg-Schulz is often credited as the founding father of the phenomenological approach to architecture.[46] One of the main historiographical contributions of this approach was to redefine acceptable primary sources in writing the history of architecture. Whereas traditional architectural history privileged so-called objective documents such as the architect's sketches, personal correspondence, and the provenance of construction materials, the phenomenological approach asserted that subjective documents, such as the historian's personal experience of the building, were also valid primary sources.

Norberg-Schulz's idea that architectural history could be written from the standpoint of direct experience had Catholic origins. Norberg-Schulz converted from evangelical Lutheranism to Catholicism in the late 1950s. For him, Catholic aesthetics appeared as a bastion against "the general disintegration of traditional forms of life," and he became deeply involved in matters of Church aesthetics, serving as official advisor to the Oslo Diocese on matters of religious art and architecture on countless occasions from the late 1950s to the 1990s.[47] He was also an admirer of Pope John Paul II, with whom he shared an interest in phenomenology.[48] As a Catholic, Norberg-Schulz secured the commission for the Marist Catholic Church and Senior Residence in Stabekk, Norway (1958–60, with architect Franz Wozak). For practical guidance, Norberg-Schulz read the writings of Rudolf Schwarz, a German Catholic church architect and theorist of modern architecture. He was interested in Schwarz's theory that architectural space could be interpreted as an existential experience through which humans found a spiritual home. [49] Schwarz applied to architecture the Catholic view of the spirit made flesh. He believed that the human body and the church building contained an invisible spirit that gave them integrity and wholeness, even if disfigured by aging.

Schwarz enabled Norberg-Schulz to elevate his own theory about invisible topologies from a psychological to an existential plane. *Existence, Space and Architecture* aimed to update the argument that all architectural representation, whether photograph, written text, or drawing, was a translation of the same topological source code. Following Schwarz, Norberg-Schulz now called topologies "existential spaces."[50] Without altering the core argument, the change in nomenclature seamlessly shifted the intellectual references used in support of his visual discourse from psychology to phenomenology. His invocation of phenomenology saved the project of topological historiography from sinking with the ship of art psychology, which had lost steam by the 1970s.[51]

To Norberg-Schulz, topologies, or existential spaces, were the invisible source code of visual architectural spaces. "Architectural space, therefore, can be defined as a concretization of man's existential space."[52] The crux of the problem was the question of "concretization." How was an architect to design according to invisible guidelines? Norberg-Schulz included illustrations as evidence of how "easy" it was to translate what the topology "wants to be" into visual representations.[53] *Existence, Space and Architecture* presented two contradictory messages: on the one hand, the text stated that topologies were a hidden code, invisible, and beyond representation; on the other hand, a parallel photo-essay used photographs to illustrate topologies.

Existence, Space and Architecture is formatted as a 22-centimeter square, suggesting (like Arnheim's Gestalt square) that it has a center and lacks a directional orientation or slant. The layout of each page was organized in three vertical columns. The outside column was reserved for footnotes and the body of the text occupied the other two. The first seventeen pages ran without illustrations, but on page eighteen, diagrams began to appear. In the midst of sentences unequivocally stating that topologies are beyond representation, a topology was diagrammatically represented as a circle with a marked center. Norberg-Schulz encouraged the reader to identify these diagrams with philosophical concepts, believing that people developed their personal identities through the intuitive recognition of a "structural similarity" between their own interior topology (existential space) and their external reality.[54] He asserted that the only way to construct oneself as an individual was to identify with objects that exhibited a clear geometrical center.

The term genius loci, which appeared for the first time in *Existence, Space and Architecture,* referred to environments saturated with centering objects, which Norberg-Schulz termed "places." Following Schwarz, he divided the size of

RIGHT and FACING PAGE: Page spread demonstrates the combined use of text and diagrams. From Christian Norberg-Schulz, Existence, Space and Architecture *(New York: Praeger, 1971), 18–19.*

these objects according to bodily experiences. First came objects for the grasping hand; his square book fell in this category. Second were houses, objects for small private movements of the entire body. Third were cities, objects containing daily walking ranges. Finally there were landscapes, objects enclosing longer experiences of mobility. Beyond the size of landscapes, Norberg-Schulz considered objects to be technically invisible in everyday experiences. The genius loci signified the visual similarity between these four sizes of objects, or places.[55]

For Norberg-Schulz's architectural audience, the argument acquired its most compelling force through the masterfully arranged photo-essay. The first square picture showed a square book, a bible, on top of a square altar rising from the ground as a solid mass. Facing the altar, priests stood or knelt in prayer, forming a perfect circle. The second picture showed a model of an oval building, a Roman amphitheater. The size of the oval building on the page was exactly the same size as the circle of priests. The third picture showed an oval city surrounded by a meandering river (Wasserburg am Inn, Bavaria). The genius loci placed the 'navel' of the world (*omphalos*) in Delphi, while the Romans considered their Capitol as *caput mundi*. For Islam the *Ka'aba* is still the centre of the world. Eliade points out that in most beliefs it is *difficult* to reach the centre. It is an ideal goal, which one can only attain after a 'hard journey'. To 'reach the centre is to achieve a consecration, an initiation. To the profane and illusory existence of yesterday, there succeeds a new existence, real, lasting and powerful.' But Eliade also points out that 'every life, even the least eventful, can be taken as the journey through a labyrinth. The sufferings and trials undergone by Ulysses were fabulous, and yet any man's return home has the value of Ulysses' return to Ithaca.'[11]

If the 'centre of the world' thus designates an ideal, public goal, or 'lost paradise', the word 'home' also has a closer and more concrete meaning. It simply tells us that any man's personal world has its centre. The *Odyssey*, however, shows that the home, too, is easily lost and that it takes a 'hard

journey' to find it again. The notion of home as the centre of one's world goes back to childhood. The first points of reference are tied to the home and house, and the child only becomes able to cross its borders very slowly. When I once asked my twelve-year-old son if he could tell me something about his 'environment', he replied: 'Then I want to start with home, because it is from there I go out to all the other places'. From the very beginning, then, the centre represents to man what is *known* in contrast to the unknown and somewhat frightening world around. 'It is the point where he acquires position as a thinking being in space, the point where he "lingers" and "lives" in the space.'[12] We also remember Archimedes' famous statement: 'Give me a place to stand, and I will move the world!'

During growth the actions of the individual are differentiated and multiplied, and new centres therefore come to supplement the original 'home'. All the centres are 'places of.

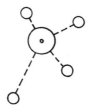

action': places where particular activities are carried out, or places of social interaction such as the homes of relatives and friends. 'The place is always limited, it has been created by man and set up for his special purpose.'[13] The actions, in fact, are only meaningful in relation to particular places, and are coloured by the character of the place. Our language expresses this state of affairs when we say that something 'takes place'. The places are goals or foci where we experience the meaningful events of our existence, but they are also points of departure from which we orient ourselves and take possession of the environment. This 'taking possession' is also related to places which we expect to find, or *discover* by surprise. It could be maintained that the gradual multiplication of the places constituting our existential place would lead to a final liberation from place attachment. We will discuss the problem of 'mobility' in more detail later, but should point out here that a structured environment depends on our ability to *recognize* it, that is, on the existence of relatively invariant places. An ever-changing world would not allow for the establishment of schemata, and would therefore make human development impossible.

A place is characterized by a certain 'size'. We should here distinguish between the immediate *Eigenraum* or 'territoriality', and the more abstract image of the places known. The *Eigenraum* has been studied by Edward T. Hall who says: 'Territoriality is usually defined as the behaviour by which an organism characteristically lays claim to an

11 M. Eliade *Patterns in Comparative Religion* 1958, p. 382

12 O. F. Bollnow *Mensch und Raum* 1963, p. 58

13 O. F. Bollnow *Mensch und Raum* 1963, p. 41.

19

was everywhere: "From the level of things to the level of nature the range widens at the same time as precision decreases. In things everything is *focused,* in nature everything *is contained.*"[56] The genius loci was the visual synthesis of four sizes of objects. As a diagram, the argument appeared as four corners (one per object size) equidistant from their central synthesis. Arnheim's Gestalt square, again! With the self-confidence of having finally arrived at a description of the architectural totality, Norberg-Schulz claimed the genius loci to be an image.

Norberg-Schulz's formulation of topological historiography carried a few negative implications. While topological historiography encouraged individual self-awareness, it surrendered the freedom of self-determination through the focus on a priori "structural similarities." Furthermore, it entailed the loss of expressive range in architectural design by limiting the definition of architecture to centering experiences. Finally, through topological historiography, the past lost all semblance of historical objectivity. Buildings figured only as evidence that the same topology had been represented at some other time and in some

(4) *Town Square* with town-hall (1559) and Jesuit church (1656 **D. Orsini**), Klatovy, Bohemia

clustering and vertical accents. In the town of Klatovy a most impressive 'double focus' is created by the towers of the town hall and the church. In general, the mass is a symbolic or ideal centre, rather than a real place of activity. It puts a stop to the horizontal extension of man's environment, and makes his need for fixed points visible.

The place of activity has roots which are just as old as those of the concentrated mass. The enclosure, in fact, may be considered man's first real attempt to take possession of the environment.

(5) **Kjell Lund** and **Nils Slaatto** *St Halvard's Church*, Oslo 1966

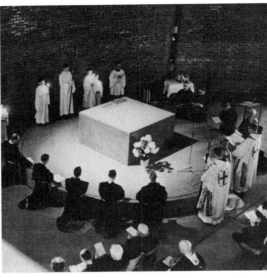

42

RIGHT and FACING PAGE: Comparison of an altar, a building, and a city, showing the common genius loci visible as a circle. From Christian Norberg-Schulz, Existence, Space and Architecture *(New York: Praeger, 1971), 42–43.*

other place, and the past ceased to be a challenge to the present. Conversely, the present became the rule and measure of the past. Norberg-Schulz's argument suggested that his understanding of architecture as the visual representation of a topology had *always* been true and was thus the foundation for all architectural thought.

Yet, the reviewers of *Existence, Space and Architecture* did not object to Norberg-Schulz's denial of the Enlightenment ideal of self-determination, the reduction of architecture's vocabulary to enclosing forms, or to the antihistorical thrust of his theory of history. Rather, the book was acclaimed as a call to resist the "loss of place" and "loss of identity" resulting from the rapid postwar growth of cities.[57] It was especially popular among those taking up the position of the local architect as a way to delegitimize cosmopolitan practitioners working outside of their urban realm. The outsider became the scapegoat blamed for devaluing the architect's social and economic status. Norberg-Schulz spurred his readers with an unfounded political message: "The *genius loci* in many cases

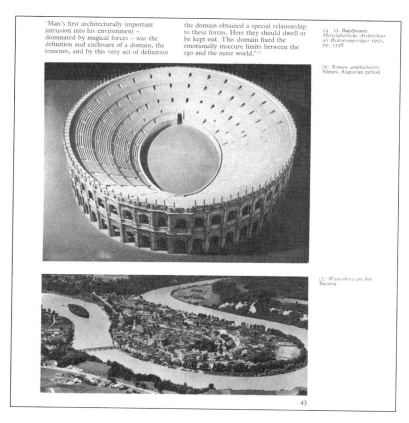

'Man's first architecturally important intrusion into his environment – dominated by magical forces – was the definition and enclosure of a domain, the temenos, and by this very act of definition the domain obtained a special relationship to these forces. Here they should dwell or be kept out. This domain fixed the emotionally insecure limits between the ego and the outer world.'[24]

14 G. Bandmann *Mittelalterliche Architektur als Bedeutungsträger* 1951, pp. 133ff

(6) *Roman amphitheatre* Nîmes, Augustan period

(7) *Wasserburg am Inn* Bavaria

43

has even proved strong enough to dominate any political, social and cultural changes."[58] The promise was clear: by subjecting themselves to the rule of the genius loci, architects could become an elite avant-garde guiding society beyond its disillusionment with modernity.

World Picture

Any critique of Norberg-Schulz's work must illuminate his engagement with the philosophy of Martin Heidegger. Previous critiques have cast him as a vulgar interpreter of Heidegger.[59] Others mistakenly equate the message of his writing with that of the photo-essays.[60] The hasty identification of his photographs with his texts ignores the question: how could Norberg-Schulz simultaneously associate the clarity of his verbal arguments with the ability to turn them into images and defend Heidegger, who offered a powerful critique of the picture as modernity's dominant intellectual paradigm?

In "The Age of the World Picture," Heidegger elaborated on his critique of metaphysics in relation to the question of representation.[61] The essay opened with a discussion of the intellectual underpinnings of the modern era, which for him began with the metaphysics of René Descartes. Heidegger identified Descartes with a historical turn in the way people understood the relationship between Being and beings. In medieval times, "to be in being [meant] to belong within a specific rank of the order of what has been created, to correspond to the cause of creation *(analogia entis)."*[62] But since Descartes' metaphysics, "what it is to be is for the first time defined as the objectiveness of representing, and truth is defined as the certainty of representing."[63] Heidegger argued that these two ways of understanding the Being of beings were irreconcilable. Modern thought was not a perfection of medieval thinking, but rather a completely different way of thinking about what it means to be. The point of the historical comparison was to establish that beings could grasp Being in different ways and, conversely, that Being revealed itself to beings through multifarious modes of thought. More importantly, it suggested that humanity's ontological understanding was always partial and historical. It could never be grasped as a whole in just one domain of thinking.

Heidegger's critique demonstrated that metaphysics tried to impart its partial understanding of what it is to be as a total grasp of the concept. To accomplish this task, metaphysics employed representation. According to Heidegger, representation was a way of "enframing" the world for oneself. That is to say, representation confined both the world to a frame (a complete object) and the person to a viewpoint (a complete subject). To represent, he explained, is "to set out before oneself and to set forth in relation to oneself. Through this, whatever is comes to stand as object and receives the seal of Being. That the world becomes picture is one and the same event with the event of man's becoming *subiectum* in the midst of that which is."[64]

The emergence of the modern concepts of object and subject as two distinct entities was integral to the understanding of the world as a picture. For Heidegger, this argument explained why, before metaphysics, there had been no "world picture" and why "the fact that [the] world becomes a picture at all is what distinguishes the essence of the modern age."[65] Heidegger's analysis of metaphysics as a method that enframed both world and humans through a world picture allowed him to ask what had been left out of the picture. He identified the most problematic aspect of metaphysics as the inability to recognize other possible ways of grasping ontology. Indeed, metaphysics could not conceive of an outside to its world picture. In metaphysics, the only way Being could come into presence (into being) was through representation.

Heidegger defined the event in which Being is revealed in beings as "truth," but he preferred to use the Greek word *aletheia* because it came closer to the meaning of truth as "revealing" that he wanted to emphasize.[66] In this sense, metaphysics could be considered a mode of accessing the truth. Yet, Heidegger cautioned that while metaphysics denied Being's ability to come into being in any way other than through a world picture, metaphysics also *concealed* the truth. Thus, Heidegger's critique challenged the idea of metaphysics as the philosophical foundation of individual freedom. Descartes' notion of self-determination required thought to be bounded and limited to a metaphysical mode of revealing the truth. Therefore, metaphysics was also a form of oppression. [67]

Norberg-Schulz's notes on his copy of Heidegger's *Poetry, Language, Thought* suggest that he was familiar with the concept of enframing and understood it as a critique of representation.[68] His annotations worked through one of Heidegger's more challenging essays: "The Origin of the Work of Art." Part of the intricacy stemmed from Heidegger's attempt to dissociate the idea of enframing from art. This was a difficult conceptual leap since enframing immediately calls to mind the artist (say, a photographer) framing a view before capturing it on the picture plane. Nevertheless, Heidegger asked his readers to consider not just individual works of art (a particular photograph or building) but art itself, understood as the essence or origin of all works of art. In other words, he tried to describe not just what a piece of art is, but how artworks come to be.

Heidegger differentiated artworks from other types of objects. An artwork, for instance, was not made to be useful. The process of making art required an artistic way of thinking, whereas the process of making useful objects required a technological mind-set. Heidegger's essay was concerned with establishing the difference between these two modes of thought.

A technological mind-set viewed everything in terms of its practical value for a future application. As such, it was an attitude commensurate with metaphysical enframing, which could only grasp Being as fixed beings (objects or subjects). Moreover, a technological mind-set concealed from itself how it viewed the world, thus falling into the dangerous fallacy that it represented the only way for a thing to be.

Against this misconception, Heidegger presented a series of exemplary acts of poetic disclosure, acts in which an entity appeared as such while simultaneously showing *how* it had come to be meaningful.[69] One example was his article: it revealed itself as being a theoretical act of questioning while simultaneously disclosing that being could be questioned. Another example was a work of art, say a photograph or a building, that established itself as this or that entity while at the same time revealing its relations to the culture and beliefs within which it achieved its artistic meaning.

The difference between enframing and poetic acts came down to how they grasped the meaning of the entities they created. By definition, meaning is finite and relational. Both enframing and poetic acts limited entities to a world of possible meaningful relationships. Through an enframing act, one found meaning by imposing the same external boundary (the world picture) on every entity and thus limiting meaning to the set of possible relationships between subjects and objects. Through a poetic act, one found meaning by allowing each being or thing to exist within its own unique world of significance, the ambiguous limits of which could not be known a priori and could be explored only through interpretation. In a "poetic act," explained Heidegger, "subject and object are unsuitable names here. They keep us from thinking precisely about this ambiguous nature."[70] He defined truth as the disclosing encounter, or aletheia, between the entity and the human work of interpreting the entity's unique world of significance.

The focus on interpretation allowed Heidegger to make one further differentiation between enframing and poetic acts in terms of historiography. An enframing act essentially repeated the same interpretation of beings (as subject or object) over and over. Its interpretation did not evolve from iteration to iteration and therefore could not develop a consciousness of its own historicity. The world picture appeared as though unrelated to history. By contrast, a poetic act required that interpretation adjust to the limits immanent in the entity itself, most notably to its changing material and temporal boundaries. Human interpretation followed the work of art in time, attempting to explore and expand the work's shifting meaning. Thus, through poetic acts, humans developed a sense of their own historical possibilities. Heidegger spoke of truth as a continuous mutual adaptation between the interpretative urge to augment meaning and the material borders it encountered; in his words, aletheia was a historical struggle between "world" and "earth."[71]

One would expect Norberg-Schulz's study of Heidegger to lead him to question his topological historiography, especially Norberg-Schulz's conflation of the thinkable with the visible. Heidegger's emphasis on the historicity of truth countered Norberg-Schulz's conception of topologies as timeless, invariant, and invisible source codes for all meaning in architecture. Yet to the contrary, Norberg-Schulz redoubled his claim that all truth in architecture rested in atemporal topologies. Moreover, he began referring to the topologies alternatively as genius loci or aletheic images, in order to emphasize their status as the real origin of visual order. Although Norberg-Schulz's notion of aletheia as truthful experience can be traced directly to his reading of Heidegger, his understanding of aletheia as a strictly visual and ahistorical phenomenon cannot. Was the idea of putting "aletheia" and "image" together an innocent misreading? To answer this question, we must reconstruct the historical moment when Norberg-Schulz studied Heidegger and analyze the relative currency of these two terms.

Aletheic Image

Norberg-Schulz's first sustained consideration of Heidegger occurred in the spring of 1974, when he read a recent English edition of *Poetry, Language, Thought*.[72] He became seriously interested in Heidegger while serving as visiting professor of architecture at the Massachusetts Institute of Technology in Cambridge, where a contentious debate regarding artificial intelligence centered on phenomenology. Marcian E. Hoff's invention of the microprocessor in 1971 raised expectations for research being conducted on machine cognition. The dissenting opinion in the otherwise celebratory engineering environment stemmed from Professor Hubert Dreyfus (b. 1929), a phenomenologist. In his 1972 book *What Computers Can't Do*, Dreyfus critiqued the metaphysical epistemological model of artificial intelligence research. He contrasted the gestalt, informal, and open-ended human thought processes with the mechanistic, formal, and closed-system operations of computer software models.[73] At first, the scientific community rejected Dreyfus's views, but then MIT scientists adopted his concepts of praxis, bodily motion, and gestalt patterning. Introduction to Phenomenology remained such a popular course and an integral part of the engineering curriculum that it was taught by mathematician Giancarlo Rota, not by a philosopher, until 2000.

The philosophy that took engineers by storm also inspired Norberg-Schulz, but his objective was not to further the project of computation. On the contrary, Norberg-Schulz invoked Heidegger's term aletheia to protect the romantic definition of the architect as authorial genius-creator against the threats of the computer. Nightmares of machine architects had plagued the profession since the early 1960s, when Serge Chermayeff (1900–1996) and his teaching assistant Christopher Alexander (b. 1936) rented MIT's new IBM 704 computer to calculate all possible "logical [building] types" for a given problem and to establish the "structural invariants" of architecture.[74] Following Dreyfus, Norberg-Schulz waged his battle against the computer on an intellectual plane. He accused structuralism and all "scientific theories" of reducing the architectural totality to a "picture frame" in the Heideggerian sense.[75] He strove to establish architectural phenomenology as more holistic than competing theories of architecture, such as Colin Rowe's formalism, Manfredo Tafuri's (1935–1994) Marxist criticism, or Donald Preziosi's (b. 1941) semiotic analysis.[76] While accusing others of enframing architecture, Norberg-Schulz proceeded to do just that, arguing truth was revealed in images.

The reluctance of Norberg-Schulz to revisit the centrality of vision suggests that he considered visual discourse to have primacy over philosophy. Indeed, what motivated him to teach at MIT was not that it was a hotbed of phenomenology, but rather that it offered him the opportunity to work with world-renowned "visual thinkers."[77] He met various times with Arnheim, who was at Harvard.[78] There was also György Kepes (1906–2001), whose profile as photographer, designer, and writer had inspired Norberg-Schulz since his graduate student years.[79] In 1967, Kepes founded the world-renowned Center for Advanced Visual Studies at MIT, which aimed to establish vision as the basis for communication between architects, engineers, artists, designers, and scientists. Kepes offered his famous Visual Design class for the last time when Norberg-Schulz was visiting. In this course, Kepes presented his theory that vision was not about seeing objects, but rather about recognizing patterns—a notion that Norberg-Schulz appropriated into his own thinking. Finally, Norberg-Schulz admired Kevin Lynch, professor of urban planning at MIT; his thesis that the visual recognition of urban patterns constituted an "image of the city" translated Kepes's ideas to an urban scale.[80]

Norberg-Schulz borrowed the word "image" as used by Lynch and Kepes to describe the effortless apprehension (or readability) of complex formal patterns. For Lynch, the image was the intersection of objective order, subjective identification of that order, and the projection of meaning into the world. As such, an image was a process, not a final product. "Since image development is a two-way process between observer and observed," stated Lynch, "it is possible to strengthen the image either by symbolic devices, by the retraining of the perceiver, or

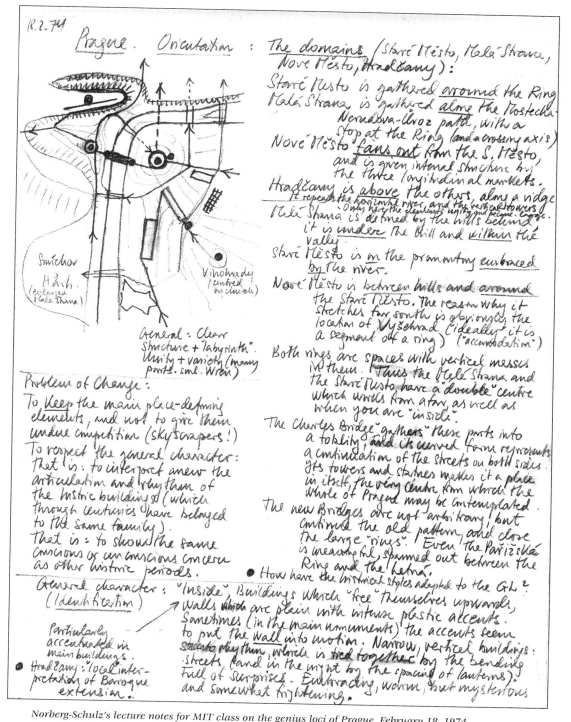

18.2.74

Prague. Orientation:

The domains (Staré Město, Malá Strana, Nové Město, Hradčany):

Staré Město is gathered around the Ring
Malá Strana is gathered along the Mostecká-
  Nerudova-Úvoz path, with a
  stop at the Ring (and a crossing axis)
Nové Město fans out from the S. Město,
  and is given internal structure by
  the three longitudinal markets.
Hradčany is above the others, along a ridge
  It repeats the horizontal river, and the vertical towers.
  Only here the elements unity and form cooperate.
Malá Strana is defined by the hills behind.
  It is under the hill and within the
  valley
Staré Město is on the promontory embraced
  by the river.
Nové Město is between hills and around
  the Staré Město. The reason why it
  stretches far south is obviously the
  location of Vyšehrad (ideally it is
  a segment of a ring) ("accommodation")
Both rings are spaces with vertical messes
  in them. Thus the Malá Strana and
  the Staré Město have a "double" centre
  which unveils from afar, as well as
  when you are "inside".
The Charles Bridge "gathers" these parts into
  a totality, and its curved form represents
  a continuation of the streets on both sides.
  Its towers and statues makes it a place
  in itself, the very centre from which the
  whole of Prague may be contemplated.
The new bridges are not arbitrary, but
  continue the old pattern and close
  the large "rings". Even the Pařížská
  is meaningful, spanned out between the
  Ring and the Letná.
● How have the historical styles adapted to the G.L.?
  "Inside" Buildings which "free" themselves upwards;
  Walls which are plain with intense plastic accents.
  Sometimes (in the main monuments) the accents seem
  to put the wall into motion. Narrow, vertical buildings:
  streets rhythm, which is tied together by the bending
  streets (and in the myst by the spacing of lanterns).
  Full of surprises. Embracing, warm, but mysterious
  and somewhat frightening.

Smíchov
Žižkov
(enlarged
Malá Strana)

Vinohrady
(centred
on church)

General: Clear
Structure + "Labyrinth".
Unity + variety (many
parts. smli. Wien)

Problem of Change:

To keep the main place-defining
elements, and not to give them
undue competition (skyscrapers!)
To respect the general character:
That is: to interpret anew the
articulation and rhythm of
the historic buildings (which
through centuries have belonged
to the same family).
That is: to show the same
conscious or unconscious concern
as other historic periods.

General character: "Inside"
(Identification)

Particularly
accentuated in
main buildings.
● Hradčany: local inter-
  pretation of Baroque
  extension.

reshaping one's environment."[81] People put their five senses to work to perceive order and could be trained to improve their skills.[82] Lynch's *The Image of the City* was extremely popular in the 1960s and 1970s because it addressed the deep postwar concern for the loss of order resulting from the rapidly changing urban morphology. Lynch laid the groundwork for retraining the visual skills of designers, and his methods were employed across the nation to help students identify the changing patterns of urban images and positively transform their environment.[83]

Kepes shared Lynch's conviction that "retraining the eye" was imperative. He insisted that only through visual understanding could humanity control the industrialized systems of production that, in his view, were turning urban cores into nodes within immense sprawling metropolises. Kepes made the grandest of statements about vision. In his famous *The Language of Vision* (1944), Kepes declared a need to tame technology and reshape it into a coherent "new vital structure" connecting all fields of knowledge. The lingua franca of this communication would be vision, since it could allegedly transmit knowledge more immediately than any other vehicle. More importantly, argued Kepes, intellectuals and idiots across the world could speak it. "Visual communication is universal and international: it knows no limits of tongue, vocabulary, or grammar, and it can be perceived by the illiterate as well as the literate."[84] Kepes initiated Norberg-Schulz into the avant-garde tradition that equates originality in aesthetic expression with purity in visual experience.

We can now better appreciate how Norberg-Schulz misread Heidegger's notion of aletheia to be a purely visual phenomenon. Following Lynch and Kepes, he believed vision to be the ontological first principle of understanding and communication. His purpose in reading Heidegger was not to criticize the conventions of modern architectural discourse. Rather, Norberg-Schulz used Heidegger as a theoretical mask to add philosophical credibility to the visual project of modernism, at the precise moment modernism seemed destined to die. The fact that modernist buildings were becoming historical made it impossible to continue to design in the modern idiom without confronting history. The danger was that the modernist way of conceiving design, as the designer's unencumbered self-projection, would collapse under the pressure of historical conventions and be reduced to copying past forms. The challenge was to open historical buildings (modern or otherwise) to the designer in a non-historical way. This was Norberg-Schulz's objective. His exchanges with Kepes, Lynch, and Arnheim led him to turn the aletheic image into an antihistorical historiography. "My *Genius Loci,*" he wrote, thinking about his new project, "would have been a bad book without this experience."[85]

Natural Identity

In 1979, *Genius Loci: Towards a Phenomenology of Architecture* repeated and perfected Norberg-Schulz's technique of running two narratives in parallel, one visual and the other textual, with contradictory messages. The text discussed the aletheic image as an a priori topological essence, which could by definition never be grasped conceptually or willed into presence. The images showed a conflicting story: through photography, the aletheic image was coaxed into recognizable visual patterns. The masterful photo-essay deployed three or four examples of aletheic images on each page: first landscapes, then pictures of cities carefully cropped to mimic the landscapes, and finally, buildings meticulously framed to evoke natural features. The rapid-fire sequence translated into print the method of information overload developed by visual artists and architects like Charles and Ray Eames. The sequence of photographs spelled out a theory that architecture was primarily a phenomenon of visual organization; only visual means could properly interpret architecture's essence. Words alone could not approximate the nature of architecture, and therefore theory demanded the visual component. For Norberg-Schulz, theory, like practice, was a visual design exercise.

The basic claim of *Genius Loci,* as stated in the introduction, was that architects were looking at the wrong images. They were seeking inspiration in the "visual chaos" of late modern architecture when they should have been looking at nature.[86] Topologies, asserted the book's introduction, "showed themselves" first in topographies as "natural patterns." Humans, continued the argument, did not invent visual logic. They originally learned it from the patterns of "visual order" in the topography of landscapes.[87] The book narrated Norberg-Schulz's idea of the history of architecture through six photo-essays, each containing roughly fifty photographs. The first depicted the origin of architecture in a sequence of landscapes. Second came bird's-eye views of cities, streets, buildings, and construction details meant to convey the human emulation of nature's visual order. The third, fourth, and fifth photo-essays were case studies of Prague, Khartoum, and Rome, cities where he felt a near-perfect identity in the visual patterns between nature, city, and architecture had been achieved. The sixth photo-essay summarized the book's argument:

other countries have an architecture wich is more unified and at the same time more varied. The themes are eminently Bohemian, but the variations are legion and give testimony to the exceptional artistic abilities of the Bohemian people. Like some other great cities, such as Rome, Prague has shaped the foreign artists who have settled there. From Peter Parler to Christoph Dientzenhofer they all became Bohemian and adapted their own cultural import to the local idiom.

What then are the natural phenomena behind the *genius loci?* We have already mentioned the rolling countryside of Bohemia, and the many surprises which break the general continuity of the land. Towards the border these surprises become dominant; wild rocks, hot springs, deep valleys and impenetrable forests bring the original forces of nature into presence. The Bohemian landscape, however, is not characterized by simple imageable elements, such as well defined valley-spaces or dominant mountains. Rather one might say that everything is simultaneously there, a fact which was noticed by Goethe: "Beautiful view over Bohemian landscapes, which have the particular character that they are neither mountains nor plains nor valleys, but everything at the same time"[9]. Obviously the whole of Bohemia does not have this "synthetic" quality. It is, however, the distinctive mark of the more characteristic parts of the country, and therefore becomes a general "Bohemian" trait. Such a generalization is natural, because Bohemia is a simple hydro-geophysical unit.

In Bohemia all the basic natural elements are present within a relatively small and well-defined area. Mountains, vegetation and water are there, not as separate "things", but mixed to form a "romantic" microcosmos. The earth in its different manifestations is exper-

98

Comparison of Bohemian rock outcroppings and curvilinear gables. From Christian Norberg-Schulz,
Genius Loci: Towards a Phenomenology of Architecture *(New York: Rizzoli, 1980), 98.*

again, Norberg-Schulz used Arnheim's diagram of a Gestalt square to illustrate the recognition of aletheic images in landscapes. Norberg-Schulz's understanding of architecture had not changed since he wrote *Intentions,* and his reading of Heidegger did not bring about a fundamental rethinking of his position.

The larger message of *Genius Loci* concerned the role of architecture in the historical formation of human identity. The notion that different types of topographies resulted in different cultures of visual organization allowed Norberg-Schulz to claim that human identity was "natural" and location-bound. Where humans copy nature's visual order, the aletheic image emerges, and "it brings about an 'increase in meaning'; that is, opens up a world by combining various and scattered elements into a unitary vision."[88] But this was not nature's visual order; it was Norberg-Schulz's disguised prejudices elevated to the plane of the natural. The talented architect-historian pictured the aletheic image, that is, photographed it and offered it as the model for all contemporary architecture. For Norberg-Schulz, photographing an aletheic image was a type of spiritually ecstatic fusion with nature. He never spoke publicly about this quasi-religious experience, but one can catch glimpses of it in sentences in *Genius Loci* that were struck from the published version, such as: "In particular I remember one evening in Jerash (Jordan) when the *genius loci* of the desert made itself present. The unforgettable experience was shared with Vittorio Gigliotti to whom this work is dedicated."[89]

In the last chapter of *Genius Loci,* Norberg-Schulz called upon architects to identify with landscapes, stop copying historical forms, and "return to the roots" of modernism in nature. The "recovery of place," he argued, could be achieved only through his "universally valid approach" of visualizing the topological structure of the landscape.[90] Norberg-Schulz's brilliant career move involved positioning himself as the high priest of a pedagogy aimed at the adulation of aletheic images. He insinuated that architects who no longer saw the true genius loci could be initiated into its mystical ways through the contemplation of his photographs. The topological truth-essence was supposedly apparent *there,* titillating on the surface of the page.

Although the idea of place-specificity seemed to undermine modernism's universalism, the opposite was in fact true. Norberg-Schulz's theory presumed a universal and ahistorical subject who learned through picturing, irrespective of the local topography he or she confronted. As such, this theory does not address how different historical cultures have interpreted natural environments and conceived their buildings. Indeed, Norberg-Schulz's architectural phenomenology

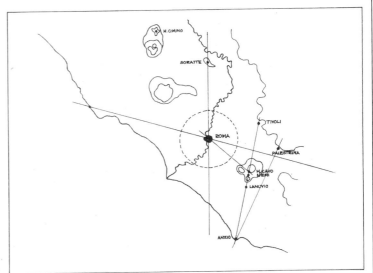

of Fortuna, that is, fate. After these excursions we may return to Rome with a basis for understanding its *genius loci*, and for explaining the meaning of the city as *caput mundi.*

2. Space

The Roman region is of volcanic origin. To the west and on both sides of the Tiber, the land is covered by a thick crust of old lava and ash which is known as *tufa*. During the millennia water courses have dug deep valleys and ravines in the volcanic crust, in Italian called *forre*[8]. The forre appear as surprising interruptions of the flat or rolling campagna, and as they are ramified and interconnected, they constitute a kind of "urban" netwoork of paths, a kind of "underworld" profoundly different from the everyday surface above. The campagna hardly offers other natural places; during the centuries the area around Rome had in fact an almost desert-like appearance. The forre therefore had a primary place-creating function, and innumerable villages have taken advantage of the protected and identified sites formed by the ramifications of the forre. (Sutri, Nepi, Civita Castellana, Barbarano, Vitorchiano, etc. etc.). In the forre one has the feeling of being "inside", a quality which is more often experienced in environments with a varied microstructure, than in the grand and perspicuous landscapes of the classical South. The forre have been extensively used during the course of history. In certain places (Norchia, Barbarano, Castel d'Asso) the Etruscans transformed the natural rocks into continuous rows of architectural façades, creating thus veritable cities for the dead. It is important to point out that the excavation of tufa rocks is an archetypal way of "building" in large parts of the Roman region. Today it is still a

ABOVE: *Diagram by Norberg-Schulz and photograph of Rome's surrounding region, showing the shared visual logic of city and landscape. From Norberg-Schulz,* Genius Loci: Towards a Phenomenology of Architecture *(New York: Rizzoli, 1980), 144.*

FACING PAGE: *Arnheim's Gestalt diagram of a square illustrates how the genius loci of a hypothetical natural place is "gathered" toward an architectural center. From Norberg-Schulz,* Genius Loci: Towards a Phenomenology of Architecture *(New York: Rizzoli, 1980), 169.*

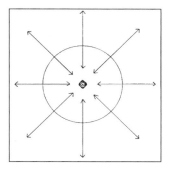

undermined local specificity by limiting its possible manifestations to a set of a priori universal archetypes. More problematically, the theory of genius loci created a place of exception where modern architects could appear tolerant of all historical cultures while acting out their prejudice against theories of history that demanded practice be historically accountable.

Intellectuality

Through the lens of Norberg-Schulz's intellectual career, we can begin to view the changes that occurred in the architectural discipline in the 1970s as modernism grappled with its own historicity and plurality. Paramount among these transformations was the emergence of the architect-historian, a figure that Norberg-Schulz played a large role in shaping. Strategically, the architect-historian aimed to wrest control of architectural history from art historians and simultaneously seize jurisdiction over architectural aesthetics from designers. This ambitious two-front battle was waged to protect modernism from becoming historical and losing its aesthetic integrity. It is significant that third-generation modernists led the charge; like Norberg-Schulz, they had come to believe the claims of aging first-generation modernists, such as Giedion, that modernism was synonymous with universal and timeless aesthetic principles. To carry out their mission, architect-historians walked a fine line, balancing the demands to become more theoretical to compete with art historians and the need to become more visually competent to contend with architects.

Norberg-Schulz exploited contradictions between textual and visual narratives to persuade readers that his personal aesthetic choices represented intuitive, timeless, and universally valid poetic truths that could not be grasped by scientific theory. Against his claim, I have demonstrated that his preferences were historically determined and only locally valid within the narrow discourse of modernism. To accomplish this, I excavated Norberg-Schulz's published texts, so to speak, to unearth the web of social, academic, aesthetic, and intellectual relations that informed his books. In the context of rejected manuscripts, private letters, friendships, his love of photography, and personal faith, the books acquire a greater significance as contributions to the history of the discipline than as self-contained products.

Topological historiography produced the aletheic image—the opposite of history—as its founding and sustaining source, thus succumbing to the contradiction of theorizing its own untheoretical source. To remain credible, topological history had to reveal the essential inadequacy of all theory. Norberg-Schulz did this by describing aletheic images through an intrinsically polysemous discourse of photo-essays and then denouncing the failure of verbal interpretations to grasp total meaning. "There can be only one language," he argued toward the end of his life, a "system of [aletheic] images," which he insisted had to remain "hidden."[91] Free from critical scrutiny, the aletheic image became reflexive, evidence of a truth that floated beyond while serving as the measure of authentic architecture.

In stripping architecture's origin of all historical ground, Norberg-Schulz raised topological historiography on a par with the manifestos of the historical avant-garde, thus securing an avant-garde aura for architect-historians. Like Giedion, Norberg-Schulz premised avant-gardism on the historian's custody of an invisible aesthetic integrity, the aletheic image, which he deemed to be the source of all genuine architecture.[92] This aesthetic integrity was the charismatic gift though which he hoped to save modernism, reducing its expressive range to differentiate its vocabulary and call attention to it. Norberg-Schulz intended his photographs to rescue modern architecture from the architects who were flooding the postwar market with buildings styled in devalued (read *historical*) modernist shapes, without pretense to higher aesthetic ideals and originality.[93] The architect-historian had an advantage over the architect in fulfilling the modernist demand to create a pure, original aesthetic: he could claim that his work, as the product of a single author, was more original than that of architects.

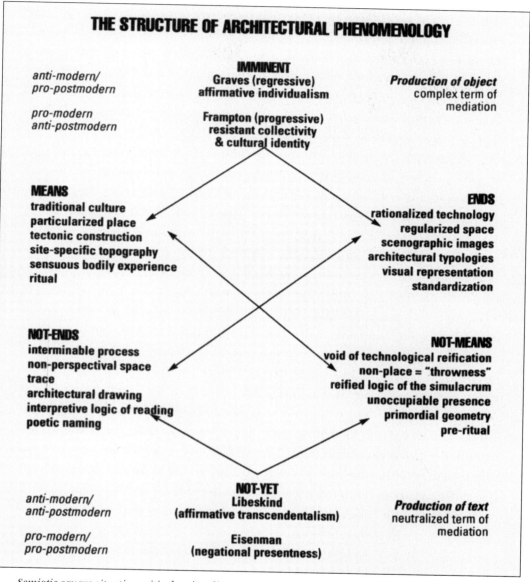

Semiotic square situating critical regionalism within architectural phenomenology. K. Michael Hays, "The Structure of Architectural Phenomenology," Newsline: Columbia University Graduate School of Architecture, Planning, and Preservation *3, no. 4 (December 1990–January 1991): 5.*

contraction to not-culture (including architectural drawing and interpretive logic of reading). In turn, civilization (understood as rationalized technology, visual representation) was placed in a relationship of contraction to not-civilization (nonplace, preritual). With diagonal lines, Hays indicated that culture and not-civilization stood in a relationship of complementarity, the same as civilization and not-culture. Following the prescribed formula of the semiotic square, Hays placed critical regionalism as a second order, so-called metaconcept, which was a compound of civilization and culture. The opposite metaconcept, the compound of noncivilization and nonculture, became the pigeonhole for Eisenman's postfunctionalist architecture of absences as well as for Libeskind's architecture of traces.

Hays made great strides in showing how architectural phenomenology's search for experience had made possible a series of postmodern intellectual positions that structured a significant part of architectural discourse (his protagonists were, after all, famous architects of their day). That is to say, he showed the discursive *effects* of Frampton's theory of experience. While one might agree with some of Hays's conclusions, for example that architectural phenomenology was not entirely free from consumer culture, one wonders why he actually remained silent on how that theory of experience was arrived at and understood by Frampton. Hays's generation owed a great debt to Frampton's older generation of architectural phenomenologists for helping redefine the nature of intellectual work in architecture as something distinct from practice. While Frampton's intellectual work, with its hint of New Left Marxism, prepared the ground for many younger scholars to later engage Adorno and Horkheimer, their contacts with critical theory also led them to recognize that their predecessors' discursive ground had mixed into it a problematic identity theory, which equated aesthetic and intellectual work, blurring the boundaries between practice and theory once more. That equation was, as we shall see, at the core of Frampton's understanding of experience as the common origin of both aesthetic and intellectual work in architecture. But rather than invoke critical theory once again as a sieve to remove the impurities of architectural phenomenology from architectural theory, and to, as it were, correct its conflation of the aesthetic and intellectual realms, we will be better served to trace the origins of Frampton's thinking about experience. Only then will we be able to gauge the degree to which his brand of architectural phenomenology was at once representative of his generation of scholars and also a personal search to recover a political thrust for both theory and practice.

His obsessive yet fragmentary treatment of the subject of experience has left gaps his critics have remarked on, interpreting them as points of weakness in his oeuvre. For instance, Fredric Jameson (b. 1934), the literary critic and Marxist political theorist, pointed out that a weakness of critical regionalism was that it did not clearly articulate its linkage of aesthetic experience to politics: "Indeed, the untheorized nature of this relationship to the social and the political movements that might be expected to accompany its development, to serve as a culture context, or to lend morale and support, is something of a problem here."[7] Jameson tried to fill in the gaps, with generous comments about how the connection between Frampton's theory of experience and politics should be read. He thought that the key was to read Frampton's theory of experience as an attempt to resist the isolation of one sense from the others by resituating individual sensory experiences within the body and in oppositional relationship to each other (e.g., visual vs. tactile). According to Jameson, Frampton's recognition of the separateness but relatedness of the senses (their plurality) resisted "the isolation of the individual sense that becomes the fundamental symptom of postmodern alienation, an isolation most often visual, but which one could just as easily imagine in terms of tactility."[8] While recognizing the progressive aspects of critical regionalism's pluralism, as expressed in its musings about sensory experience and the celebration of the local, Jameson echoed Hays's concern about how Frampton's theories dovetailed with the larger internal dynamics of capitalism.[9] In truth, however, Jameson's attempt to fill in Frampton's thinking tells us more about Jameson than Frampton. Rather than trying to repeat Jameson's projective operation, I will try to excavate the connections, in and below the level of published discourse, in Frampton's biography.

Frampton's turn toward experience and politics began first as an architecture student in the 1950s and became more explicit after a visit to New York in 1964 when he discovered Hannah Arendt's book *The Human Condition* (1958). These events framed his experience of an entirely new, alien, and alienating urban environment and gave him the intellectual tools with which he first tried to make sense of that new reality. While the New York visit and Frampton's lifelong fascination with Arendt are well known, the nature of the transformation they produced in his thinking can only be understood against the background of his personal history. Frampton did not write a coherent treatise on the core questions posed by his thinking about the relationship between aesthetic experience and politics. Instead he wrote many essays that approached the subject from different and often unrelated angles. Looking back at his own career, he remarked half-jokingly: "It is said that architects always design the same building. In a sense I have always rewritten the same essay."[10] It is true that Frampton was not shy about repeating his arguments and even went as far as to reuse sections of previous essays in new ones. Still, rather than one essay, what we find are groupings of essays around particular questions or themes. Given this fact, it is best not to isolate particular essays for close readings. Instead, I propose to examine two groupings of his writings. As we shall see, Frampton's treatment of architectural experience as containing a political dimension is most overtly worked out in his essays on Arendt: "Labour, Work and Architecture" (1969), "Industrialization and the Crisis of Architecture" (1973), and "The Status of Man and the Status of His Objects: A Reading of *The Human Condition*" (1978). These essays also contain less obvious clues regarding Frampton's understanding of architectural historiography, as structured by repetitive failures to achieve the experiential-cum-political potential of architecture. A second set of essays articulate Frampton's hope that these repetitive crises would eventually be surmounted in a final eschatological moment when architecture, under the right political conditions, would reach its full potential as the common experiential foundation for the individual development of fully human lives, that is, lives capable of experiencing a shared social reality. The most significant essays in this second group are: "On Reading Heidegger" (1974), "Constructivism: The Pursuit of an Elusive Sensibility" (1976), "Place, Production and Architecture" (1980), "Prospects for a Critical Regionalism" (1983), reworked into the more concise "Towards a Critical Regionalism: Six Points for an Architecture of Resistance" (1983), and "Rappel à l'ordre: The Case for the Tectonic" (1990). Experience also figured prominently in these later essays, but it was reworked through Frampton's reading of the eschatological phenomenology of French philosopher Paul Ricoeur. This eschatological turn is the hinge that differentiates Frampton's early works from his late thinking about experience certainly, but also about politics.

My grouping of articles according to the question of experience cuts against the grain of Frampton's own recent classification of his oeuvre in terms of "history, theory and criticism."[11] I am less interested in the overt content of the writings than in their shared assumptions about the nature of intellectuality in architecture, and in the central place that Frampton gives to experience in that formulation. This said, Frampton's understanding of the nature of intellectuality in architecture cannot be arrived at by focusing narrowly on close readings of texts. A much richer account emerges when we expand the frame to relate those close readings to the particulars of his life and career. Such biographical context opens up new interpretive paths through his writings, helping us better appreciate the manner in which he rethought architectural intellectuality as something separate but never entirely free from practice, and as something that involved not just the mind, but the entire sensing body. The task of piecing together biographical details, social history, and intellectual history was made possible by Frampton himself, who agreed to be the subject of protracted oral history that I conducted with him over the course of two years. What follows benefits from the strengths, and suffers from the weaknesses, of all oral histories, not the least of which is the problem of privileged access turning into ventriloquism. I trust my voice will be recognizable as I try to reclaim the value of Frampton's thinking for our present situation, while guarding against some of its shortfalls.

The Foundation in Labour

Frampton was born on November 20, 1930, in Woking, Surrey, a small dormitory railroad town 51 kilometers southwest of London, and was brought up in Guilford, a town eight miles away. His mother came from a family of toolmakers, and his father was a carpenter-builder who owned a modest construction company in Guilford, where he built suburban homes. As an only child, Frampton grew up hearing his father sing the praises of Charles Voysey (1857–1941), a local arts and crafts architect in the school of William Morris, whose attention to craftsmanship and detail was the source of much admiration. At his father's workshop, he learned about carpentry and the proper working of tools. His library still contains a nineteenth-century book on woodworking machinery that he received from a machinist at the shop. "I liked going there very much in fact," he recalled. "The smell of the wood in production, sawdust. The smell of glue and of paint and all the rest of it. That was a great pleasure."[12] Beyond the workshop, Frampton recalled his childhood life in Guilford as being structured around certain landmarks, such as the town church, the fire station, and a pseudo-Japanese public park. Aware of the remarkable similarity between his description of his childhood interests and his adult concern with craftsmanship and with buildings that served as orienting enclaves within the built environment, Frampton denied that his early memories could in any way stand "as some sort of predestined thing about architecture."[13] But who is to say where an obsession comes from? We only really know where it leads us, and Frampton's retelling of his own lifelong interests kept leading him back to his childhood. The landmarks of his childhood English suburb shaped his adult understanding of the architectural relationship between the public and private realms. Significantly, Frampton's childhood home was ambivalently both private and public. In 1939, his parents fell on hard times and had to move into the rooms above his maternal grandparents' "public house" or pub in Woking. The building was originally an eighteenth-century brick farmhouse faced with a more refined addition toward the street to house the pub itself. It is worth noting that this model of a private functional building behind a public representational façade returned throughout Frampton's career to mark the division between the concepts of building and architecture. "Behind the classic front lies the working farm," he wrote in reference to Palladian Villas. "The split between architecture and building is reflected in this division. The backs of villas with their dependencies are *buildings,* while, without a doubt, the interiors and fronts of the villas are *architecture.*"[14] His association of architecture with notions of the public and building with ideas about private life followed closely the separation between the private life he led in the farmhouse and the public life that went on in the pub. Frampton's home figured in his recollections as an enclave of both privacy and community life set in the context of a lifeless suburb:

> Suburbanization was, I thought, a nightmare. And it was relevant in the sense that the town of Woking . . . basically had become a commuter town . . . One of many other dormitory suburbs, of course feeding white-collar, service-industry labor into the capital city and out again every morning and evening. So that, you know, as a child I picked up on that.[15]

From an early age, Frampton showed dissatisfaction with the nineteenth-century transformation of the countryside into suburban environments. "My romantic ideal I suppose was really about the late eighteenth and early nineteenth century but with regard to agriculture as the primary means of production."[16] At age seventeen, against his father's wishes that he become a scientist, he decided to become a farmer on the grounds that "the really authentic life was agriculture."[17] He apprenticed with a farmer in West Meon, then returned to live at the family pub and found employment at a local farm. Despite the postwar introduction of American combine harvesters in the United Kingdom, farm work remained more physically taxing than he had expected. Exhausted after two years, he came to the conclusion that he did not have a body capable of such physical exertion. The degree of bodily toil was also a reason Frampton ruled out becoming a carpenter-builder like his father. Somewhat defeated, he opted for a less physically demanding career. He was attracted by the more intellectual work associated with the architectural practice of arts and crafts architects like Voysey.

After a year learning drafting at the local Guilford School of Art, Frampton was admitted to the Architectural Association in London in the autumn of 1950. His choice of school had to do in part with his perception that the AA's pedagogy embodied the arts and crafts ideals of Voysey. The AA, founded in 1847, had evolved in the late nineteenth century very much under the ethos of the arts and crafts. The school emblem was designed by Walter Crane (1845–1915), an associate of William Morris, bearing a typically arts and crafts motto: "Design with Beauty, Build in Truth." Frampton saw the AA as "an old arts and crafts institution turned avant-gardist, whereas the Bartlett [the Faculty of the Built Environment at University College London] was a somewhat petrified school, still linked to classicism."[18]

Frampton's use of the term "avant-gardism" was code for a particular brand of modernist architecture that had developed in Britain during the postwar years under the aegis of the London County Council, the city's influential municipal authority, which was particularly well represented at the AA. Many of the AA's professors also worked in the offices of the LCC, such as Anthony and Oliver Cox, Frampton's second-year teachers.[19] By the 1950s, the LCC had come to embrace a specific type of modernist architectural aesthetics that showcased the use of traditional building materials, especially brick, in a way that referred consciously to the functionalist projects of the Swedish welfare state. The connection to Sweden's socialists was seen as coherent with the LCC's long history, dating back to its auspicious beginnings in 1889, which was closely associated not just with Labour politics (Progressives dominated the agency until 1907), but also with the towering figure of William Richard Lethaby (1857–1931), who had served in the agency as art inspector and been responsible for drastic changes in art and architectural education during the 1890s. As both an influential architect and architectural historian, Lethaby was a pivotal figure in the transformation of the late arts and crafts ideals into central tenets of the modern movement in the United Kingdom. "Functionalism" was the term that enabled him to connect the arts and crafts to modernism. He defined functionalism as the idea that architecture should not be merely for aesthetic enjoyment and that it should serve the pragmatic needs of its inhabitants. He also endorsed the notion that architectural design should not be taught through the imitation of historical styles. Both of these ideas were familiar to modernists, and Lethaby combined them with more properly arts and crafts tenets, such as that design excellence came from an intimate working knowledge of tools and materials. The practical know-how of craftsmanship could only really be involuntarily transmitted through hands-on work. In his influential text "The Foundation in Labour" (1917), he blamed architects for being too intellectual and cautioned that too much "brain-work" would lead to the catastrophic detachment of architectural design from construction work and to its eventual downfall into a self-referential visual game. He thought the situation had been made worse by the mechanization of the building industry, which was ultimately controlled by intellectuals who had no real understanding of the manual act of building. It was important, thought Lethaby, to keep architects from "forming a camp" with intellectuals against manual workers.[20] "We have to set up a sympathetic and understanding contact between all brain-workers and the completer men who work both with hands and brain."[21] To accomplish this, he proposed that all professionals and intellectuals be required manual work as part of their training: "No one should be allowed to pass into 'brain-work' such as stockbroking without his year of manual drill; and others—Members of Parliament, architects, and all kinds of pastors and teachers—should, I think, be asked to have two years to show their good faith. If there were this basis of actual experience, then, perhaps, we might hope to control the machines before they tear civilization to bits."[22]

Lethaby's legacy was not without its critics outside of the AA and the LCC, especially in politically conservative architectural circles. For instance, H. S. Goodhart-Rendel (1887–1959), a conservative architectural historian who was at one time president of the Royal Institute of British Architects (RIBA), attacked Lethabian functionalism for being too accommodating of industrial construction and for losing sight of the human inhabitant:

> Functionalism may be regarded as a close architectural analogue of Puritanism, with its insistence upon moral values, its distaste for aesthetic values, its righteous slow-wittedness, and its abhorrence of gaiety. Like Puritanism it offered the consolations of assured virtue to those whom a naughty world might otherwise abash . . . It was first preached in England by Professor W.R. Lethaby many years ago, but enjoyed no vogue until it was restated more recently by M. Le Corbusier, and by him put into practice . . . Although the theory of Functionalism was Lethaby's and therefore English, it nevertheless seemed for many years as though the country of its origin was the only part of Europe in which it never was to be put into practice. If in Lethaby's own strange buildings all was done for convenience and nothing for looks, the convenience must have been that of the builder rather than that of the occupier.[23]

Lethaby's construal of manual labor as an experiential foundation for intellectual work was ultimately a denunciation of the industrial division of labor. But, as his critics pointed out, it was also a way of accommodating it by creating a better integration between labor and management, builders and architects, based on a common set of experiential references. In line with Lethabian ideals, the AA curriculum encouraged students to spend at least one summer working on a building site. Frampton complied with an enthusiasm fueled by the sense that the authentic life, which he once searched for in farming, could be found in the manual labor of building. The time he spent on the construction site was understood as a form of community service. These two words, community and service, had been brought together by Lethaby as core values of architectural education. And they were, he argued, Christian values:

> We must gather together a teaching about life which recognizes that life is founded on work . . . It may not be denied that Christianity did include within itself a body of teaching in regard to the slave, the labourer, the poor. It was, to some degree at least, the scheme of thinking of working men.[24]

Lethaby thought that by teaching architects about the Christian value of labor they would eventually help forge a civilization "based here and now on common labour, a common life, and a common aim."[25]

The socialist ideals of the arts and crafts, such as that architects should maintain commitments outside of their self-interests, gained renewed popularity in British architectural circles during the postwar years as a result of the publication of Edward P. Thompson's (1924–1993) celebrated first book *William Morris: Romantic to Revolutionary* (1955). As a social historian and political activist, Thompson was one of the leading intellectuals of the British New Left, the political movement that led British society through its profound restructuring into a welfare state under the Labour party.[26] Thompson promoted the British arts and crafts, and Morris in particular, as an example of how to juxtapose creative practice with a socialist engagement in political reality. Many architects in the circles of the AA and the LCC, whose engagement in the project of a socialist architecture was modeled closely on the Swedish model, saw the book as an opportunity to strengthen the homology between Sweden and the United Kingdom. "Let's face it," James Stirling told Frampton, "William Morris was a Swede!"[27]

While the focus on Morris helped to play up the socialism of the arts and crafts, it also helped to strategically take attention away from Lethaby, and to

The Royal Festival Hall, designed by LCC architects Holland, Hannen & Cubitts, for the Festival of Britain (London, 1951), viewed from Hugerford Bridge. From "Royal Festival Hall," Special Edition: The Architectural Review 109, no. 654 (June 1951): 343.

play down the Christian underpinnings of the arts and crafts. At the time, in the context of the tumultuous process of decolonization that ended the British Empire, New Left intellectuals were trying to accommodate the pluralization of cultural and religious identities evident in British cities into socialist thinking. The British New Left emerged in the late 1950s as a reorientation of Marxist politics, away from the party line of the USSR, and toward a greater sensitivity for the diverse interests of local constituencies. Under Thompson's pen, this attentiveness to the local developed into a celebration of grassroots mobilization within civil society. In his influential book *The Making of the English Working Class* (1963), Thompson critiqued the prevailing Marxist analyses of economic forces as directly productive of historical change and of nineteenth-century class consciousness as a correlative of industrial systems of production. Thompson argued that Marxists had turned the working class into a static object of study and missed the particular interests, experiences, and agency of individuals who struggled to create a collective identity for themselves. The popularity of Thompson's book initiated a wide scholarly interest in a new type of history narrated from below.

At the AA however, Frampton learned a more conventional historiographical model from the hand of Sir John Summerson, who still interpreted architecture as the product of a reduced canon of architects, and for whom without architects, there remained mere buildings. There were unresolved tensions between the AA's Lethabian studio pedagogy and the teaching of architectural history, which in the charged climate of the school acquired political overtones: "The AA," recalled Frampton, "had a strong leftist tendency inside the school, although there was also the opposing position."[28] The relationship between architecture and building became a trope around which the individual political positions of faculty and students were articulated and understood. In studio, Frampton recalled, "we were encouraged to read Rasmussen's *London.*"[29] The choice of Steen Eiler Rasmussen (1898–1990), a Danish architect, introduced an alternative way to interpret historic architecture based on direct experience, not on the historian's knowledge of facts. Rasmussen's *London* (1937) was a counterpoint to Summerson's *Architecture in Britain 1530–1830* (1953). Influenced by Gestalt psychology and phenomenology, Rasmussen analyzed Georgian architecture in terms of experiential patterns: a particular cadence of window openings, a rhythm of compressing and expansive spaces, and the alternating concealment and disclosure of forms according to the visitor's movements.[30] The contrast with the historian's stylistic descriptions in terms of flared lintels, escutcheons, balustrades, and plasterwork was dramatic. Under Rasmussen's pen, it appeared possible to use Georgian architecture as a source for contemporary design, by emulating its particular experiential patterns, without having to imitate its style.

The idea that two buildings with entirely different outward appearances could be based on the same experiential pattern fed into the ongoing discussion about socialist British architecture, providing theoretical justifications to those in search of architectural aesthetics beyond the LCC's traditional brick construction. The first significant breaks away from brick occurred around the time

OVERLEAF: Image pairing showing the continuity of building forms and architectural experiences from the nineteenth to the twentieth century, as presented in Steen Eiler Rasmussen's London, the Unique City, *first published in 1937. Rasmussen helped to popularize the photo-essay in architectural publications. From Steen Eiler Rasmussen,* London, the Unique City *(Cambridge, Mass.: MIT Press, 1982), 248–49.*

House in Downshire Hill, Hampstead. Beginning of nineteenth century

climate. They were provided with balconies although it was
evident that no one would ever venture to sit on them. (They
had generally rail floors, so that decency must have made it
impossible for a lady wearing a crinoline to stand on them.) In
sitting in the room and looking out of the large windows,
people wished to have the same feeling of freedom as when
sitting in the verandaed houses of the tropics. In the drawing-
rooms of the house they wanted to feel in close contact with

248

House am Rupenhorn, Berlin (Gebr. Luckardt). Beginning of twentieth century

the trees of the park or square. In housebuilding the precise and the smooth, the plain and the refined was still their aim. It showed what could be created by modern means, and as an effective contrast to the barren block of the building the living trees and plants were used, still more living against the concise form of the dead cubes. The balconies were intended for flowers and creepers which made the streets of London look like the hanging gardens of Babylon.

when Frampton entered the AA, with the 1951 Festival of Britain, which was being organized by the Labour party on the South Bank of London to celebrate the centennial of the first world fair, the Great Exhibition in the Crystal Palace. Many of Frampton's teachers were involved in designing buildings for the festival, and he visited the grounds under construction as part of class trips. Significantly, the most important precedent for the Festival of Britain was the Stockholm Exhibition of 1930, famously remembered for Gunnar Asplund's (1885–1940) and Sigurd Lewerentz's (1885–1975) introduction of functionalist and constructivist aesthetics to Sweden. The signature structures of the Festival of Britain, The Dome of Discovery by Ralph Tubbs (1912–1996), The Skylon by Hidalgo Moya (1920–1994) and Philip Powell (1921–2003), and The Royal Festival Hall by LCC architects Holland, Hannen & Cubitts, revived the aesthetics of the Stockholm Exhibition, presenting the possibility of a socialist British architecture made with modern materials like concrete, plate glass, and steel.

The Festival of Britain, and the academic debates that surrounded it, had a profound and far-reaching effect on Frampton. It awoke his interest in constructivism and his belief that it represented a "more rigorous modernity" than was possible through traditional brick construction.[31] He became involved with a loose social network of young architects, splintering out of the LCC, who also sought to develop the new aesthetic legitimized by the Festival of Britain: "I mean architects like Alan Colquhoun, for example, who did work in the LCC. Or Peter Carter, who later would work in Mies's office in Chicago [and who] also worked in the LCC. Also, Colin St. John Wilson at some point."[32] Eager to learn more about constructivism, but unable to travel, he turned to books and journals, studying the photographs, and skipping over the texts written in foreign languages that he did not speak. Together with his classmate Peter Land, he assembled these photographs into a visual exhibition on Dutch constructivism, focused primarily on the work of Johannes Duiker (1890–1935) and Bernard Bijvoet (1889–1979).[33] "Although this wasn't Russian constructivism," said Frampton, "Duiker could be seen as someone partly influenced by Russian constructivism, anyway by structure, construction, the overt expression of it."[34] Constructivist ideas about structural expression were governed by tenets such as the rejection of art for art's sake and the idea that architecture should be a form of social service, which dovetailed well with the undercurrent of Lethabian pedagogy at the AA. Constructivism appeared to Frampton as a particularly successful aesthetic resolution to the constellation of sometimes contradictory ideas that he associated with the authentic life: the foundation on physical labor, the communication through intellectual work, the inwardness of private life, and the communal nature of public engagement. For the following two decades, Frampton returned constantly to constructivism to illustrate the possibility of an aesthetic that could connect architecture and life:

> The importance of the term "Constructivism" seems to have lain not in itself, but rather in the extremely volatile and elusive sensibility it came to evoke. Beyond any doubt, this sensibility played a major role in transforming our way of viewing the world and, if nothing else, it modified our expectancy with regard to the nature of artistic production.[35]

He only began to drop the word "constructivism" by the early 1980s, when his research into that "elusive sensibility" was subsumed into his notion of critical regionalism. Although the introduction of the term critical regionalism appeared as a sudden breakthrough, it was actually the result of a gradual increase in the relative importance he assigned to constructivist aesthetics as an experiential surplus linking architecture, life, and social reality. Frampton's mature conception of experience was certainly informed by his readings in philosophy. But it is important to distinguish what he brought to these readings from the readings themselves. By the time Frampton read Arendt, he had already formed this peculiar personal understanding of experience as a surplus. He developed this idea largely through his practice as a graphic designer, a fact that casts unusual light on the nature of architectural intellectuality in the 1950s and 1960s as an ambiguous realm encompassing both aesthetic and written works.

Graphic Design

Frampton was trained as an architect to think that every argument should be able to play itself visually, and conversely, that every aesthetic arrangement was an intellectual argument. Many of the architects of his generation who were also interested in analyzing the experience of architecture documented it through traditional architectural means such as measuring buildings, taking photographs, and drawing diagrams, plans, and sections. Rassmussen's photo-essays were influential in this regard, as would later be those of Kevin Lynch and Norberg-Schulz. Comparatively, Frampton did very little in terms of first-hand documentation, preferring to rely on existing drawings and photographs. More than most architects, however, Frampton developed sophisticated visual skills for analyzing buildings from printed documents. He honed these skills as technical editor of *Architectural Design,* where he succeeded Theo Crosby (1925–1994) from 1962 to 1965. Working closely with the editor, Monica Pidgeon (1913–2009), Frampton received dozens of architects' portfolios every month, which he carefully scrutinized in search for examples of that elusive constructivist sensibility. During these years, Frampton began to reflect on the nature and capacity of print media not only to represent a building, but to actually construct a new sort of experience of the building, more intense in many ways than the direct experience itself. To really comprehend the experience of a building, he thought it was necessary to drastically increase the number of photographs of it, to highlight material textures as evidence of changing light conditions, and to include more close-ups of details, not just the usual wide shots of the street facades. The striking outcome of his practice as an editor was that Frampton began to theorize graphic design as a means to transform an essentially visual medium (print) into a tactile experience. His discriminating eye discerned photographs taken with different camera makes and formats, the types of film used, the paper on which they were printed, and so on:

> I was one of the first editors to publish pictures of Stirling and Gowan's Leicester Engineering Building. Most of the photographs we used on that occasion were taken by Richard Einzig with a plate camera. The difference between Einzig's images and a number of high-speed alternative shots we had in hand was very marked. As opposed to the dramatic darks and lights of the latter, the specific textures of metal, glass, and brick were almost palpable (tactile) in Einzig's almost shadowless pictures.[36]

The tactile experience that Frampton wanted to provide was meant to "compensate for the inevitable misinformation" offered by other editors of architectural journals who, in his view, yielded to "the imperatives of the mass media" and reduced their coverage of buildings to one or two general shots.[37] He thought that the widespread practice of superficial coverage had come to shape how architects went about experiencing buildings and ultimately influenced the way buildings were built—to be perceived only from afar. "And here we have the strange general tendency of our times: the trend to stress information at the expense of experience."[38] An editor worth his salt had a responsibility, if not to expose the constructive weaknesses of excessively visual buildings, at least to turn the focus back onto the experience of architecture by recognizing those buildings that rose above the norm in their attention to tactile experience.

Frampton's demotion of the visual in favor of tactility was his response to a wider set of British cultural debates concerning the estrangement of youth from traditional social norms and their desire to rediscover a more authentic social reality. The debates were variously interpreted within architectural discourse, often in reference to the towering figure of Sartre, who was incredibly popular among British youth.[39] His existentialist philosophy of action influenced Alison and Peter Smithson's (1928–1993 and 1923–2003, respectively) theorization of new brutalism as a rediscovery of social reality through direct experiences of new types of gathering spaces (e.g., streets in the sky), typically rendered in unfinished materials, such as concrete, steel, or brick.[40] At the AA, professors also struggled to cast their pedagogy in experiential terms, as a more honest engagement of social reality than that possible in traditional "real world" architectural practice.[41] Although Frampton was not particularly drawn to Sartre, Frampton's pursuit of a more authentic experience of architecture through architectural photography and graphic design cannot be entirely divorced from the cultural context in which his search appeared legitimate and worthwhile. Nevertheless, he did not read phenomenological philosophers at the time. Rather, phenomenology appeared to him as a set of aesthetic architectural preoccupations expressed in the visual structure and organization of professional journals. "I was a big admirer of Ernesto Rogers's *Casabella,*" he recalled:

> What is amazing is the magazine itself, *Casabella,* the format, the size of the images, and the emphasis that is put in his attempt to recover the lost roots of the modern movement . . . There were special issues by Rogers on Behrens, and Mendelsohn . . . I admired the intensity with which this decision had been taken and the graphics of the magazine emphasized the tactile value of the work. That is what impressed me . . . I admired the plastic results in the magazine, so to speak. I thought it manifested the kind of decisive editorial position that I admired and which I tried to, in a naïve way, emulate.[42]

Frampton could not read Italian, but he nevertheless "read" *Casabella Continuità* as a visual argument about the phenomenological rediscovery of reality through experience. Architectural images functioned as a lingua franca for him, which he tried to emulate and perfect through his own work. Significantly, Frampton did not read Ernesto Rogers's many writings about architectural phenomenology in *Casabella.* He knew of important translations of Rogers's articles such as "The Phenomenology of European Architecture" (1964), mainly

Above: a view of the boiler house flue, above the roof of the aerodynamics laboratory. The flue is designed to spout off any corrosive deposit formed at its head

Below: a view up through a staircase opening to the roof of the electrical laboratory. The spiral stair constructed out of steel sheet and tube leads from the direct haulage galley up to the top laboratory

Above: a view of the aerodynamics and electrical laboratories situated at high level above the heavy structural laboratories. The unglazed ends of the trusses over the lower laboratories show on the right. The trusses are glazed on alternate faces with opaque and translucent plyglass. The walls of the upper laboratories are faced with opaque plyglass

Below: interior of the aerodynamics laboratory showing the junction of the diagonal trusses with the orthogonally set, enclosing brick wall

Graphic design layout by Kenneth Frampton in the shape of a cross: four close-up views of the Leicester University Engineering Building by James Stirling and James Gowan. From Kenneth Frampton, "Leicester University Engineering Building," Architectural Design 32, no. 10 (1962): 484.

Nelle due pagine / Dans ces deux pages / In these two pages: Le Corbusier, Il Carpenter Center per le arti figurative alla Harvard University, Cambridge, Mass. Nella pagina di fronte, colonna a destra / Dans la page ci-contre, colonne à droite / Opposite page, right column: Sert, Jackson & Gourley, Centro medico Holyoke alla Harvard University.

Graphic design layout by Ernesto Rogers in the shape of a cross: four close-up views of Carpenter Center, Cambridge, Massachusetts, by Le Corbusier. From Donlyn Lyndon, "Filologia della Architettura Americana," Casabella Continuità, *no. 281 (1963): 24.*

through his friend Joseph Rykwert, a Polish-born British architect and historian who later also became an influential architectural phenomenologist, and who had worked for Rogers in the 1950s. But for Frampton, the visuals remained a more direct and effective means of communicating an argument about architecture than writing. That is to say, visuality was for him a form of intellectuality.

Following the *Casabella* model, Frampton increased the size of photographs in *Architectural Design* and bled them to the edges of the page. His graphic design style was also influenced by his association with the British constructionist group of artists including Anthony Hill (b. 1930), John Ernest (1922–1994), Stephen Gilbert (1910–2007), and Kenneth Martin (1905–1984) and Mary Martin (1907–1969), who were also in the circle of *The Structurist,* a journal devoted to art as a building process and to the search for a neoconstructivist visual language connecting architecture, photography, design, painting, sculpture, music, and literature. The structurists formed a part of the wider transatlantic postwar discourse on the synthesis of the arts, which remained at the core of modernist architectural theory from Le Corbusier to Carlos Raúl Villanueva (1900–1975).[43] Frampton published structurist works in the back of *Architectural Design* under the loose rubric of art. The other major influence was the Swiss constructivist painter and graphic designer Richard Paul Lohse (1902–1988), who believed graphic design to be indistinguishable from political activity, in line with the tradition of agitprop Russian artists. During World War II, Lohse was an active member of the resistance, providing support to immigrants. He also staged more public acts of resistance, such as the 1938 exhibition of Russian and German constructivist artists in Zurich. Lohse was a critical influence on Frampton, encouraging him to think of the connection between the arts as something experientially structured, but also politically charged.

Constructivist graphics presented a decidedly modernist, even utopian, goal for human life, holding the promise that, in the future, individual experience and social reality might actually coincide. This belief was reinforced by Frampton's London circle of structurist artists, through which he discovered the writings of the American painter Charles Joseph Biederman (1906–2004). Frampton was particularly drawn to Biederman's argument in *Art as the Evolution of Visual Knowledge* (1948) that constructivist art had arrived at its maximum expression in the work of the Dutch constructivist painter Piet Mondrian (1872–1944), because he had been able to introduce an intuitive element into constructivist painting. In Mondrian, Frampton recognized a quest to find subjectivity on the other side of objective (i.e., mathematically proportioned) painterly construction, as an experiential surplus that could not be done away with. "This had an enormous appeal for me," said Frampton. "In a way I have to say it still does. It is linked in my mind with this interest in graphics."[44]

During his years at *Architectural Design,* Frampton also worked part-time as an architect in the firm of Douglas Stephen and Partners, where he was given the responsibility of designing an eight-story concrete and glass housing tower in Craven Hill Gardens, Bayswater, London (1964). Like his structurist friends, Frampton became interested in constructivism as an experiential lingua franca between his graphic design work and his more conventional practice as an architect. This search for a constructivist thread between the arts sparked his interest in the Swiss Max Bill (1908–1994), whose work bridged architecture, painting, graphic design, and typeface design. Frampton admired particularly that Bill did not seek to unify the arts by imposing on all of them a particular style, in the manner of a nineteenth-century *Gesamkunstwerk.* Rather, the aesthetic unity of Bill's multidisciplinary practice came from his ability to abide by, with the strictest economy, the objective conditions of production employed in the material construction of each work, while simultaneously making that process yield a "surplus" of gratifying sensory experiences: "These nuances of material expression that arise out of the substance itself, return us to the intrinsic quality of Bill's fine art where, for all of the objectivity of the concept, the phenomenological attributes of the material itself are exploited rather than suppressed."[45]

Constructivism provided the frame for Frampton to reorient the interest he had developed in experience through his graphic design work back toward the act of building. In his writings, sensual experiences began to be invoked to serve a unifying purpose, something equivalent to nineteenth-century stylistic decoration, and having the same relationship of "surplus" to the building's structure. For instance, what attracted him to Bill's work was the presence of a specific sensual experience, say a tactile roughness of surfaces, throughout the building.[46]

Frampton was not immediately able to achieve this type of experiential coherence in his own work. At Craven Hill Gardens, there was an unresolved tension between the exterior and the interior of the building. The design of exterior elevations was still conceived stylistically, to appear within the modernist idiom of new brutalism: this was most apparent in the direct expression of the unfinished reinforced concrete cross-wall construction, but also in the volumetric separation of the stair core from the main body of the building. To make the connection to new brutalism more overt, Frampton published it

Craven Hill Gardens, residential block of split-level maisonettes, Bayswater, London, 1964.
Designed by Kenneth Frampton for the firm of Douglas Stephens and Partners. Photograph
courtesy of Michael Carapetian.

alongside Alison and Peter Smithson's The Economist Building (London, 1964), Alan Colquhoun and John Miller's Secondary School (Stratford, 1964), and James Stirling and James Gowan's Leicester Laboratories (Leicester, 1964).[47] However, an entirely different logic governed Frampton's design of the interior units. There, decisions were not based on style but rather on creating a specific type of historically charged bodily movement within the spaces: the crossover scissor section was abstracted from the vertical arrangement of spaces in Georgian townhouses, a return to a cultural experiential pattern that Rasmussen would have understood.

If Craven Hill Gardens did not succeed in presenting a unified experience between interior and exterior, then it is possible to read Frampton's publication of the building as an attempt to achieve that unity through another medium. Exploiting the analogy between the front cover of *Architectural Design* and the building's façade, he turned the interior into the exterior, prominently displaying a sectional axonometric drawing of the interior scissor section on the face of the issue. More precisely, the graphic choice to represent the interior with a diagonally oriented drawing visually brought forth the primary organizing experience of the interiors—the diagonal movement up and down the scissor stairs—while reviving the preferred drawing mode of Dutch constructivism. The emphasis on the diagonal structuring of the page served to set up a relationship of equivalency between the visual graphic design and the haptic experience of the stairs, both as means of psychological orientation. There were less obvious ways in which the elision of the difference between visual and haptic was pursued in the reportage itself, such as the use of Michael Carapetian's sharp, oversized photographs to render the textured surfaces of the building, which, given the format of the journal, quite literally had to be held in hand in order to be looked at. All this allowed Frampton to present Craven Hill Gardens according to the logic of an experiential coherence that was not quite there in the building. Indeed, Frampton's careful graphic constructions were never meant to be merely neutral documentations of buildings, or direct representations. Instead, they aimed to transform the photographs and drawings extracted from the building itself into works of graphic design worth experiencing in and for themselves. Graphic design achieved the production of an experience that was in excess of the building itself, yet remained intimately tied to it. If in constructivist works the achievement of that surplus experience was tantamount to the elevation of building into architecture, then graphic design could also make architecture from buildings.

Frampton's graphic work gives us a different kind of access to a central theme in his writings: the distinction between building and architecture.[48] If we take his graphic design work seriously, then we cannot help but note that buildings did not appear to him to be fully graspable as architecture until they were drawn, photographed, graphically laid out, and published. This media-driven understanding of the relationship between building and architecture, which Frampton was fully conscious of,[49] has been recently theorized as enabling the complete dissociation of architecture from building, and the circumscription of architecture entirely to the sphere of publications, films, and exhibitions.[50] Frampton resisted the idea that building could be excluded from architecture and media. Instead, he searched for the unifying thread between all three domains. In his work, graphic design appeared as a new synthesis of building and architecture, which attempted to resolve the tensions and contradictions between the two on the plane of experience.

Working at *Architectural Design* also had the effect of increasing Frampton's profile not only within the local London scene but also internationally. He joined the circle of James Stirling (1926–1992), which met on Saturday mornings over beers in Soho's Yorkminster Pub and included the likes of Douglas Stephens, Robert Maxwell, John Miller, Tony DeLorenzo and others.[51] He also met Peter Eisenman, then pursuing a doctorate under Colin Rowe at Cambridge.[52] In 1964, Eisenman invited him to participate in the Committee of Architects for the Study of Environments (CASE), an association for young academics to collaborate on applied projects with New York policy makers.[53] The meeting brought together an elite group of young and intellectually inclined architects, many of whom were trained at America's Ivy League schools: Eisenman and Richard Meier (b. 1934) at Cornell; Michael Graves (b. 1934), John Hejduk (1929–2000), and Henry Millon (b. 1927) at Harvard; Robert Venturi and Donlyn Lyndon at Princeton; Charles Gwathmey (1938–2009) and Vincent Scully at Yale; and Stanford Anderson (b. 1934) at Berkeley, then at Columbia. The trip proved to be a defining moment in Frampton's life, for reasons that would become apparent to him only later. He brought with him his interest in working out the question of the relationship between building and architecture at a critical moment of intellectual ferment. In the American context, this question seemed to be at the crux of contemporary architectural theory: Venturi was trying to work out the distinction by differentiating between program and style in what would become his theory of the decorated shed; Eisenman, Meier, Graves, and Gwathmey were looking to establish the unity

Robert Venturi, "I Am a Monument," 1966. Courtesy of Venturi, Scott Brown, and Associates, Inc.

between architecture and building through style alone, reviving the modernist language of the 1910s.

In these American intellectual and aesthetic formulations, Frampton recognized "the predicament of modern architectural theory,"[54] as diagnosed by his teacher, Sir John Summerson. In his RIBA address, "The Case for a Theory of Modern Architecture" (1957), Summerson argued that whereas classical architecture had established the unity between architecture and building in terms of stylistic integrity, the modern movement had displaced style as its principle of order in favor of a socially determined program. Frampton saw the attempts of American architects to turn back to style as fundamentally antimodern. This was clear to him in the case of Venturi and Moore's interest in premodern style, but it was also the case in the neomodern revival of Eisenman, Meier, and the others. Instead, Frampton proposed a constructivist alternative, rejecting style for style's sake, and seeking the unity between building and architecture through "the structural system which, to a large degree, transcends the Summersonian opposition between the paradigm and the programme."[55] However, unlike the constructivists, he did not find unity in the construction process itself, but rather in the experiential surplus, indeed the pleasure, derived from a properly articulated building unit:

> Such hedonistic values manifest themselves in Le Corbusier's 1935 Week-End House despite the overriding presence of the vault as a structural unit. A world is established with which, at a secondary level, qualitatively different conditions emerge. Through changes in floor surface, in light and in enclosing material, distinct realms are created . . . All these induce significant and delicate transformations to the human experience within a confined area . . . Thus, variations in the vault treatment articulate the built form so that it is able to assert itself as an existential precondition for "lived" meaning. The formulation of meaning in such terms returns us to archaic values of a preclassical era, regardless of any concern for the preeminence of the programme or the paradigm. Our changing existence as men in relation to nature is surely the final meaning of the Week-End House, a meaning which seems to transcend the opposition of architecture and building through achieving a synthesis at another level of being.[56]

Experience appeared in this passage not only as the future synthesis of architecture and building in a poststylistic moment, but also as its roots in a deep medieval past before the classical notion of style. In other words, experience figured as an elision of traditional historiography, making the synthesis of architecture and building also into that of future and past. While passages such as this were common in Frampton, they coexisted with meticulous chronologies in which he abided by the strictest historiographical standards. Not only did Frampton leave these contradictions unresolved in his texts, he actually exploited them as mirrors of what he believed to be the unresolved tensions between contemporary architecture and building, the former bent on a postmodernist search for unity through past styles, and the latter focused only on satisfying social programs. Amid the general pall, he occasionally identified the potential of certain works to synthesize these two poles. In their isolation, they stood more as promises of a future, more authentic experience of reality than as reality itself.

Frampton's early works suggest that the surplus experience of reality seemed achievable to him through the graphic working of buildings into architecture. A telling example was his article "Maison de Verre," on which he worked intermittently between 1965 until it was published in *Perspecta* in 1969. Symptomatically, the project began out of his frustration in learning that the Maison de Verre (Paris, 1928–1932), Bernard Bijvoet (1889–1979) and Pierre Chareau's (1883–1950) masterwork, had not been adequately published and was therefore not understandable to him as architecture entirely:

> I knew it from photographs . . . I was very interested in it but I hadn't seen it . . . Very beautiful drawings were published in *Architects and Building News* . . . They were very intriguing plans in any case, with very beautiful drawings which had been laid out, drawn with mechanical instruments, but inked in by hand very carefully to give it a certain quality . . . The house was very important to me because it embodied a kind of sophisticated constructivism in a sense, and that's what interested me a lot."[57]

In July 1965, Frampton resolved to document the house himself, calling upon his architect friends Michael Carapetian, to take photographs, and Robert Vickery, to help him with the drafting. He produced a forty-nine-page graphic design exercise, which pushed the limits of anything ever published in *Perspecta* and in most American journals in terms of the sustained attention to one single building. The article included 119 illustrations, five of them in color, more than most contemporary books on architectural history, ranging from exterior shots of the façade, details of the doorbells, views of the stairs, close-ups of the operable windows, views of the different flooring systems, multiple pictures of moving panels, a focus on the bidets and the perforated metal screens shielding them, foldout plans, sections, and axonometrics, all with a sharpness of focus and crispness of line to make the essay yield a surplus experience from mere ink on a page. Interspersed among them were biographies of Bijvoet and Chareau, a 1933 article on the house by Paul Nelson, and Frampton's own writing. The graphic design performed what the text only described. "The 'functionalism' of the Maison de Verre," he wrote, "is permeated by such metaphorical ideas at every level. A great deal of its equipment and mechanization is poetic and symbolic rather than strictly functional."[58] The graphic excess exhibited on every page was meant to turn the building into a poetic experience, which stood polemically against the habitual economy of

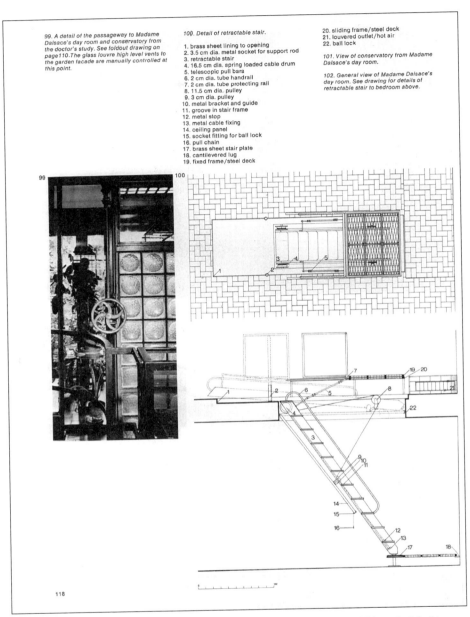

99. A detail of the passageway to Madame Dalsace's day room and conservatory from the doctor's study. See foldout drawing on page110.The glass louvre high level vents to the garden facade are manually controlled at this point.

100. Detail of retractable stair.

1. brass sheet lining to opening
2. 3.5 cm dia. metal socket for support rod
3. retractable stair
4. 16.5 cm dia. spring loaded cable drum
5. telescopic pull bars
6. 2 cm dia. tube handrail
7. 2 cm dia. tube protecting rail
8. 11.5 cm dia. pulley
9. 3 cm dia. pulley
10. metal bracket and guide
11. groove in stair frame
12. metal stop
13. metal cable fixing
14. ceiling panel
15. socket fitting for ball lock
16. pull chain
17. brass sheet stair plate
18. cantilevered lug
19. fixed frame/steel deck
20. sliding frame/steel deck
21. louvered outlet/hot air
22. ball lock

101. View of conservatory from Madame Dalsace's day room.

102. General view of Madame Dalsace's day room. See drawing for details of retractable stair to bedroom above.

118

Graphic layout by Kenneth Frampton of pages 118 and 120 with middle foldout (in black), showing views and drawings of the retractable stair in the master bedroom of Maison de Verre. From Kenneth Frampton, "Maison de Verre," Perspecta 12 (1969): 118, 120.

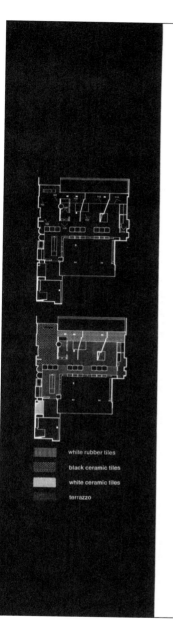

white rubber tiles

black ceramic tiles

white ceramic tiles

terrazzo

103. Interior detail: guest bathroom. Signal light and tube light mounted on vertical conduit.

104 and 105. In master bedroom: detail views of retractable stair. In the master bedroom, note in addition detailing of "curtain wall" panelling to garden facade. Any condensation accumulating in the panel may drain out via gargoyles into an interior gutter built into the edge of the tiled floor.

106. The master bedroom looking towards the storage wall. See axonometric of the whole house.

107. The master bedroom looking towards the curtain wall with the retractable stair in the rearground.

103

104

105
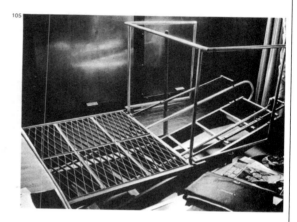

120

architectural publications. Frampton described the house in terms that could equally portray his article:

> In the Maison de Verre there is a kind of surplus, it is functional and direct, but it always goes beyond what is required . . .There are aspects of the Maison de Verre where you could say that the functionalism is a kind of surplus functionalism.[59]

Frampton never measured another building, but he did continue to pursue the production of experiential surplus through graphic design. Frampton's search for experience was part of the broader culture of experientialism of the late 1960s, which had important ramifications within architectural theory. The idea that architectural theory could be entirely reformulated on the basis of a new phenomenological understanding of experience had caught hold of many architects in Frampton's intellectual circle. Most noteworthy was Joseph Rykwert, who in October 1968 founded The History and Theory of Architecture course at the University of Essex, a program specifically geared to practicing architects. [60] Rykwert polemically presented his program as the antithesis of the Courtauld Institute of Art at the University of London, where architectural history was taught as the study of precedents for design. Rykwert was interested in integrating historical context into design, but not as a formal precedent. Rather, he understood historical context as a background of experience which preceded the architect's design proposal.

Rykwert's notion of historical context was not far from Labatut's and that of others at Princeton, where Frampton was teaching at the time. The difference was that at Princeton the search for authentic experiences of architecture aimed at reconciling modernism with its own history, whereas at Essex the interest in authentic experience was motivated by a wholesale rejection of modernism. The Essex school was more intellectually rigorous than Princeton, but also more ideological. Rykwert and his colleagues upheld phenomenology as the only intellectual framework capable of guiding the architect's search for authentic experience. The other influential promoter of this hard-line position was the architect Dalibor Vesely, a Czechoslovakian dissident, who was as brilliant as he was dogmatic.[61] As a student of the famed Czech phenomenologist Jan Patočka, Vesely was well qualified to teach courses like "The Phenomenology and Psychology of Perception; Their Implications for Methods of Design."[62] Vesely also employed graphic design as a means to document architectural experiences. His students' drawings were beautiful renditions of lighting conditions, textures and movements collapsed into fragments of building plans and sections. But unlike Frampton, Vesely was an antimodernist who made radical claims, for example, that phenomenology could clean modernism from the architect's mind and help him achieve original and unmediated experiences of architecture.[63] Essex became an international point of reference for architectural phenomenology, drawing the likes of Norberg-Schulz as external examiners, and spawning a new generation of antimodernists.[64] Although Frampton was in contact with Rykwert and Vesely and sincerely admired them, his political labour leanings and his commitment to modernism were also antagonistic to theirs, which led him to keep his distance and to chart his own course in his architectural search for authentic experience.

Toward the end of the 1960s, Frampton became deeply influenced by the anti-institutional student revolts that took hold of North Atlantic societies. Aware of capitalism's ability to subsume all opposition into itself, the radical student groups of the sixties emphasized transgression as resistance. Experience became a code word for the rediscovery of reality unmediated by capitalist distortions, and a youth culture of experientialism emerged in an effort to keep the path toward unalienated existence open. The search for experience became part of the tactics of provocation aimed at violating traditional rules and codes of liberal culture. Frampton joined student demonstrations and participated in marches on Washington, D.C. The turning point in his own rethinking about surplus experience as something political was a trip to Berlin in December 1967, to attend a four-day conference on architectural theory at the Technical University of Berlin, only months after Benno Ohnesorg, a student, was shot dead by plainclothes police at a demonstration against the Shah of Iran. Immediately upon his return to Princeton, Frampton made a striking collage, which he called *Berlin Grafik!* (1967).

At a basic level, the collage was simply a version of the conference program. *Berlin Grafik!* was structured into four separate boards, according to the conference's four days of panels. At another level, however, the collage represented Frampton's attempt to draw forth a surplus experience from the program. Overlaying the initial division according to time, a secondary set of four diagonal black lines weave the panels (and the days) together. These lines dominate the composition, skewing the orientation of the conference program, and indeed of all the other documents, according to their own oblique logic. Formally, these lines serve a clear graphic purpose to overlay a new frame of reference, within which various rectangular pieces of paper fall into line with one another. From afar, the collage displays a striking unity of form. Upon closer inspection, we discover each piece of paper to be an independent written or visual document, containing its own explicit content. The kinds of documents vary. There are documents pertaining to architectural discourse narrowly understood, such as an architectural drawing by a student from Berlin, or the program of the conference itself. There are also simple proofs of travel: hotel stubs, an airline towel, telegrams confirming the flight of Colin Rowe and Frampton. Then there are records of leisure activities: the wrapper of a cigarette pack, a nightclub program, tickets to a museum, a card from the "Small Revolutionary Library," a matchbook cover advertising Berlin's Paris Bar. Finally there is political propaganda: the manifesto of *Der Sozialistische Deutsche Studentenbund* (Socialist German Student Union), which lurks ominously behind the conference program, newspaper clippings of student protests, a postcard of the Berlin Wall at the Brandenburg Gate, the cover of *Unabhängige Aktions Gemeinschaft* (Independent Community Action). While the discrepancies and contradictions between these documents remain clearly visible, *Berlin Graphik!* brings them all together into unifying visual form. In this way, Frampton was able to accomplish the functional task of providing information about what happened during the conference, but also to yield a surplus experience from that information. The key revelation of *Berlin Graphik!* was that it represented a breakthrough from Frampton's understanding of surplus experience. Here it was cast as that which brings together all the various facts and disparate events in a meaningful unity: the experience of reality itself. Moreover, the ability to experience reality now appeared to Frampton as something deeply political: "It was an important moment for me . . . Why did I put this [collage] together? Because I had been politicized by the United States."[65] He felt that in the United States the direct experience of reality was denied to individuals, so that a recovery of the experience of reality was also a political move against the forces of America's capitalist society.

Nothing in the collage itself refers to the political situation in the United States; there are references only to Greece's military junta and the German student riots. However, the experience in Berlin made Frampton realize what had happened to him in the two years since he had moved to the United States to teach at Princeton. "The students blocked the session," he said, recalling the shock and thrill he experienced in Berlin, "and on the one side [of the auditorium] there was a slogan 'ALL BUILDINGS ARE BEAUTIFUL' and on the other side 'STOP BUILDING.' "[66] The latter slogan seemed to him to express a resistance to the unplanned capitalist development he felt was rampant in American suburbia. The first slogan appeared to him like a denial of the aestheticism of architecture based on style. He read it as a return to the constructivist placement of art at the service of society, which in that case meant the Russian revolution. By employing neoconstructivist graphics to aestheticize the events in Berlin, Frampton was also attempting to bring to consciousness an intellectual link between the student protests and the Russian revolution. This was, in other words, his attempt at art in the service of social revolution: "What I liked about this graphic art is that it was a materialist product that escaped this whole question of what is fine art, bypassed it completely."[67]

While *Berlin Grafik!* was clearly a protest against the capitalist, style-driven modern architecture of the postwar period, its constructivist style can also be read as an attempt to accommodate dissent within the language of modernism. Indeed, Frampton did not reject modernism wholesale. Rather, he sought to return it to what he thought were its true materialist origins, a moment when style and social service were indistinguishable. In Frampton, there was a great deal of idealization of constructivism. He was often willing to overlook that it was not as free of stylistic considerations, or as organically linked to the whole of Soviet society, as he might have liked. Nevertheless, *Berlin Grafik!* was a breakthrough for Frampton in the sense that it allowed him to think of the surplus experience produced through graphic design as something political.

Politics

Berlin Grafik! enabled Frampton to work out ideas about the political dimension of surplus experience visually before he elaborated them in writing. If constructivist aesthetics were the framework for his visual investigations, the writings of Hannah Arendt served as the intellectual structure that helped him organize his writing on the subject. In particular, Frampton was drawn to Arendt's *The Human Condition* (1958), which he read in 1964, roughly at the time of his first visit to the United States.[68] Beginning with "Labour, Work and Architecture" (1969), his first major scholarly essay, Frampton returned to interpret Arendt at two key moments of his life: He wrote "Industrialization and the Crisis of Architecture" (1973) for the inaugural issue of *Oppositions* as a manifesto of his theoretical position on architecture; he wrote "The Status of Man and the Status of His Objects: A Reading of *The Human Condition*" (1979) upon completion of the manuscript of his first major book, *Modern Architecture: A Critical History* (1980), as a theoretical complement to what was a straightforward architectural history textbook. Taken together, these articles theorized surplus experience as a fundamental human experience that resolved the contradictions between building and architecture. The essays also argued that surplus experience had been degraded and denied in the modern era by misguided politics: under capitalism or Communism, politics looked either after consumption or production, instead of after the wholesomeness of human experience—so that it had become impossible to reconcile building and architecture anymore.

Frampton's idea of surplus experience as the synthesis of building and architecture predated his reading of Arendt. Apart from his visual investigation of it, one can also find it in his early critical essays for *Architectural Design*.[69] For instance, he praised James Stirling for creating a surplus experience at the Leicester University Engineering Laboratory. Stirling had gone beyond the client's functional requirements, increasing the size of the entrance hall to the lecture theater, and thus had created a "social core" to the building. This oversized entrance hall, wrote Frampton, "may be seen as an heroic and liberating attempt to reconcile the essential conflict existing between two distinct cultures of the environment," [70] architecture and building.

As her book's title indicates, Arendt theorized "the human condition from the vantage point of our newest experiences and our most recent fears."[71] By definition, the human condition referred to those elemental activities that were within the range of every human being. She identified them as labor, work, and action. Significantly, she left out thinking, "the highest and perhaps purest activity of which men are capable,"[72] because not all men fully achieved it. Arendt's analysis of the human condition also explained the relationship between these three fundamental activities. Frampton's first essay on Arendt attempted to overlay her categories onto his own, equating labor with building, work with architecture, and action with surplus experience—a move that, as we shall see, allowed Frampton to begin to think of the relationship between his three categories in political and historical terms.

According to Arendt, labor referred to the bodily activity required to stay alive, an effort bound up in the natural metabolism of the living body and its

FACING PAGE: James Stirling and James Gowan, Leicester University Engineering Laboratory, Leicester, England, 1962. Photograph by Brecht-Einzig. From Douglas Stephen, Kenneth Frampton, and Michael Carapetian, British Buildings 1960-1964 *(London: A. and C. Black, 1965), 75.*

cycles of consumption and reproduction. Labor's product was biological life, and left no durable traces behind except life itself. Following Marx's definition of men as *animal laborans,* Arendt pointed out that humans were capable of "surplus labor" in excess of what they required to stay alive. Their strength was not exhausted in producing the means for their own subsistence and survival, "but is capable of producing a 'surplus,' that is, more than is necessary for its own 'reproduction' . . . Through violent oppression in a slave society or exploitation in the capitalist society of Marx's own time, it [surplus labor] can be channeled in such a way that the labor of some suffices for the life of all."[73]

Identifying surplus labor as something that could be alienated from individuals by third parties made Marx (as well as Locke, Smith, and others) consider it the root of capitalist economies. The question for Marx as for Arendt was, how could humans redeem themselves from labor in a way that was not oppressive (i.e., without enslaving others)? Arendt diverged from Marx, pointing out that his definition of freedom from labor was contradictory. On the one hand, he claimed that labor was an "eternal necessity imposed by nature,"[74] and on the other hand, he wrote that labor had to come to an end before freedom could take its place. Marx made labor and freedom from labor mutually exclusive. Arendt proposed that there was a more nuanced analysis of how humans achieved freedom from labor, while continuing to exercise the labor required to stay alive. This analysis involved distinguishing labor from work, two words that are often used interchangeably but that Arendt differentiated etymologically. Work involved the production of artificial tools and instruments to ease the labor of the life process.[75] The main difference between the products of labor and those of work was that the former were consumed in the process of making them (the labor of digestion produced energy that lasted only long enough to be used up by the body), whereas the latter endured beyond their creation. Work produced durable products by reifying labor into, say, a hammer or a frying pan, and thus offering humans an artificial world that was more stable and permanent than themselves. In so doing, work freed humans from the painful experience of labor, without abolishing the pleasurable experience of labor, and without enslaving other humans. Experience was a key term in Arendt's analysis of the relationship between labor and work. By focusing on it, she was able to provide a more nuanced description of labor and to move beyond some of the contradictions in Marx's analysis.

The comforts provided by work applied only to the body. Arendt insisted that work and its products did not comfort the mind at all. The mind found comfort in meaning, and the material products of work were meaningless of themselves. The experience of work, she wrote, was "the most fundamental experience of instrumentality," in which the ends justified the means and justified also "the violence done to nature to win the material, as the wood justifies killing the tree and the table justifies destroying the wood."[76] Within the sphere of work, everything appeared to the mind as an instrument to achieve something else. In other words—and here is the crux of Arendt's argument—work enslaved the mind to think of every entity instrumentally, even itself, as a means to an end, something not meaningful in itself. Work imprisoned the mind within a "dilemma of meaninglessness."[77] Arendt explained that many philosophers, notably Kant, had attempted to theorize the freedom of the mind from work by thinking of thinking as work, that is, instrumentally, turning the mind into an end in itself. This move, she thought, mistook the bondage of the mind to the instrumentality of work for its freedom. The idea of the subject as an end in itself "actually is either a tautology applying to all ends or a contradiction in terms. For an end, once it is attained, ceases to be an end and loses its capacity to guide and justify the choice of means, to organize and produce them."[78] To consider the subject as an end in itself was precisely to deprive it of the freedom to think for itself. If philosophy was a search for the meaning of life, then according to Arendt it was in deep trouble, because it had become unable to think itself out of the dilemma of meaninglessness.

For Arendt, freedom from work meant freedom from the experience of oneself as a means to an end. But just as freedom from labor could not be won through labor alone and needed to be achieved through work, freedom from work could not be achieved through work alone and could only be achieved through a different activity, namely action. "To act," she wrote, "means to take an initiative, to begin . . . Because they are *initium*, newcomers and beginners by virtue of birth, men take initiative, are prompted into action."[79] Because at an existential level every human subject was unique, a human action was tantamount to the creation of something completely new, a setting into motion of a process heretofore unseen. Action, therefore, was, according to Arendt, the human experience of freedom. All action was free action, entirely unpredictable by virtue of its newness, and as such a liberation from the experience of work as a means to achieve a predictable end.

As the title of Frampton's article made clear, "Labor, Work and Architecture" equated architecture with Arendt's notion of action. Under this scheme, Frampton seemed to be theorizing architecture as a human experience of freedom from necessity and toil, rather than as a physical artifact. However, in the text itself the identification of architecture with action was not so clear. Frampton muddled Arendt's terms of work and action by identifying architecture with both at different times. He did nonetheless unequivocally equate building with labor. The resulting theoretical structure he presented was: first, building as the satisfaction of only the basest biological requirements for life, then, architecture as a liberation from building achieved by attending to higher functional requirements such as visual coherence (i.e., style), and lastly, architecture again, a surplus architecture, if you will, free from both utility and style. The identification of architecture with both work and action created such a blatant contradiction in Frampton's theory that it cannot be overlooked, especially given that the core argument in *The Human Condition* was, precisely, to undo the conflation of labor, work, and action. As Arendt wrote of Marx: "Such fundamental and flagrant contradictions rarely occur in second-rate writers; in the work of the great authors they lead into the very center of their work."[80] In Frampton's case, the contradiction leads us back to his notion of surplus experience, which he remained ambiguous about, sometimes describing it as identical only to architecture, other times as the synthesis of building and architecture—a third category akin to action. Before reading Arendt, Frampton had referred to that third category as surplus experience. This notion of surplus experience is the thread that runs from his early graphic works, through his mid-career writings on Arendt, to his later work on critical regionalism. To keep this thread in focus, I will continue to refer to it as surplus experience. I say this only to foreground the fact that the clarity with which his search might appear today, historicized through my own writing, was not so evident to him. "Nobody is the author or producer of his own life story,"[81] wrote Arendt:

> Action reveals itself fully only to the historian, who indeed always knows better what it was all about than the participants. All accounts told by the actors themselves, though they may in rare cases give an entirely trustworthy statement of intentions, aims, and motives, become mere useful source material in the historian's hands and can never match his story in significance and truthfulness. What the storyteller narrates must necessarily be hidden from the actor himself, at least as long as he is in the act or caught in the consequences, because to him the meaningfulness of the act is not the story that follows. Even though stories are inevitable results of action, it is not the actor but the storyteller who perceives and "makes" the story.[82]

In "Labor, Work and Architecture," we find Frampton groping away from graphic design toward a verbal definition of surplus experience as a new synthesis of building and architecture. Contrary to Arendt's definition of action as "not tangible, since there are not tangible objects into which it could solidify,"[83] Frampton insisted that surplus experience could be solidified into material form: "In doing this, I would submit, we shall need to distinguish carefully both culturally and operationally between acts of 'architecture' and acts of 'building' and to discretely express both 'labor' and 'work' within each building irrespective of its scale."[84]

The resulting synthesis, he argued, would "make a viable *res publica.*"[85] He borrowed this term directly from Arendt, who defined the public realm as the existential condition of being among equals.[86] Although Arendt defined action as one of the necessary conditions for the existence of the public realm, she pointed out that speech was also necessary for its appearance—something Frampton overlooked. Action and speech were related but different experiences, both constitutive of the public realm in different ways. Action allowed humans to experience themselves as unique (as instantiations of newness), while speech immediately revealed humans to exist socially among others. Action and speech revealed the human condition to be one "of plurality, that is, of living as a distinct and unique being among equals."[87] Arendt sought a new model of subjectivity that could break out of the pure inwardness to which metaphysics had reduced the self—a pursuit also involving many of Heidegger's other students, like José Ortega y Gasset. Through her phenomenological analysis of the experiences of action and speech, she demonstrated that the subject could only know itself as both unique and constituted intersubjectively. To discover themselves as unique subjects, humans had to confront others through action and speech. "In acting and speaking," she wrote, "men show who they are, reveal actively their unique personal identities and thus make their appearance in the human world."[88] The word "appearance" here is key. For Arendt, the confrontation of humans through action and speech made the res publica appear as such. "The space of appearance," as she called this immaterial public realm,

comes into being wherever men are together in the manner of speech and action, and therefore predates and precedes all formal constitution of the public realm . . . Its peculiarity is that, unlike the spaces which are the work of our hands, it does not survive the actuality of the movement which brought it into being, but disappears not only with the dispersal of men—as in the case of great catastrophes when the body politic of a people is destroyed—but with the disappearance or arrest of the activities themselves.[89]

Despite Arendt's insistence that the public realm appeared as the result of an intersubjective, intangible experience of action and speech, Frampton insisted on translating it as the physical product of work: "The very act of human public appearance depends upon 'work' as the sole agency through which the relative permanence of the human world, testifying to human continuity, may be established."[90] Frampton's insistence on this point is striking, especially given that much of Arendt's book is devoted to a critique of metaphysics for falsely construing action as work. It revealed the degree to which Frampton was still beholden to the structurist notion that all human experiences could be constructed in material and visual terms.

Indeed, if we turn our attention to the illustrations, we find a revealing layer of information about Frampton's new conception of surplus experience. Here was a sudden shift in the portrayal of the synthesis of building and architecture: the image sequence added a temporal vector that projected it at once into the deep past of human history, as an essential human experience, and into the deep future, as the utopian promise of an architectural practice redeemed from the contradictions between building and architecture. The illustration sequence began with a plan of the ancient Greek city of Hippodamia (fifth c. BC), then transitioned to a view of medieval Siena, flashed back to the ancient Roman Augusta Raurica (44 BC), cut to a Zulu Kraal settlement, flashed forward to Toni Garnier's Cité Industrielle (1904) and Frank Lloyd Wright's Broadacre City (1932), turned to a few contemporary Japanese megastructures, and closed with a plan of Kyoto in the eighth century. The images flew in the face of traditional historiographical categories such as chronologies, distinctions between ancient and modern, or regional divisions into east and west. Frampton was searching for a new historiographical model. He immediately drew the conclusion that reading Arendt meant dispensing with architectural history as it was taught by architectural historians:

Architectural history, as it is traditionally taught in architectural schools, is essentially still a primer course in the masterworks of western architecture. As such it concerns itself with the "works" of architecture as opposed to those anonymous structures that have always arisen out of the never ending process of biological "labor."[91]

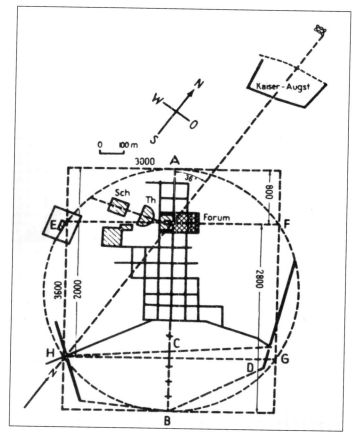

ABOVE: Zulu Kraal. From Kenneth Frampton, "Labor, Work and Architecture," in Meaning in Architecture, *ed. Charles Jencks and George Baird (New York: George Braziller, 1969), 157.*

RIGHT: Diagram of the Roman town of Augusta Raurica, 44 BC. From Kenneth Frampton, "Labor, Work and Architecture," in Meaning in Architecture, *ed. Charles Jencks and George Baird (New York: George Braziller, 1969), 157.*

Charles Moore, Piazza d'Italia, New Orleans, 1979, copyright Norman McGrath.

Architectural history "necessarily prejudices the young student architect,"[92] he wrote, making him or her focus only on architecture and ignore
building. If surplus experience was the synthesis of architecture and building,
then it necessarily required a new way of writing history that included both.
Having made a first attempt through his illustrations, Frampton made his second
attempt at a new historiography in writing with "Industrialization and the
Crisis of Architecture." The article was intended as a manifesto for the new
journal *Oppositions,* which Frampton cofounded with Eisenman and Mario
Gandelsonas in 1973. They wanted to capture a specific cultural moment of
intellectual ferment in architecture, coinciding with the world oil crisis and the
decline in architectural commissions, when architects began to rethink the aims
and purposes of their profession. The question was whether the best way forward
was to pursue new utopian models or to return to historical precedents—in
other words, whether theory or history was the key to the future. The 1970s saw
a proliferation of other small journals that also explored the tensions and
contradictions between theory and history,[93] most notably *Arquitecturas Bis* in
Barcelona, *Architese* in Zurich, and *Lotus* in Milan.[94]

This context is important because it explains both the changing nature
of architectural intellectuality and why Frampton's writings hit a nerve with
architectural audiences. The larger discussion about whether contemporary architecture should be theoretical or historical was played out in the microcosm of
Oppositions, especially in the confrontations between Eisenman and Frampton.
"The cross-purposes were beyond belief," recalled Frampton. "Anyone reading
this magazine with some attention can recognize that there wasn't really much
common ground between these people."[95] Eisenman reproached Frampton for
derailing his attempt to make a "theoretical" journal, and for making *Oppositions* "too historical":[96] "We were starting out to build a modernism in America,
and unfortunately Postmodernism, as it came to be in this country, was one
of the effects of *Oppositions.* That is, it had exactly the reverse effect . . . For some
reason it spawned the Charles Mooreses, The Michael Graveses, etc."[97]

The suggestion that Frampton's work in *Oppositions* led to postmodernism
gave the journal too much credit, and Frampton too little. Charles Moore had
reached the peak of his fame ten years before the founding of *Oppositions,* and
Frampton's historical writings were in fact a reaction to the postmodernist
emphasis on architectural style (at the expense of building). Even if Frampton's
interest in experience as a way to access the history of architecture echoed that
of Charles Moore, he loathed Moore's theatrical use of the classical style as a

mask for poorly crafted buildings. He undermined Moore's and Venturi's authority by suggesting that they had misunderstood their master Louis I. Kahn's experiential relation to historic architecture:

> For Kahn, "historicist" monumentality meant an orientation toward the *underlying structure* of traditional forms. Thus he remained committed to transforming these forms rather than reducing them to the status of being mere references which made rather obvious allusions to historical precedents, and it may well be that it is this subtle distinction which accounts for his eclipse from current discourse.[98]

The frictions between Eisenman and Frampton were also a reflection of the tensions in the larger intellectual field, as structuralism began to undermine the postwar hegemony of existentialism. While Frampton remained committed to Arendt and by extension Heidegger and the phenomenological tradition, Eisenman was interested in Noam Chomsky's *Syntactic Structures* (1957), which had revolutionized theoretical linguistics by proposing that humans had an innate ability to understand the formal structure of language.[99] Chomsky's theory of language maintained the sense of an original meaning being rooted in human experience and was therefore still palatable to phenomenologists. But the reception of structuralism also included Ferdinand de Saussure's (1857–1913) idea that language was a system external to human beings, arising instead from the power structure of society.[100] The extrication of language from human experience was anathema to Arendt's notions of action and speech, and did not attract Frampton, who continued to press the phenomenological agenda in *Oppositions* with articles such as "On Reading Heidegger" (1974).

While serving to advance architectural phenomenology, *Oppositions* also served to disseminate a new structuralist model of signification. Through his teacher Colin Rowe, Eisenman discovered and promoted Claude Lévi-Strauss (1908–2009), who had extended Saussure's model of language to all human practices in *Les structures élémentaires de la parenté* (*Elementary Structures of Kinship*, 1949). Other seminal texts of structuralism, such as Roland Barthes's "Le degré zéro de l'écriture" (1953), were more explicit attempts to break with phenomenology and existentialism. Also Michel Foucault's *Les mots et les choses: Une archéologie des sciences humaines* (1966) argued that the phenomenological notion that disciplinary knowledge could emerge from prereflexive bodily experiences was a fallacy. Foucault's *Surveiller et punir: naissance de la prison*

(1975) went further, arguing that the body itself was constructed and understood through discourse.[101] The architectural reception of structuralism's model of signification encouraged reevaluations of architectural historiography's assumptions, such as the identity of meaning and architectural style. Why, in the case of 1920s functionalism, for instance, were ship handrails assumed to mean efficiency in construction?[102] The notions of stylistic coherence or formal consistency which had so preoccupied postwar critics such as Banham came loose, as did the entire history (and meaning) of modern architecture. *Oppositions* exposed the historicism that had governed modernist historiography, exposing its assumptions about the coincidence of meaning and stylistic expression.[103]

Frampton's own turn toward history occurred as part of this larger rethinking of the methods of architectural historiography. "Industrialization and the Crises in Architecture" represented his own take on how architectural history should be written. The plural in "Crises" was somewhat misleading, because he really discussed them all as one fundamental human experience: the painful separation of building from architecture, repeated over time. According to his historiography, the first architectural crisis was experienced in 1747, when the French divided the profession of engineering from that of architecture with the foundation of the École des Ponts et Chaussées. French engineering specialized in the process of making utilitarian structures, leaving French architecture adrift to be concerned only with theories of style. Architecture, he wrote, "had henceforth to seek for its now fragmented object in the theoretical deliberations of the *Académie Royale.*"[104] Disconnected from building, architecture degenerated into utopian, speculative, unbuildable projects, such as those of Boullée. Architecture and building had been divided, but architecture remained more culturally important than building engineering. The second architectural crisis happened roughly a century later, with the building of the Crystal Palace for London's Great Exhibition of 1851. The Crystal Palace was essentially designed by Charles Fox, a railway engineer, even though the architect Joseph Paxton took most of the credit. For Frampton, this was the symbolic moment when building engineering overtook architecture in terms of cultural significance. "With the Crystal Palace," he wrote, "the question of 'how' began, at a public level, to take precedence over the issue of 'what.'"[105] The instrumental thinking of *homo faber,* to use Arendt's term, and his singular obsession with the "how" of things, had become commonplace in European culture by the mid-nineteenth century. "Equipped with a surplus of means over needs,"[106] he wrote, architects tried to dress utilitarian buildings with "instant culture," applying meaningless historicist styles to them.

By doing so, bourgeois culture reduced architecture to the worthless pretentiousness of kitsch. For him, the emergence of architectural kitsch was evidence of a desperate attempt by architects to compensate for the "disintegration of the public realm" by stylistically recreating, however deceitfully, the image of past "coherent and authentic culture."[107] The third crisis was World War I, when "industrial production and consumption acquired a new and horrific meaning, namely the mass production and the mass consumption of men."[108] This crisis completely "burst the bubble" of architectural styles within which the bourgeoisie had constructed for itself the image of a meaningful culture. Borrowing from Roland Barthes, Frampton described this moment when architecture lost all of its cultural significance as "an architecture degree zero," a time when a "cultural break" took place "in which the traditional cultural system is totally vitiated, resulting in a 'black hole' so to speak within which an unforeseen sociocultural complex begins to accrete."[109] After the third crisis, for all practical purposes, there was no viable experience of architecture left, and all that was left was building.

With these three crises as anchoring points, Frampton organized the history of building and architecture according to an Arendtian framework. Just as Arendt had argued that the experience of action had been liquidated in the modern world, Frampton described the disappearance of architecture. For Arendt, the problem was that action was being confused with work, and work with labor:

> Action was soon and still is almost exclusively understood in terms of making and fabricating, only that making, because of its worldliness and inherent indifference to life, was now regarded as but another form of laboring, a more complicated but not a more mysterious function of the life process.[110]

By analogy, Frampton interpreted that surplus experience was being confused with architecture, and architecture with building. This was the reason for "the fundamental ambiguity of the term 'architecture'"[111] as he saw it. Arriving at this interpretation was like a sudden breakthrough for him. It strengthened his conviction that he had been right all along, and that his years working to understand the relationship between architecture and building were paying off. Arendt awoke a fervor and purpose in his intellectual life to search for the architectural equivalent of action, to define that which gave rise to the public realm, something more than just architecture or just building: surplus experience.

Frampton struggled with this question for much of the 1970s, groping through various articles toward a definition of surplus experience. His search took two decisive and interrelated turns, one toward history and the other toward politics. These two turns represented a fundamental intellectual reorientation, but also, and just as importantly, a change in the direction of his professional life: he relinquished the practice of architecture to become an architect-historian[112] and began advocating for a politically engaged history of architecture. Both of these conceptions of experience, as historical and political, can be found in Arendt,[113] and Frampton interpreted them to his own ends.

His turn toward history began as an attempt to rectify the "prejudice"[114] of traditional architectural historians to write only about architecture and never about building. As such, Frampton was part of a long tradition of architects, from Giuseppe Pagano (1896–1945) to Bernard Rudofsky (1905–1988), who argued for the importance of including vernacular buildings in the history of architecture. But Frampton went deeper. It was not just a matter of expanding the canon by including vernacular buildings in standard architectural histories. The problem was more fundamental. Interpreting Arendt, he portrayed modern architectural historiography as beholden to instrumental thinking[115] and only able to speak of architecture (work) as a form of building (labor). What was once architecture—the public dimension of building—had been completely pushed out of architectural history in favor of engineering. Architecture proper was simply no longer talked about. But why? Historians, and everyone else for that matter, could not talk about what they had not experienced, and architecture had not been available as an experience since the crisis of 1851! Architecture, as something public, had fallen victim to the larger "disintegration of the public realm" that Arendt had diagnosed.[116] In other words, the disappearance of architecture from architectural history was due to the general existential condition of humans in the modern age, their alienation from the public realm into their private lives of labor. Frampton, who never lost his allegiance to Labour welfare-state politics, tied the loss of the public realm to capitalist privatization, lashing out against its architectural apologists, like Melvin Webber (1920–2006) and Venturi, for providing "slogans devised to rationalize the absence of any adequate realm of public appearance within modern suburbia."[117]

Frampton's turn toward history was an attempt to rediscover architecture on the other side of building. But this was not easy, because the experience of architecture qua architecture was no longer available in a contemporary "laboring society," which looked upon everything as building. "We still fail," he bemoaned, "to make any satisfactory distinction between architecture and building." This was "dramatic proof of the paradoxical Heideggerian thesis that language, far from being the servant of man, is all too often his master."[118] However, if his theory was true, that when building and architecture were joined they appeared in the form of surplus experience, then it could perhaps be possible to reverse-engineer surplus experience, and to *experientially* recover architecture as something different from, but latent within, building. This required a fundamental reorientation of architectural historiography, away from the rote recounting of changes in architectural styles or construction technology and toward a recovery of the surplus experience of architecture. At a practical level, it meant that historians should attend to the constructive details of buildings, especially the articulation of building units,[119] rather than the overall shape and style of the structure. In essence, Frampton proposed a historiography based on his long-standing interest in constructivist aesthetics.

But Frampton now portrayed constructivist aesthetics in more decidedly phenomenological terms, likening the historiographical retrieval of surplus experience to Arendt's philosophical attempt to rescue the human experience of action from its degradation in the modern world: "The instrumentalization of action," wrote Arendt, "never really succeeded in eliminating action, in preventing its being one of the decisive human experiences, or in destroying the realm of human affairs altogether."[120] For Arendt, the experience of action was redeemed by speech, by putting it into words that told a story. Action, in other words, required the work of the historian to be disclosed as meaningful: "He who acts never knows what he is doing . . . and meaning never discloses itself to the actor but only to the backward glance of the historian who himself does not act."[121] In the same way, to recover surplus experience, and to understand its meaning as architecture, required the work of a new type of historian, capable of sensing the surplus experience of buildings and putting it into words as history. To forge the new architectural historiography meant "to postulate first, *nature* as manifest in the processes of applied science (i.e., engineering) and then *history* as the sociopolitical determination of man—as the two irreducible determinants of building."[122]

In this passage, Frampton made reference to seeing his turn toward history as political. Again, he was interpreting Arendt, for whom action was the existential source of politics. Through the experience of action, humans discovered both themselves as unique and their reality as something they shared with equals. "Without trusting in action and speech as a mode of being together, neither the reality of one's self, of one's own identity, nor the reality of the surrounding world can be established without a doubt . . . The only character of the world by which to gauge its reality is its being common to us all."[123] Only when this shared reality was discovered through a proper experience of action could there be politics, understood as the capacity to collectively and freely respond to the problems in our shared reality. As recent scholarship has emphasized, Arendt's political philosophy was based on the primacy of the aesthetic experience of action.[124] For phenomenologists, her analysis of public-political life "reacquaints us with the thick dimensionality of political life born of the mutual active witnessing between particular others who share the world."[125] Without this shared sense of reality, politics degenerated into totalitarianism. Nazism, for instance, tried to extinguish this shared sense of reality by making the destruction of human particularity into its political ideal.

If Arendt placed a political premium on the aesthetic experience of the particularity of human action, Frampton assigned political value to the aesthetic experience of the particularity of constructivist building details. Unlike regular mass-produced construction details, constructivist details turned industrial construction into one-of-a-kind joints. This uniqueness provided the surplus experience in which structures could be rediscovered as both plural and singular, public and private, architecture and building. However, Frampton warned, the possibility of constructivist details was itself contingent on the existence of a conducive political reality:

> Whether architecture, as opposed to building, will ever be able to return to the representation of collective value is a moot point. At all events its representative role would have to be contingent on the establishment of a public realm in the political sense.[126]

One cannot overstate the importance of Arendt in Frampton's rethinking of surplus experience in terms of history and politics. As a result of his protracted engagement with *The Human Condition* during the decade of the 1970s, he embarked on the path to develop a new historiography, based on the careful examination of structural joints and details in search of an elusive surplus experience on which to hang a new history of architecture and building. Frampton developed his new historiography most conclusively during the late 1970s and 1980s, in articles such as "Constructivism: The Pursuit of an Elusive Sensibility" (1976), "Place, Production and Architecture" (1980), "Towards a Critical Regionalism" (1983), and "Rappel à l'ordre: The Case for the Tectonic" (1990).

Eschatological Historiography

"Constructivism: The Pursuit of an Elusive Sensibility" presented the architecture and graphic design of Soviet artists like Rodchenko, Vertoz, Tatlin, and others working at the Vkhutemas school as the origin and promise of a truly modern architecture.[127] Constructivism embodied Soviet society's will to organize "the given material on the principles of tectonics, structure, and construction; the form becoming defined in the process of creation by the utilitarian aim of the object."[128] The article was meant as a corrective to contemporary architectural histories of modern architecture, notably that of Banham, which had completely ignored constructivism.[129] Frampton also began to seriously research the offshoots of Soviet constructivism, such as the German Werkbund and the Dutch constructivists, and to contrast them with other avant-gardes. Initially, he could afford the time for this research, thanks to a contract from Thames and Hudson Ltd. to write what would become, almost a decade later, *Modern Architecture: A Critical History* (1980). As he unearthed and selectively curated the origins of modern architecture to fit his constructivist sensibilities, he noticed that each constructivist origin was really not an origin at all, but rather a series of self-contained events that had failed to engender and sustain a lineage. Frampton came to understand that he was facing a larger historiographical question: How did all these origins of modern architecture relate to one another historically? This question became Frampton's obsession during the 1970s. He refused to accept the received idea that modernism was just a direct byproduct of industrialization and the thought implied by Johnson and Hitchcock that once the factories were set up and running, the international style would follow.

Instead, Frampton began developing a new master narrative for modernism, which gave more importance to the role of autochthonous building cultures in receiving and shaping the modernization of building construction. This was a dramatic reorientation of architectural history, which paved the road for later non-Western and postcolonial studies of modernism. Building cultures were not only geographic, they were also social, political, and temporal. They could be as large as a country and produce constructivist aesthetics for decades (e.g., the

FACING PAGE: By carefully juxtaposing stills of Vertov's The Man with the Movie Camera *and Rodchenko's graphic design work, Frampton tried to demonstrate the continuity of the constructivist aesthetic across creative disciplines, including architecture. From Kenneth Frampton, "Constructivism: The Pursuit of an Elusive Sensibility,"* Oppositions, *no. 6 (Fall 1976): 38.*

19. *Image from* The Man with the Movie Camera. *Dziga Vertov, 1929. The split screen image implodes the Bolshoi theater on itself.*

20, 21. *Images from* The Man with the Movie Camera. *Dziga Vertov, 1929. Frames showing the film and its own 'montaged production'.*

22, 23. *Cover designs for the magazine,* Lef. *Alexander Rodchenko, 1923.*

24. *Cover design for the magazine,* Kino-fot, *No. 4, 1922. Alexander Rodchenko, 1922.*

38

19.

20.

21.

24.

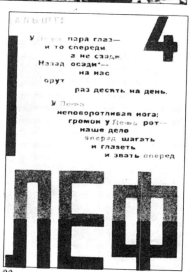

23.

22.

Soviets) or as small as a school, with a period of activity of a few years, such as the Hochschule für Gestaltung under Max Bill and Tomás Maldonado:[130]

> By appropriate extension, an architectural school can certainly be conceived of today as a cultural "region"; and it is precisely the self-cultivation of this region which will enable it to resist without falling either into reactionary hermeticism on the one hand or into the media juggernaut of universal civilization.[131]

Surplus experience could develop only under the right political conditions, in places where individuals developed fully human lives, that is, lives capable of experiencing action as a shared social reality. He looked on the Soviet constructivists as the prime example of a society where such political and existential conditions were present. "For a brief moment," he wrote about the Soviet constructivists, "the mid-18th century division between architecture and engineering loses its significance. Art now rises into the ascendant as the potential embodiment of unalienated value and the artist briefly re-emerges as the highest form of the *homo faber*."[132] For him, constructivism stood "at the threshold of a promise that remains unresolved."[133] That promise was none other than the moment when humans could properly experience the difference between building, architecture, and surplus experience.

Unlike the present tendency to always pluralize "modernisms," Frampton retained the view that all the building cultures where surplus experience was manifest were part of a single phenomenon of the resistance of surplus experience in a hostile world dominated by instrumental civilization. Wherever modern architecture was detached from "primary" building culture, it was incapable of evading "the false naturalness of bourgeois ideology,"[134] and quickly degenerated into mere building.

The real historiographical breakthrough came in 1983, when Frampton found a new name for surplus experience: critical regionalism.[135] He presented critical regionalism as a historiographical framework and "critical category"[136] for understanding the relationship between all the various isolated building cultures of surplus experience to each other. But despite Frampton's explanation, critical regionalism was received as an architectural style, rather than a method for writing and grasping history. Frampton's writing in many ways encouraged the conflation, as it catered to the disposition of architects to think that everything learned must be expressible visually.

In "Towards a Critical Regionalism: Six Points for an Architecture of Resistance," Frampton synthesized more than twenty years of work into six bullet points. The first three described the cultural, political, disciplinary, and existential conditions facing architects—an altogether bleak diagnosis. Hope was quickly recovered in the last three, more prescriptive bullet points, where Frampton laid out specific recommendations for how to design buildings that could provide surplus experiences and thus stand up against the current state of affairs. It is worth recalling those six points before we proceed to unpack them and to examine the historiographical model they constituted.

Frampton's description of the contemporary situation facing architects began with an analysis of 1) *culture and civilization* as interrelated forms of social and political belonging that only made sense in dialectical opposition to one another. But, according to Frampton, these had become unhinged from each other in the nineteenth century, then more dramatically in the 1930s with the rise of reactionary nationalisms, which liquidated culture and erased the distinction between the social and the political. In so doing, reactionary politics also liquidated the progressive promise of modernization offered by what Arendt described as the dialectics of mutual challenges between social reality and political representation. He followed with 2) *the rise and fall of the avant-garde,* an analysis of the destructive effect that the dissociation of culture from civilization, of the social from the political, had on the discipline of architecture in general, and architectural avant-gardism in particular. After the 1930s, avant-gardism, in the sense of an architectural practice politically committed to improving social reality, was no longer possible. The reason for that impossibility appeared in 3) *critical regionalism and world culture.* The avant-garde could not accomplish its mission to transform social reality because it had become impossible for architects to know social reality as such. Contemporary politics veiled local social realities under a web of technological mediations (television, newspapers, and sometimes architecture) that portrayed the impression of a "world culture." Technology was being used politically to sublimate "a desire for direct experience through the provision of information." The stage was set for the last prescriptive three points, in which Frampton argued that for architecture to recover its ability to positively transform society, politics had to be brought back in touch with the real needs of society. And the most pressing need of society was to recognize itself as something real. The first step in that political realignment was to use technology to help people have real experiences of the social. To embark on this search for experience was, for Frampton, a deeply political choice to go against the grain of contemporary "world culture." The troubling situation was that, especially in the rapidly suburbanizing and sprawling postwar American environment, most people found few places to experience social reality directly. In 4) *the resistance of the place-form,* Frampton encouraged architects to design buildings as low-rise, high-density enclaves where people could see and feel themselves living as part of a larger social group. He favored large places of public assembly, such as theaters, galleries, and oversized hotel atriums. In residential developments, he advocated shared communal spaces such as courtyards in the center of perimeter blocks. Frampton thought that properly designed communal spaces should also be grounded in the aesthetic traditions of craftsmanship of the place, to remind the actors in the social drama played out in that particular communal space of the larger material culture of which they partook. The architectural aesthetics of place was the subject of 5) *culture versus nature: topography, context, climate, light, and tectonic form.* The key term "tectonic" referred to the detailing of buildings in such a way as to elevate mere construction technology into a refined architectural aesthetic, a surplus experience expressive of the particular society's political attitude toward the region of land it shared. Since, according to Frampton, most of the Western world was bent on dividing the land, not sharing it, it followed that the tectonic could appear only in rare places, where a political commitment to social land-use programs was already in place. In those places, architects could critically interpret regionalism by giving it tectonic aesthetic expression in their buildings. Critical regionalism was an aesthetic choice for architects, but it was also a political commitment to the cause of improving society. The key differentiating factor of critical regionalist buildings was that their tectonic aesthetic provided a different sort of aesthetic experience from other buildings, one in which people could experience directly their relationship to each other as parts of a shared local society, to the place they inhabited in common, and to the technology that sheltered them and kept them alive. Frampton believed this directness of experience set architecture apart from the deceptive technological mediations of "world culture." His manifesto ended with 6) *the visual versus the tactile,* a call to architects to design buildings that presented people with authentic experiences of reality. Frampton ranked the bodily senses in terms of their empirical trustworthiness. Vision was the least trustworthy sense, as it involved a "distancing from a more direct experience of the environment." To know reality required being in close contact with it, to touch it, hear it, smell it, and taste it. He wrote:

In this way, Critical Regionalism seeks to complement our normative visual experience by readdressing the tactile range of human perceptions. In so doing, it endeavours to balance the priority accorded to the image and to counter the Western tendency to interpret the environment in exclusively perspectival terms. According to its etymology, perspective means rationalized sight or clear seeing, and as such it presupposes a conscious suppression of the senses of smell, hearing and taste, and a consequent distancing from a more direct experience of the environment. This self imposed limitation relates to that which Heidegger has called a "loss of nearness." In attempting to counter this loss, the tactile opposes itself to the scenographic and the drawing of veils over the surface of reality.[137]

Critical regionalism asked architects to cultivate relationships to particular places as a way to improve the lives of the people in those places. Cultivation required preliminary preparations: the architect had to first experience the local social reality. Frampton thought that social reality was embodied in material culture, in which he included architecture as a paradigmatic part, something that "can only be decoded in terms of *experience* itself."[138] The surplus experience of architectural material culture thus figured as the origin and foundation of aesthetic cultivation.

The importance that critical regionalism ascribed to experience was ethically rooted in an analysis of how difficult it was to achieve: the reduction of public space under the urban conditions of sprawl menaced people's ability to experience social reality and to develop human lives based on healthy socialization. To follow Frampton, most architects were also caught in this stunted existential and social situation. However, a few fortunate ones had the benefit of working in regions with municipal governments committed to maintaining a public interest in the built environment. The prospects for a humanizing critical regionalism were with these fortunate architects for whom the experience of social reality was still available. In pursuing critical regionalism, these architects made a choice that was simultaneously aesthetic and political, helping to make the experience of social reality available to a greater number of people.

Returning to the question of historiography, critical regionalism also functioned, indeed one could even say *primarily* functioned, at least so far as Frampton's own praxis was concerned, as a critical category for organizing the history of architecture. This much Frampton made clear when he included it as a chapter, revealing it to be the organizing principle of the second edition of *Modern Architecture*. As a historiographical method, critical regionalism collapsed the history of modern architecture into a single recurring event: the advent of a political building culture capable of nurturing the individual development of fully human lives—that is, lives capable of experiencing a shared social reality. The organizing historiographical principle of critical regionalism was not chronology, but rather the recurrence of a primordial experience of the self as unique and plural, and of the built environment as private and public, building, and architecture. Critical regionalism arranged architectural history in an entirely new way. Instead of following a teleology of development or a logic of purposeless change, it presented the history of modernism according to an eschatology of multiplication. That is to say, critical regionalism presented "authentic" modern architecture as the end of "the crises" and therefore of modernism. Critical regionalism theorized the writing of architectural history as the study of the multiple endings of modernism with the ultimate aim of comprehending the meaning of its history. It was an eschatology, like the Christian theological science concerned with the four last things (death, judgment, heaven, and hell).

At the suggestion of his friend Dalibor Vesely, Frampton modeled critical regionalism on one of the late twentieth century's foremost eschatological thinkers: the French phenomenologist Paul Ricoeur (1913–2005). During the postwar years of decolonization, Ricoeur wrote a series of critical essays analyzing the predicament of nations rising from "underdevelopment." In "Universal Civilization and National Cultures," he focused on the effects of modernization on traditional culture from the point of view of communication.[139] Modernization, he thought, was hypothetically a beneficial advancement, insofar as it promised to forge a universal civilization where everyone could understand each other in "authentic dialogue." But in reality, he argued, modernization failed to deliver on its promise because, paradoxically, it actually eroded people's ability to make sense of their life. Like Arendt, Ricoeur thought the trouble was really in the system of thought underpinning modernization: Cartesian rationalism. Secular reason was a universal system that could not tolerate the concept of uniqueness, of something existing totally outside of the system. Thus, reason could not adequately interpret the uniqueness of individual human life. It only assigned it a value relative to other unique lives, thus denying their singularity. This relativism, he thought, was fundamentally in conflict with the mystery of human life.

By contrast, traditional cultures explained the uniqueness of life precisely as a mystery, establishing the meaning of individual existence on the basis of myths. Ricoeur thought the fundamental problem of the postwar period was "how to become modern and to return to sources; how to revive an old, dormant civilization and take part in universal civilization."[140] Compounding the problem, according to Ricoeur, was that reason and myth, the systems of thought governing modernization and traditional culture, respectively, were totally incompatible. The key to solving the problem was to negotiate between both systems "in hope" that they would "in the end" be reconciled. This "in the end" was for him quite literally the end of history, an absolute eschatological horizon that gave new meaning to life.

Frampton saw in Ricoeur a clarification of his own thinking. "By the opposition between Civilization and Culture," stated Frampton, "I intend, after Paul Ricoeur in his essay 'universal Civilization and National Culture,' the resistance to locally grounded cultural form as opposed to the phenomenon of universal technology."[141] His lifelong ambivalence about the modernization of construction and the detachment of architects from the building site now appeared to him in monumental proportions as part of a global crisis dividing civilization and culture. Ricoeur's understanding of this struggle as one of communication and interpretation also helped Frampton to connect his ideas to the postmodernist architectural debates about whether the meaning of buildings could be interpreted according to historically determined linguistic paradigms. Influenced by Ricoeur's phenomenology, Frampton couched the whole question of architectural communication, and indeed of one's ability to read or "decode"[142] buildings historically, in terms of bodily experience.

Since his days as a young farmer, Frampton had always conceived of bodily experience as the source of an authentic life. Now well into his fifties, Frampton turned toward bodily experience as a more authentic way than traditional historiography to understand architectural history. To fully grasp the intellectual and political import of that move, we must analyze the eschatological argument on which it was based. The key is Ricoeur's phenomenological thesis that reason and myth, the two mutually exclusive ways of thinking, originated from two

OVERLEAF: The composition is weighed heavily toward the images, such that the article shows as much as describes how architectural tectonics express the ground and landscape on which the buildings sit. From Kenneth Frampton, "Mario Botta and the School of the Ticino," Oppositions, no. 14 (Fall 1978): 16-17.

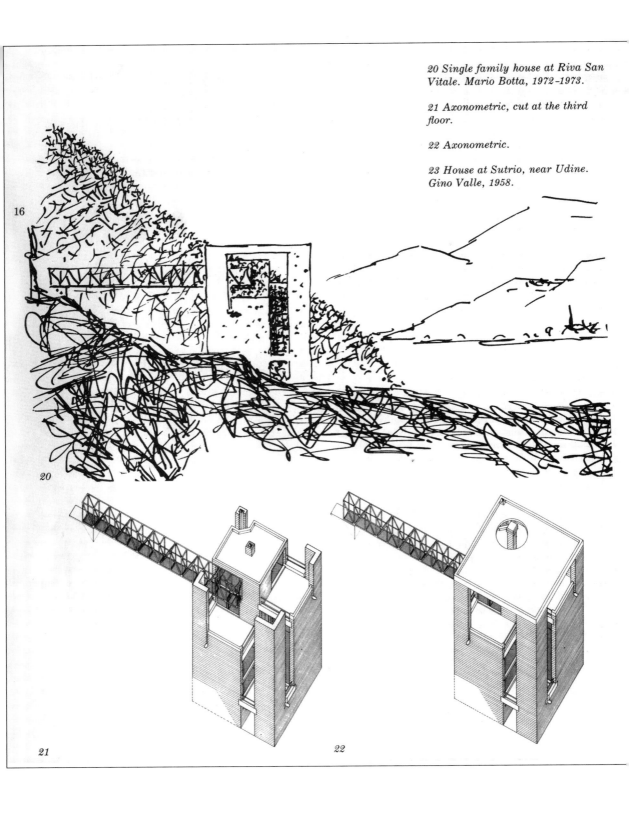

20 Single family house at Riva San Vitale. Mario Botta, 1972–1973.

21 Axonometric, cut at the third floor.

22 Axonometric.

23 House at Sutrio, near Udine. Gino Valle, 1958.

16

20

21

22

23   24

24 *House project for a painter, Tuscany. Léon Krier, 1974.*

25 *Single family house at Ligornetto. Mario Botta, 1975–1976. Axonometric.*

26 *Perspective sketch showing relationship of the form to both the landscape and the village.*

17

atria open to the air. Like Le Corbusier's use of the *piloti*, such an approach presupposes the elevation of the principal rooms to the first floor.

Unlike the neo-Corbusian houses built in the region by Snozzi, Ruchat, and Galfetti (Galfetti's Rotalini House at Bellinzona of 1961 may be considered as inaugurating the Ticino movement), Botta's houses are never contoured into the site, but instead declare themselves as clear primary forms set against the topography and the sky. Their surprising capacity to harmonize with the agrarian landscape seems to derive directly from their *analogical* form and finish, that is to say, from the concrete block from which they are invariably built and from the simple primary box-like forms which, together with the proportions adopted, allude directly to the traditional barns from which they are derived and to which they evidently refer. The intractable problem of achieving a satisfactory resolution between rationalist formal principles and an analogical commitment to the vernacular—the current problem of accessibility in modern architectural culture (particularly at the private level)—seems to be resolved in Botta's work through his strategy of according the vernacular shell precedence over the Rationalism of the interior. To this end the steel fenestration articulating the domestic space is always withdrawn from the facade into those recessed and shaded terraces by which his barn-like forms are penetrated. Apart from the imposed rationality of the flat roof, the inherently abstract quality of the traditional agrarian structure, long since celebrated by Bernard Rudofsky in his book *Architecture Without Architects*, is here capitalized upon as much as possible. The primitive architectonic nature of such structures even in their traditional form is surely the associational device through which Botta is able to pass from the vernacular referent of the exterior to the stoic and astringent order of his rationalist interiors; to the black slate, white-washed block, radiant wall panels, and to Escher-like staircases by which his modernist space is structured. It is by means such as these that Botta is able to evade the false naturalness of bourgeois ideology of which Steinmann wrote, after Roland Barthes,[3] in his seminal essay of September 1976 "Reality as History—Notes for a Discussion of Re-

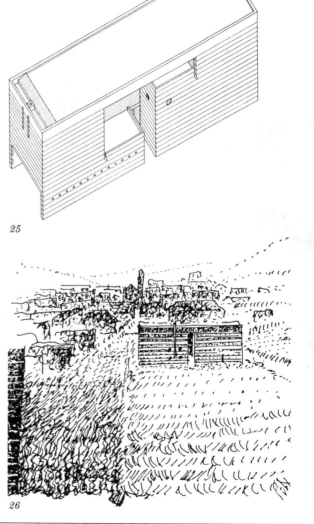

25

26

essential human experiences: the experience of the absolute and of finitude. These two experiences were antithetical. Therefore, he concluded, human existence was limited by and torn between these two experiential poles and the two modes of interpretation they made possible. The essential human condition was to be "broken" between life understood either as an absolute or as finite.

It is not obvious how Frampton was able to turn this description of existence, which purported to be ahistorical, into a theory of history. What, in other words, gave this timeless understanding of existence a historical tendency or direction? For Frampton, as for Ricoeur, it was the hope of reconciliation in the end that gave history an eschatological direction. Ricoeur was more explicit than Frampton in stating where that hope came from. Ricoeur, who was raised a Protestant like Frampton, believed that the life of Christ on earth gave that hope. Christ lived as man and God, unique and absolute. His promise that humanity would be redeemed in the end gave hope that a reconciliation between reason and myth was possible and would eventually happen. Ricoeur thought that the solution to the paradox of how to become modern while returning to mythic cultural sources was foretokened when "the wrath of God" was satisfied on the Cross.[143] Christ was the promise that the broken dual nature of man would be redeemed in a future total reconciliation of man with himself and man with man, which could only happen at the end of history.[144] In Christianity, the eschatological hope of redemption is an affirmation of faith. It escapes reasoned analysis. Its exegesis is carried out through physical rituals, such as communion, during which people experience themselves, even if only for a brief instant, as finite and absolute. The experience of religious ritual nourishes the hope in a final and definitive moment of redemption.

Critical regionalism ritualized experience, codifying a hagiography of buildings (by Mario Botta, Tadao Ando, Alvaro Siza, and others) and instructing how attention should be directed within them in order to grasp the experiential surplus of the building. In particular, Frampton argued that attention should be directed at the construction joints of buildings. Starting especially with "Rappel à l'ordre: The Case for the Tectonic" (1990), Frampton used the term tectonic, from the Greek *tekton,* signifying carpenter or builder, to refer to the appearance of surplus experience, or critical regionalism, in construction joints.[145] Tectonic form was meant to be nonstylistic. It was simply the expression of the transfer of loads from the sky onto the earth. Although perhaps a simple structural operation, this transfer was symbolically and ontologically charged for Frampton. The cosmological opposites of sky and earth, he wrote, "still constitute the experiential limits of our lives."[146] These poles appeared as symbols of the broken ontological nature of (Christian) men, torn between the eternal spiritual life of heaven and the mortal life on earth:

> Indeed, these forms may serve to remind us, after Heidegger, that inanimate objects may also evoke "being," and that through this analogy to our own corpus, the body of a building may be perceived as though it were a physique. This brings us back to . . . the joint as the primordial tectonic element, as the fundamental nexus around which building comes into being, that is to say, comes to be articulated as a presence itself.[147]

The construction joint was, for Frampton, "a point of ontological condensation rather than mere connection."[148] To witness it as such was to apprehend "the phenomenological presence of an architectural work."[149] It was to experience the synthesis of building and architecture, of the private and the public, of the haptic and the visual. In sum, the phenomenological experience of the structural joint offered hope that all irreconcilable opposites might be redeemed in the end. This experience was at the crux of the transformation of critical regionalism from an aesthetic into a historiography:

> With the tectonic in mind it is possible to posit a revised account of the history of modern architecture, for when the entire trajectory is reinterpreted through the lens of *techne* certain patterns emerge and others recede. Seen in this light a tectonic impulse may be traced across the century, uniting diverse works irrespective of their different origins.[150]

The work of connecting buildings from different periods and places under the aegis of critical regionalism denied the traditional architectural historiography of the "evolution" of styles and building techniques. As a theory of history, the eschatological thrust of critical regionalism supposed that until the end of architectural history there could really be no critical regionalism, no fundamental historical change in modern architecture. Critical regionalism was therefore presented as an *arrière-garde* position. It was a clear wish for the end of architectural history, so that architects could cross "the threshold of a promise that remains unresolved."[151] By the same token, critical regionalism presented itself as the agent of the end of architectural history, bringing the resolution of that promise within tantalizing reach in the experience of the tectonic joint.

Bourgeois Taste

Frampton placed the four decades from the end of World War II to 1985 under the aegis of critical regionalism. As a period in architectural history, it coincided with the lead-up and emergence of postmodern architecture, and with momentous transformations within architectural intellectuality. These were also the four decades marking Frampton's own personal turn from practicing architect to historian. His trajectory shows architectural intellectuality during that time to be an ambiguous realm between the aesthetic and the conceptual, architectural drawing and lecturing, graphic design and writing. He had been trained with the dispositions of the architect to think that the value of intellectual work in architecture was only its pragmatic application in practice. Critical regionalism represented that ambiguous realm and gave it coherence by placing it under the aegis of a single principle: hope. It was an affirmation of faith in the unity of the aesthetic and intellectual facets of architectural praxis. If, according to Ricoeur, hope was the existential foundation of all disciplines, because it allowed for the acceptance of contradictory truths as constitutive and promoted the search for their synthesis,[152] then critical regionalism perfectly embodied the tensions and contradictions of the discipline of architecture during the 1970s and 1980s. As intellectual work, or so-called theory, became increasingly divorced from aesthetic work, critical regionalism offered hope that the two might be reconciled in the end.

One cannot lose sight of the fact that this treasured synthesis could only come at the cost of architectural history as we know it. Within the eschatological historiographical model, critical regionalism was always already—originally and finally—evidence of the end of the old architectural history. The search for a new architectural history, beyond styles and building technology, was not taken up by other historians. Indeed critical regionalism was mostly received as a style, despite Frampton's best efforts to argue that it was not.

Critical regionalism was variously interpreted by vulgarizers as the putative center of ahistorical architectural exegeses during much of the 1980s. In the hands of second-rate thinkers, critical regionalism lost much of its subtlety. Divorced from Frampton's careful Arendtian considerations of surplus experience as both unique and plural, critical regionalists affirmed only their "local" uniqueness. In so doing, they fell into the trap that Frampton was trying to help them avoid: they were invited back from the repressed margins into the center of architectural discourse at the price of exacting from them the language of the center. Thus, under the semblance of displacing the center, marginal architects entered into a complex discursive mechanism of tokenism, to use Gayatri Spivak's term: "The putative center welcomes selective inhabitants of the margin in order better to exclude the margin. And it is the center that offers the official explanation; or, the center is defined and reproduced by the explanation that it can express."[153]

Critical regionalism became a movement, with annual congresses, memberships, and regular publications.[154] But what held these social groups together was something other than the search for a new historiography. They were drawn together by their disillusionment with the "star system" that modern architecture had become, and by their marginality in that system. They constituted a group linked by their shared aesthetic sensibility for "marginal" modern architecture. Ideologically, the rise of critical regionalism as a social movement perpetuated the tradition of bourgeois thought whereby the fragmentation of social order was compensated by a sense of communal unity at the level of the aesthetic. As the British Marxist philosopher Terry Eagleton has noted, this construction of aesthetic experience carried with it a theory of privacy and publicity, interiority and exteriority that was crucial in constructing the universal subjectivity that the ruling class required for its ideological solidarity.[155] Transformed and debased into an aesthetic preference, critical regionalism was reduced by its vulgarizers into little more than evidence for the social affinity created by bourgeois taste. This was perhaps a sad confirmation of Frampton's analysis that critical regionalism could not exist without a radical transformation of the public sphere of politics.

After Architectural Phenomenology

Architectural phenomenology radically transformed architectural historiography, expanding traditional theories of history beyond mere writing conventions to include a more ambiguous experiential intellectual realm expressed through photography, graphic design, camouflage studies, and in short, a wealth of visual techniques imported from architectural practice. Yet the intellectual history of architecture has once again become surprisingly text-centric. Contemporary textbooks and compendia on the history of architectural intellectuality invariably mention phenomenology as a major movement and include the writings of architectural phenomenologists.[1] What is transmitted in these reprints are the words, but not their visual context. A lot of information is lost through this operation, such as the original graphic layout, image quality, and size. The assumption is that architectural intellectuality is exclusively textual. Presenting the texts ripped from their historic visual context grants them the autonomy from aesthetics that is precisely in question.

The problem of decontextualization is compounded by the fact that the presentation of architectural ideas is seldom tied to the social history of the discipline. Yet, it was the social struggle to legitimize a more inclusive, and indeed ambiguous, understanding of architectural intellectuality that motivated architectural phenomenologists to engage and transform architectural history. A history of architectural intellectuality that accounts for the multiple ways intellectual work manifests itself, in light of the social struggle to recognize those alternative practices as legitimate forms of understanding, has been sorely missing from our field.

Whether we agree or not with the claims about architectural intellectuality made by architectural phenomenologists is not the issue. The question is to properly account historically that those claims were made, and to grasp the manner in which they were put forth. The history of architectural intellectuality would be distorted if we had begun our inquiry with the assumption that words are the only thing that goes into theories of architectural history. What was written is clearly important, but it is only a part of what was really going on in architectural discourse.

Architectural phenomenology involved the rise of a generation from within another, individuals, institutions, and dates: the prewar generation of Labatut; the postwar generation of Moore, Norberg-Schulz, Frampton; and the American university system during the 1960s and 1970s. But architectural phenomenology was not willed into being by these individuals and their social circles. Within architectural phenomenology, these names designate not just persons or subjects, but a way of dealing with a particular concern—just as the names of some musicians are associated with certain genres of music. These architectural phenomenologists did not consciously collaborate with one another to create architectural phenomenology. They did not write a collective manifesto. Architectural phenomenology emerged as the intersection of what mattered to these individuals and how these concerns functioned, or were functionally woven together in architectural discourse.

What mattered to architectural phenomenologists was intellectuality, bodily experience, and history. Each of these matters had a long history within architecture. But architectural phenomenologists wove them into a new coherence, making them appear inseparable. Architectural phenomenologists functionally wove these three matters together primarily through publications, courses at schools of architecture, and the social unity that comes from a shared mark of distinction, which in this case was becoming architect-historians. Architectural phenomenology functioned through platforms that, as Jean-Louis Cohen has pointed out, are the mechanisms of affirmation and constitution used traditionally by the avant-garde, namely the social sect, the school, and the press.[2] But we should be careful not to depict architectural phenomenology as an avant-garde. The word avant-garde denotes a consciously willed phenomenon, even an oedipal sense of killing one's predecessors, that we would be hard-pressed to find in architectural phenomenology. Indeed the history of architectural phenomenology calls into question the bestowal of the power to change discourse on avant-garde groups. The profound impact of architectural phenomenology on the transformation of architecture's cultural order during the 1970s reveals the blind fetishism of those who insist on reducing architectural history to self-identified groups of architects. Architectural phenomenology shows the 1970s turn toward history, which was so central to postmodernism, to be imbricated in matters of intellectuality and bodily experience. The rethinking of architectural intellectuality effected by architectural phenomenology was partly an attempt to resolve long-standing tensions and contradictions between existing architectural discourses on history and bodily experience.

Modern architects' understanding of experience was a product of crucial nineteenth-century debates in physiology, psychology, and philosophy.[3] By that time, scientists had proven that the bodily senses were unreliable and that they could therefore not claim an essential objectivity or epistemological certainty. Technology played a crucial role in raising doubts about the trustworthiness of the senses. Machines like the tachistoscope, developed in the mid-nineteenth century as a laboratory instrument that flashed images before subjects in short but precisely controlled exposure times, helped quantify how long it took for a visual stimulus to be recognized as a percept, establishing that visual perception was not instantaneous and that its accuracy varied greatly as a function of how long subjects were allowed to see the image. Experiments such as this had important intellectual repercussions, especially within the philosophical branch of epistemology. How could one know reality if the senses were unreliable? The new technological manipulation of the body presented an epistemological crisis.

Jonathan Crary has extended Foucault's and Deleuze's critiques of Husserl[4] to argue that phenomenology was part of a broader series of attempts within Western culture to cope with the technological splintering of the unity of aesthetic experience. The phenomenological emphasis on focusing attention on the manner in which experience was given in consciousness emerged precisely at the time when science and technology revealed aesthetic experience to be malleable, discontinuous, susceptible to fatigue, and prone to distraction. A person's ability to hold his or her attention on something became synonymous with his or her ability to cope with the distraction, mental disorder, and nonproductivity induced by the technological age. Husserl transposed this discourse of attention from the empirical to the transcendental. Following Crary, Husserl could tolerate modern experience only "if there was a guarantee that beneath it, over it, or embedded in it was access to the primordial oneness of consciousness."[5] Phenomenology served to mend together, once again, the intellectual and bodily experience.

As architectural phenomenologists tried to sort out the relationship between architectural experience and intellectuality, they found themselves having to confront the empirical questions that Husserl had so craftily deferred. The tools through which architects understood attention were not the same purely conceptual instruments used by Husserl. The dispositions of architects led them to think that something was learned only when it could be played out visually or in buildings. To pay intellectual attention to experience, for architects, meant to represent it properly, either through two-dimensional drawings, collages, and photographs, or through three-dimensional models and buildings. The question of representation immediately brought technology, now understood as various forms of media, back as the very thing that provided the common source of both the intellectual grasp and the visual experience of architecture. Within architectural phenomenology, technology functioned as both the enabling element and the dividing rift between the matters of intellection and experience.

This double understanding of technology had been in operation in architectural discourse since the early twentieth century. By World War I, Western architects had developed a sophisticated discourse about which construction technologies developed the architect's attention best and could serve as the antidote to those technologies that "fragmented" experience. On one end of the spectrum were staunch reactionaries, like the American Beaux-Arts architect Ralph Adam Cram, who argued that instead of the "careless" and "inattentive" modern construction methods, architects should return to the care and attention to detail of traditional craftsmanship.[6] On the other end were those "progressives" who thought that the dislocating effects of modern technology on the senses could be assuaged through visual technologies, like graphic design or "styling." Peter Behrens's work for AEG in Germany first advanced this notion in Germany, later influencing the ideology of the Bauhaus.[7] In the United States, Albert Kahn's work for Ford, and the wider discourse of "industrial democracy" developed during World War I, also fed on a similar belief in the restorative power of architectural design.[8] There were also those, like the Soviet constructivist architects, who put forth photography and cinema as the technologies that could put the world of experience back together. It was this understanding of photography as having a restorative experiential function that attracted Kenneth Frampton to constructivism.

Photography was also brought into functional relation with history and bodily experience by architectural historians, like Giedion, who taught architectural phenomenologists. He argued that to properly write the history of modern architecture the historian's vision had to become mechanical.[9] Significantly, he *illustrated* his point, cutting up his photographs as if to demonstrate the technological fragmentation of his experience, and then reconstituting the fragments into beautiful collages to show his capacity to achieve a new technological synthesis of the intellectual, experiential, and historical. We've seen the degree to which this woven photo[historio]graphy was influential for architectural phenomenologists like Norberg-Schulz, who took it to new levels of intensity in their books. Architectural phenomenology was not so much a representation of real architectural experiences. Rather, it was a discursive fabrication of a new sort of technologically mediated architectural experience.

More than a discourse about authentic architectural experience, architectural phenomenology aspired to *deliver* authentic experiences of architecture through various textual and graphic media. This aspiration was most overt in Frampton's use of photography to enhance the normal perception of buildings and create experiences in surplus of those available in reality. He ascribed a central role to photography in the almost magical operation that turned mere building into architecture. Significantly, he lamented the fact that the experience of buildings in real life was not as rich and intense as the experience of the pictures: "When much modern building is experienced in actuality, its photogenic quality is denied by the poverty and brutality of its detailing."[10] A good building demanded, held, and focused attention like a photograph.

Although architectural phenomenologists actively employed media technologies, their position toward technology was ambivalent. They recognized the centrality of visual media in architectural production and consciously worked to perfect its deployment within architectural discourse. But they opposed the careless use of photographs, fearing they would reduce architecture to mere information. Instead, in their essays and slide lectures, they employed photographs in carefully orchestrated visual essays that presented arguments about the coherence of particular architectural experiences. Each image was meant to trigger a sensual response, and the whole choreographed to give the feeling of total immersion in the architecture: a beam of light raking a wall to cue vision, a close-up of a rough texture as tactile signal, cascading water to prompt hearing, snow to evoke temperature, and so on. Images were staged as new kinds of focused architectural experiences meant to stimulate the senses and captivate attention.

By staging these representations of architectural experience within the existing format and conventions of architectural history publications, architectural phenomenologists were able to exploit the natural tendency of readers to draw inferences from the apparent relationship of elements on a page. The visual and the textual were drawn into each other in such a way that it became impossible to grasp their meaning in isolation. To decode the historical narrative presented required a kind of creative reading that called upon the reader's familiarity with the conventions of visual literacy in architectural design culture and played by its rules. The need for creative reading involved the readers so as to make them feel they had a unique experiential access to the historical message presented about architecture. Deploying the traditional protocols for designing architecture into the new context of reading and interpreting architectural history challenged the protocols of traditional art historiography. Architectural phenomenology marked positively what had been traditionally stigmatized: an incoherent historiography. Architect-historians broke free from the tradition of art history the way architects break free from their critics: by creating intrinsically polysemous works beyond all discourse and declaring the inadequacy of all discourse. In this way, architectural phenomenology also introduced an element of anti-intellectualism into the very process of intellectualization that it partook in.

The form of anti-intellectualism that was absorbed into architectural phenomenology became, in the context of the postmodern turn toward history, also a negation of architectural history. Their call to "return to the sources" of architecture, allowed them to turn against the art history establishment the weapons it used to justify its hegemony over architects, in particular asceticism, rigor, and disinterestedness. As a result, architectural phenomenologists participated in the transformation of architectural education, institutionalizing new standards of intellectual rigor, and it is not by coincidence that Labatut, Moore, Norberg-Schulz, and Frampton were each involved in the creation of new curricula for masters' and PhD programs in architecture. By the late 1980s, architect-historians had become ubiquitous in architecture schools. By then, architectural phenomenology had done its work: giving academic legitimacy to architectural intellectuality.

During the decades of its ascendancy, architectural phenomenology played an important role in maintaining the validity of certain modernist intellectual frameworks within postmodernist discourse. For instance, while postmodernism raised the antimodern specter of a historical consciousness, architectural phenomenology offered the modern notion of essential experience as the means to defeat it. Architectural phenomenology helped reconcile the postmodernist fascination with history and the modernist repulsion from it.

Architectural phenomenology also prepared the ground for postmodern architectural theory to claim its autonomy from practice, something that the postwar generation of architectural phenomenologists resisted. In 1988, the *Pratt Journal of Architecture* produced a special issue pitting the "old" architectural phenomenologists against the new. The journal was literally split down the middle, with the articles by the old guard in the front and those by the heretical young architect-historians in the back, including Stephen Perella (who edited the journal), Hilde Heynen, John Knesl, and Mark Wigley. In his editorial, Perella argued for a "non-foundational," progressive and "phenomenological" revision of the 1970s "foundational/conservative" appropriation of phenomenology in architecture. "A body of architectural thought," he announced ominously, "has been affected by a widespread Heideggerian influence." [11] He openly avowed his intention to displace the "conservative" architectural phenomenology of Christian Norberg-Schulz, Kenneth Frampton, and Alberto Pérez-Gómez, who he claimed were to blame for this Heideggerian malaise in architectural pedagogy. He accused them of misreading Heidegger as a way to cast personal authenticity as the essential origin of discourse. He thought "conservative" architectural phenomenologists reified the manifold nature of context into a fixed concept, which they then employed in the service of arguments for harmoniousness, semiautarchic resistance, or poetic dwelling.

The "old" architectural phenomenologists fell right into the trap. They replayed their worst clichés, pitching phenomenology as the only way to recuperate the "fullness" of experience and save humanity from the crisis of modernity. Mark Schneider, a professor at the University of Houston's School of Architecture, argued that people experienced reality in a "fragmented" way, so "mental," "false," and "abstract" that it kept them from finding themselves.[12] He argued that it was the task of architectural phenomenologists to employ their "superior" vision to produce wholesome experiences. The supposedly fragmented, distracted, technologically mediated, and schizophrenic experience of modern subjects *required* the phenomenological search for stable limits. Architectural phenomenologists engaged in paranoid searches for the "purifying fullness of reality." John Lobell, a professor of architecture at Pratt Institute, lambasted "monumental architecture" for blocking "the flow of consciousness" and breaking an experiential "umbilical union" between world and people. He urged architects to regain their place in the centering womb of reality, to "penetrate into phenomena, into the dialogue [of experience] itself."[13] Dalibor Vesely was also included in the journal representing the old guard. Vesely argued that phenomenology was the way for architects to achieve authentic experiences of reality, to leave behind the "highly sublimated, intellectual, and abstract world" of science, and win back "the tendency to see things the way that people used to see them, as designers or painters."[14] He claimed that phenomenology's *response* to modern experience was to provide a restorative "cleansing" of experience: "One can think of it as an inevitable dimension or hygiene of the modern mind. It is a catharsis one must go through in order to restore one's own experience."[15]

Significantly, the new contenders undertook to displace the "old" architectural phenomenologists by claiming that they had a better grasp on phenomenology. For Perella, the question was whether or not Heidegger's "later" thinking could inform the "earlier" in such a way as to prevent the reification of authentic experience. Heynen argued that Frampton and Norberg-Schulz had produced "uncritical" readings of phenomenology. In contrast to this, Heynen argued that a second, more "critical" understanding of Heidegger had been carried out by her generation of scholars, including Wigley and Francesco dal Co (b. 1945), who had stressed Heidegger's description of the impossibility of dwelling in the modern era, and compared them to similar diagnoses by Theodor Adorno. Heynen therefore questioned the value of Heidegger to architects concerned with "rooted" dwelling and associated phenomenology with Nazi ideology.[16] These attacks on "conservative" architectural phenomenologists replayed within architecture some of the accusations put forth against Heidegger within philosophy in the aftermath of the 1983 "Heidegger Affair." Perella, Knesl, Heynen, dal Co, Wigley, and others appropriated and transformed the discursive techniques and social positions of power made available by architectural phenomenology. They claimed the positions of old architectural phenomenologists by exposing the inconsistencies and "disquieting aspects" within their discourse.[17]

John Knesl, professor of architectural design and theory at Rensselaer Polytechnic Institute, denounced the "spiritualization" of architecture by architectural phenomenologists as an attempt to resurrect the classical ideal of unity. There was no truth, he argued, in the promises that postmodern architecture could embody meanings that would "ground" human spirituality and result in individual fulfillment. These arguments were for him founded on a specious notion of identity as closure, a correlate of which was the equally erroneous idea that meanings were ideal entities. Following Foucault, Knesl argued that meanings were artifacts of power relations "and the corresponding signifying systems, to organize the practices by which it [power] must work to maintain itself."[18] For Knesl, the possibility of resisting power was contingent on one's capacity to critique both identity and its systems of signification precisely as institutionalizations of power. If one ignored this fact, if one operated under the delusion that identity was an ahistorical constant, then one was operating in complicity with the power establishment. Knesl accused architectural phenomenologists of this very thing. He believed that by spiritualizing architecture they were trying "to restore to the powers and conditions of today, the legitimation provided by the great classical metaphysical referents: man, nature, and history."[19] Surprisingly, as if remorseful of his oedipal drive, Knesel tried to reconcile Foucault with architectural phenomenology, overlooking that Foucault understood his genealogical epistemology to be opposed to the phenomenological understanding of the immediacy of knowledge.

Wigley suggested that the superficiality with which previous architect-historians had engaged phenomenology was an index of their subservience to cultural conventions about hierarchy, structure, solidity, and the primacy of practice. He displaced (and deferred) the notion that any "foundational" meaning of the architectural object could be attained outside of discourse, thus demoting practice. Once this younger group displaced the earlier "conservatives," they began instituting a "nonfoundational" approach to phenomenology, which prepared the ground for the introduction of poststructuralist theory. More significantly, the emphasis on a nonfoundational architectural theory was code for the autonomy of theory from its traditional "foundation" in practice. The architect-historian began to turn into the figure of the autonomous architectural theorist.

It is important to emphasize that not all architectural theorists of the generation born in the late 1940s and 50s were opposed to the work of older architectural phenomenologists. The mantle of resistance to the poststructuralist revision of architectural phenomenology was taken up by figures like Alberto Pérez-Gómez (b. 1949), head of PhD studies at McGill University in Montreal. Pérez-Gómez became the most influential thinker of a younger generation of architectural phenomenologists, including David Leatherbarrow and Helen Powell, who sought to extend the work of their predecessors.[20] Pérez-Gómez studied architecture in Mexico, where he was exposed to the writings of Ortega y Gasset, and completed his studies at Essex under Rykwert and Vesely. Many of the themes that defined the early phases of architectural phenomenology also shaped his 1979 dissertation, later published under the title *Architecture and the Crisis of Modern Science* (1983), in an obvious reference to Husserl.[21] Like Frampton, Pérez-Gómez portrayed architectural phenomenology as the way to surmount the contradictions of modernity. For Pérez-Gómez, modern architecture had its roots in neoclassicism, which in turn was the culmination of a long Cartesian tradition to make architecture into a science by imposing abstract mathematical theoretical models upon practice. For him, Jacques-Nicolas-Louis Durand's (1760–1834) attempt to reduce architectural design to the "science" of combining interchangeable modular parts according to functional requirements signified the negation of the poetic artistic content of architecture, which could be restored only through a phenomenological return to authentic experiences of buildings.[22] Pérez-Gómez's search for an undistorted experience of architecture in history was the subject of much criticism from members of his own generation, mostly inspired by Tafuri, for distorting historiography in an "operative" way.[23]

As architectural phenomenology came under the closer scrutiny of the new poststructuralist architectural theorists, the old architectural phenomenologists retreated into sectarian social circles. Associations such as EDRA (Environmental Design Research Association) appeared as umbrella societies for architects interested in phenomenology to network.[24] By the early 1990s, new publications began to appear that kept the flame of architectural phenomenology alive. For instance, philosopher and geographer David Seamon founded the *Environmental and Architectural Phenomenology Newsletter* (1990) and established the *SUNY Series in Environmental and Architectural Phenomenology*.[25]

Significantly, as architectural phenomenology appeared to lose its footing in architecture, philosophers came to the rescue. Harries encouraged architectural phenomenologists with infinitely quotable pronouncements like: "Architecture is at least as likely to edify as philosophy."[26] The "ethical function" of architecture, he argued—replaying the old clichés—was to get society beyond modernity's "arbitrariness" by making people *feel* the "wholeness" of the "original" language of the senses and the imagination.[27] For Harries, architecture was the best way to teach the process of spiritual self-discovery on which he premised the "discovery of meaning."[28] Michael Zimmerman, a phenomenologist who became interested in architecture while teaching at Tulane University in the 1970s, identified "egoism" with a dismembered experience of reality. In his article "The Role of Spiritual Discipline in Learning to Dwell on Earth" (1985), Zimmerman argued for an "ego-less attunement to Logos."[29] Contradicting his own theory, Zimmerman argued elsewhere that only those architects capable of imposing their egoistic visions on the world had been capable of creating places where people could still experience the spiritual and emotional dimensions of existence.[30]

Other phenomenologists shifted allegiances, withdrawing their support for the old architectural phenomenologists. Don Ihde, dean of the School of Humanities and Fine Arts and professor of philosophy at SUNY Stony Brook, wrote about a "new" architectural phenomenology that was more intellectually postmodern.[31] Also shifting allegiances, philosopher Edward Casey, another professor at SUNY Stony Brook, critiqued Norberg-Schulz's notion of place as a steadfast essence. Rather, Casey argued that place emerged out of, or became "implaced," as part of an unfolding, dynamic process of "embodiment,"[32] a phenomenon he identified with the architecture of Peter Eisenman and Bernard Tschumi (b. 1944). Casey claimed this "non-foundational" understanding of place was present in Bachelard's writings on the "poetic imagination."[33] Casey drew a line from Bachelard to Jacques Derrida's late 1980s collaborations with architects Eisenman and Tschumi. He ignored the long history of intersections between phenomenology and architecture in order to identify his own philosophical project with those architects deemed avant-gardists in the late 1990s. Casey's selective and instrumental account of the intersections between architecture and phenomenology obscured more than it revealed. His suggestion that the emergence of place in Tschumi's architecture is best understood as a type of Bachelardian embodiment of "intimate immensity" [34] would have been more convincing in relation to the work of Charles Moore. After all, Moore played a bigger role in disseminating Bachelard in architectural circles. Casey's rewriting of the history of architectural phenomenology is evidence of how social struggles distort knowledge. His genealogy of architects was an attempt to validate his own position in relation to the changing social structure of architecture, of who was "in" and who was "out."

Although its centrality in architectural theory has been much diminished, architectural phenomenology continues to be the primary discursive mode for dealing with questions of perception and affect. With its promise to recover the fullness of a lost experience of reality, architectural phenomenology became the catch basin for all disillusionment with modernity. In the early phases of postmodern thought, architect-historians exploited that disillusionment to establish their authority. They cast themselves as the ideal observers of architecture by claiming that immediate experience was not immediate at all, but rather that reality was always hidden behind veils of self-deceptions and distorting technological manipulations. They claimed that the immediate experience of buildings required a level of aesthetic competency only they had achieved, but that everyone could learn.

Architectural phenomenology produced new architectural standards of intellectual, aesthetic, and historiographical competency. Through its objective and discursive mechanisms, it organized the attention of architects toward what mattered (aesthetic experience, history, and theory) and structured the functional relationships between these matters. It posited a transhistorical, preverbal experiential language as the synthesis of these matters and as the source of all architectural expression. This interest in preverbal language was instrumental in opening architects to the emergent discipline of structural linguistics and to semiotics. While the idea that this preverbal experiential language of architecture could be expressed in many styles opened modern architects to historic architecture and spawned postmodernism, the phenomenological ideal of aesthetic purity dovetailed into the modernist discourse of abstraction and survived the demise of the postmodern style.

Today, architectural phenomenology undergirds the sensualist neomodernist fantasy of an essential experiential origin to architecture. Paradoxically, the theoretical project that began as a search for a historically conscious modern architecture achieved its opposite. These lessons are paramount to theory today, when the postcritical pursuit of architectural expression outside of history and culture is again on the rise. If a critical historiography can be provisionally sketched out, along Bourdieu's definition, as an attempt to "explore the limits of the theoretical box in which one is imprisoned . . . to provide the means for knowing what one is doing and for freeing oneself from the naïveté associated with the lack of consciousness of one's bounds,"[35] then to acknowledge the history of architectural phenomenology is also to recognize that we are not entirely free from its grasp.

Notes

Introduction

1. Murray Fraser, "All Phenomenology and No Substance," *The Architect's Journal* 382, no. 17 (March 23, 1995): 42–43.

2. Ole Bouman and Roemer van Toorn, "I Am Trying to Save the Phenomenology of Architecture: Interview with Oswald Mathias Ungers," *Archis* 2 (February 1993): 58–65.

3. See especially Anthony Vidler, *The Architectural Uncanny* (Cambridge, Mass.: MIT Press, 1992). The book collected a series of lectures first presented at the Architectural Association in London in 1989.

4. Herbert Spiegelberg, *The Phenomenological Movement: A Historical Introduction* (The Hague: Nijhoff, 1982), 473.

5. Ann Fulton, *Apostles of Sartre: Existentialism in America, 1945–1963* (Evanston, Ill.: Northwestern University Press, 1999), 135.

6. John McCumber, *Time in the Ditch: American Philosophy and the McCarthy Era* (Evanston, Ill.: Northwestern University Press, 2001).

7. Dermot Moran, *Introduction to Phenomenology* (London: Routledge, 2000), 204.

8. For an account of the theological turn in phenomenology see Dominique Janicaud, *Le tournant théologique de la phénoménologie française* (Combas: Éditions de L'Éclat, 1991).

9. David Farrell Krell, "A Malady of Chains: Husserl and Derrida on the Origins of Geometry and a Note to the 'Archeticts' of the Future," *Architectural Design* 67, no. 5–6 (May–June 1997): 12–15.

10. Mark Wigley, *The Architecture of Deconstruction: Derrida's Haunt* (Cambridge, Mass.: MIT Press, 1993).

11. Mark Wigley, "Heidegger's House: The Violence of the Domestic," *Columbia Documents of Architecture and Theory D* 1 (1992): 91–121.

12. See Mark Jarzombek, *The Psychologizing of Modernity: Art, Architecture, History* (Cambridge: Cambridge University Press, 2000). Significant inroads into the history of the reception of phenomenology in architectural discourse have also been made in Hilde Heynen's "Worthy of Question: Heidegger's Role in Architectural Theory" (1993), later reworked into her book *Architecture and Modernity* (Cambridge, Mass.: MIT Press, 1999). Heynen critiqued Norberg-Schulz and Frampton for what she saw as their one-sided reading of the concept of dwelling as being-at-home and their disregard of Heidegger's notion of "homelessness." Also important is K. Michael Hays's "The Structure of Architectural Phenomenology" in *Newsline: Graduate School of Architecture Planning and Preservation, Columbia University* 3, no. 4 (December 1990–January 1991): 5, which compared how Kenneth Frampton, Daniel Libeskind, Peter Eisenman, and Michael Graves understood the relationship between subject and object phenomenologically.

13. See Michael Benedikt, *For an Architecture of Reality* (New York: Lumen Books, 1987), and Benedikt, *Deconstructing the Kimbell: An Essay on Meaning and Architecture* (New York: SITES/Lumen Books, 1991).

14. Zeynep Çelik, "Kinaesthetic Impulses: Aesthetic Experience, Bodily Knowledge, and Pedagogical Practices in Germany, 1871–1918" (PhD diss., Massachusetts Institute of Technology, 2007).

15. Harry Francis Mallgrave and Eleftherios Ikonomou, "Introduction," in *Empathy, Form, and Space: Problems in German Aesthetics 1873–1893,* ed. Julia Bloomfield, Kurt W. Forster, and Thomas F. Reese, trans. Harry Francis Mallgrave and Eleftherios Ikonomou (Santa Monica, Calif.: Getty Center for the History of Art and the Humanities and Chicago: University of Chicago Press, 1993), 1–85.

16. Giulio Carlo Argan, *Walter Gropius e la Bauhaus* (Torino: G. Einaudi, 1951), 11. My translation.

17. Reyner Banham, "Neo-Liberty: The Italian Retreat from Modern Architecture," *Architectural Review* 746 (March 1959): 231.

18. Ernesto Nathan Rogers, "Tradizione e attualità nel disegno," *Zodiac* 1 (1957): 272, trans. by Jorge Otero-Pailos. See also the general discussion of tradition, 95–102, 247–51, 269–74.

19. Ernesto Nathan Rogers, "L'evoluzione dell'architettura: Risposta al custode di frigidaires," *Casabella Continuità* 228 (June 1959): 2–4.

20. Ernesto Nathan Rogers, "The Phenomenology of European Architecture," in *A New Europe,* ed. Stephen R. Graubard (Boston: Houghton Mifflin, 1964), 438–42.

21. On the reasons why Italian architects turned from phenomenology to critical theory, see Vittorio Gregotti and Jorge Otero-Pailos, "Interview with Vittorio Gregotti: The Role of Phenomenology in the Formation of the Italian Neo-Avant-Garde," *Thresholds* 21 (Fall 2000): 40–46. For a good overview of the Italian debates on the relationship of modernism to history, see Luca Molinari, "Between Continuity and Crisis: History and Project in Italian Architectural Culture of the Postwar Period," *2G* 3, no. 15 (2000): 4–11.

22. Jorge Otero-Pailos, "Ernesto Rogers and Enzo Paci: Tradition as Lifeworld," in "Theorizing the Anti-Avant-Garde: Invocations of Phenomenology in Architectural Discourse, 1945–1989" (PhD diss., Massachusetts Institute of Technology, 2001).

23. Jacques Maritain to Labatut, March 13, 1961, Box 7, Jean Labatut Papers, Princeton University Department of Rare Books and Special Collections, trans. by Jorge Otero-Pailos.

24. Jean Labatut, "History of Architectural Education through People," *JAE: Journal of Architectural Education* 33, no. 2 (November 1979): 21–24.

25. Sigfried Giedion, "The New Monumentality," in *New Architecture and City Planning,* ed. P. Zucker (New York: Philosophical Library, 1944), 547–68.

26. Pope Pius XII, *Mediator Dei,* November 20, 1947, in *Papal Archives of the Holy See,* http://www.vatican.va/holy_father/pius_xii/encyclicals/documents/hf_p-xii_enc_20111947_mediator-dei_en.html.

27. Wild was instrumental in the founding of The Society for Phenomenology and Existential Philosophy (SPEP) in 1962, and many faculty members of the philosophy department were members. The SPEP held its annual meeting at Yale in 1968. See James M. Edie, "Introduction," in *New Essays in Phenomenology,* ed. James M. Edie (Chicago: Quadrangle Books, 1969), 7.

28. John Daniel Wild, *The Challenge of Existentialism* (Bloomington: Indiana University Press, 1955), 166.

29. Ibid., 5–6.

30. Jarzombek, *The Psychologizing of Modernity: Art, Architecture, History.*

31. Rudolf Arnheim, rebuttal to Monroe C. Beardsley, "On Arnheim's 'Visual Thinking,'" *Journal of Aesthetic Education* 5, no. 3 (July 1971): 186. Arnheim's clearest elaboration of his theory, written after Norberg-Schulz's own clarification, is found in *Visual Thinking* (Berkeley: University of California Press, 1969).

32. Martin Heidegger, "The Age of the World Picture," in *The Question Concerning Technology and Other Essays,* trans. William Lovitt (New York: Harper and Row, 1977) 115–54.

1. A Polygraph of Architectural Phenomenology

1. Hippolyte Taine's principles of art and architecture history are most clearly spelled out in *The Philosophy of Art* (London: H. Baillière, 1865). For a critical assessment of Taine's contribution to art history, see Thomas H. Goetz, *Taine and the Fine Arts* (Madrid: Playor, 1973), and Jean Thomas Nordmann, *Taine et la critique scientifique* (Paris: Presses universitaires de France, 1992).

2. "La realidad no es dato, algo dado, regalado-sino que es construcción que el hombre hace con el material dado." José Ortega y Gasset, *En torno a Galileo,* ed. José Luis Abellán (Madrid: Editorial Espasa Calpe, 1996), 50.

3. Ortega y Gasset, "La idea de la generación," *En torno a Galileo,* 71–94.

4. For an excellent exegesis of Ortega y Gasset's notion of interindividuality, see Julián Marías, *El método histórico de las generaciones,* in *Obras completas,* Vol. 6 (Madrid: Revista de Occidente, 1961), 64–67.

5. "En el 'hoy,' en todo 'hoy' coexisten, pues, articuladas varias generaciones y las relaciones que entre ellas se establecen, según la diversa condición de sus edades, representan el sistema dinámico, de atracciones y repulsiones, de coincidencia y polémica, que constituye en todo instante la realidad de la vida histórica. Y la idea de las generaciones, convertida en método de investigación histórica, no consiste en más que proyectar esa estructura sobre el pasado." Ortega y Gasset, *En torno a Galileo,* 88.

6. Precedents for the development of a polygraphic historiography can be found in Mark Jarzombek's notion of "critical historiography," as presented in *The Psychologizing of Modernity: Art, Architecture, History* (Cambridge: Cambridge University Press, 2000). See also Beatriz Colomina, *Domesticity at War* (Cambridge, Mass.: MIT Press, 2007). Carlos de San Antonio Gomez has also advanced a promising analysis in terms of generations in *El Madrid del 27: Arquitectura y vanguardia: 1918–1936* (Madrid: Comunidad de Madrid, Consejeria de Educación, Secretaría General Técnica, 1998).

7. For Pierre Bourdieu's critique of Foucault and the Frankfurt School, see his "Principles for a Sociology of Cultural Works," in *The Field of Cultural Production: Essays on Art and Literature,* ed. Randal Johnson (New York: Columbia University Press, 1993), 178–81.

8. Illuminating descriptions of the theory of the field are collected in Bourdieu, *The Field of Cultural Production.*

9. For a good explanation of the concept of *habitus* with reference to architecture, see Hélène Lipstadt, "Theorizing the Competition: The Sociology of Pierre Bourdieu as a Challenge to Architectural History," in *Thresholds* 21 (2000): 32–36.

10. The process by which modern architects came to wrest the position of architectural historians from unwilling art historians has been examined, from a sociological perspective, by Hélène Lipstadt in "Celebrating the Centenaries of Sir John Summerson and Henry-Russell Hitchcock: Finding a Historiography for the Architect-Historian," in *The Journal of Architecture* 10, no. 1 (2005): 43–61. Lipstadt maintains that architect-historians claimed to be both insiders and outsiders vis-à-vis the disciplines of architecture and history. Thus, they established for themselves a powerful position of elite cultural producers, unattainable by either architects or historians.

11. Herbert Spiegelberg, *The Phenomenological Movement: A Historical Introduction* (The Hague: Nijhoff, 1982), 18.

12. Dermot Moran, *Introduction to Phenomenology* (London: Routledge, 2000).

13. Edmund Husserl, *Formal and Transcendental Logic,* trans. D. Cairns (The Hague: Nijhoff, 1969), 234.

14. Edmund Husserl, *Logical Investigations,* trans. J.N. Findlay (London: Routledge and K. Paul; New York: Humanities Press, 1970), 252.

15. See the English translation of *Philosophie als strenge Wissenschaft* in Edmund Husserl, *Phenomenology and the Crisis of Philosophy: Philosophy as Rigorous Science, and Philosophy and the Crisis of European Man,* trans. Quentin Lauer (New York: Harper and Row, 1965), 71–147.

16. Edmund Husserl, *Ideas Pertaining to a Pure Phenomenology and to a Phenomenological Philosophy,* Vol. II, trans. F. Kersten (The Hague: Nijhoff, 1982), 16.

17. See Edmund Husserl, *Cartesian Meditations,* trans. Dorion Cairns (The Hague: Nijhoff, 1977), originally published in 1931.

18. Moran, *Introduction to Phenomenology,* 10.

19. Christian Norberg-Schulz, *Intentions in Architecture* (Cambridge, Mass.: MIT Press, 1965), 62–63.

20. For Maritain's views on intuition as they were presented to architects and artists, see Jacques Maritain, *Creative Intuition in Art and Poetry* (Princeton: Princeton University Press, 1977).

21. Spiegelberg, *The Phenomenological Movement,* 395.

22. Heidegger's relationship to Husserl's phenomenology is well explicated in Thomas Sheehan, "Husserl and Heidegger: The Making and Unmaking of Their Relationship," in *Psychological and Transcendental Phenomenology and the Confrontation with Heidegger (1927–1931),* trans. Thomas Sheehan and Richard E. Palmer (Boston: Kluwer Academic Publishers, 1997), 1–32. See also Spiegelberg, *The Phenomenological Movement,* 336–71.

23. Heidegger first expressed these views in his 1919 lectures in Freiburg on "The Idea of Philosophy and the Problem of World View." See Moran's analysis of these lectures in *Introduction to Phenomenology.* 204–5.

24. Heidegger critiqued Husserl's philosophy as idealist at various junctures in *Being and Time,* including: "If what the term 'idealism' says, amounts to the understanding that Being can never be explained by entities but is already that which is 'transcendental' for every entity, then idealism affords the only correct possibility for a philosophical problematic. If so, Aristotle was no less an idealist than Kant. But if 'idealism' signifies tracing back every entity to a subject or consciousness whose sole distinguishing features are that it remains indefinite in its Being and is best characterized negatively as 'un-Thing-like,' then this idealism is no less naïve in its method than the most grossly militant realism." Martin Heidegger, *Being and Time,* trans. John Macquarrie and Edward Robinson (New York: Harper Collins, 1962), 251–52.

25. Ibid., 2.

26. See, for instance, Michael E. Zimmerman, *Heidegger's Confrontation with Modernity: Technology, Politics, Art* (Bloomington: Indiana University Press, 1990). Zimmerman studied the relation of Heidegger's thinking on technology to the reactionary politics of his time and to the German intellectual tradition from Hegel to Marx. Zimmerman contended that to properly evaluate Heidegger's thought one must decenter its totalizing tendencies by examining its own indebtedness to realities and histories outside of itself.

27. In their translation of *Being and Time,* Macquarrie and Robinson chose the word "historicality" to denote Heidegger's particular use of the German word *Geschichte,* usually meaning simply history, in the literal sense of the German word *Geschehen* (to occur, or to happen). "Historicality" signifies the actual happening of events, or history in the making.

28. Hannah Arendt, "The Concept of History," in *Between Past and Future: Eight Exercises in Political Thought* (New York: Penguin Books, 1977), 41–90.

29. See especially Part II of Hans-Georg Gadamer, *Truth and Method* (New York: Seabury Press, 1975).

30. Kenneth Frampton, "Place, Production and Architecture: Towards a Critical Theory of Building," *Architectural Design* 52, no. 7–8 (1982): 44.

31. Christian Norberg-Schulz, *Existence, Space and Architecture* (New York : Praeger, 1971), 18.

32. The journal *Places,* edited by Donlyn Lyndon and William Porter, captured the spirit of the times with its title and did much to advance postmodern positions deeply influenced by architectural phenomenology. See, for instance, Donlyn Lyndon and William L. Porter, "Place Debate: Piazza d'Italia, Editor's Introduction," *Places: A Quarterly Journal of Environmental Design* 1, no. 2 (Winter 1984): 7.

33. Martin Heidegger, "The Origin of the Work of Art," in *Poetry, Language, Thought,* trans. Albert Hofstadter (New York: Harper and Row, 1971), 17–81.

34. For Heidegger's meditation on *das Gestell,* the technological framework through which he believed modern society looked upon the whole of reality, see "The Age of the World Picture," in *The Question Concerning Technology and Other Essays,* trans. William Lovitt (New York: Harper and Row, 1977).

35. Christian Norberg-Schulz, "Architecture and Poetry," *The Dallas Institute of Humanities & Culture Newsletter* 1, no. 3 (August–September 1982): 17–19.

36. Maurice Merleau-Ponty, *L'Oeil et l'esprit* (Paris: Éditions Gallimard, 1964).

37. See, for instance, Steven Holl, "Archetypal Experiences in Architecture," *Architecture and Urbanism,* special issue on Holl (July 1994), 121–36; and Steven Holl, "Pre-Theoretical Ground," *Columbia Documents of Architecture and Theory D* 4 (1995), 91–121.

38. Hans-Georg Gadamer, *Truth and Method,* trans. Joel Weinsheimer and Donald G. Marshall (New York: Seabury Press, 1975), 84.

39. Ibid., 277.

40. Ibid., 293.

41. Ibid.

42. Kenneth Frampton, "The Status of Man and the Status of His Objects: A Reading of *The Human Condition,*" *Architectural Design* 52, no. 7–8 (1982): 6–7.

43. Kenneth Frampton, "Architecture in Print: A Dialogue with Kenneth Frampton," *Design Book Review* 8 (1986), 11.

44. Heidegger's "The Rectorate 1933/34: Facts and Thoughts," although allegedly written in 1945, was published in 1983, in accordance with his request to his son Herrmann that it be released at a "propitious time." The essay was received as an attempt by Heidegger to defend his involvement in the Nazi party. Inadvertently, it sparked a series of historical investigations that effectively exposed the mendacious character of his remarks, the first of which was Victor Farias's *Heidegger et le nazisme* (Paris: Verdier, 1987), followed in Germany by Hugo Ott's *Martin Heidegger: Unterwegs zu Seiner Biographie* (Frankfurt: Campus, 1988). By 1998, similar studies followed within the Anglo-American academy by Richard Rorty, Richard Wolin, Thomas Sheehan, and Michael E. Zimmerman, among others.

45. Gilles Deleuze, *A Thousand Plateaus: Capitalism and Schizophrenia,* trans. Brian Massumi (Minneapolis: University of Minnesota Press, 1987).

2. Eucharistic Architecture

1. "The Thomas Jefferson Memorial Foundation Medal in Architecture," *Modulus* 9 (1973): 56–57.

2. Jean Labatut, "Conversations with Jean Labatut, Interview by Michael Wurmfeld," in *Princeton's Beaux Arts and Its New Academicism: From Labatut to the Program of Geddes, an*

Exhibition of Original Drawings over Fifty Years, the Institute for Architecture and Urban Studies, January 27 to February 18 (Princeton Junction, N.J.: PDQ Press, 1977), 1–17.

3. Guy Hartcup, *Camouflage: A History of Concealment and Deception in War* (New York: Scribner's, 1980).

4. Not every artist in the Service de camouflage was a certified cubist, but most were conversant with the visual principles it advanced and of their usefulness for disguising structures. Some artists like André Dunoyer de Segonzac were influenced by cubism before the war (see his *Le déjeuner sur l'herbe,* 1912–13) but later turned toward more figurative styles. Others like André Mare worked more clearly in the cubist tradition. It is also important to note that cubism was not the only source of visual theory for camouflage artists. Especially in the United Kingdom and the United States, which founded camouflage units in 1916 and 1917, respectively, artists were influenced by studies of protective coloration in nature first carried out by Abbot H. Thayer (1849–1921), a prominent U.S. painter. See Roy B. Behrens, "The Theories of Abbott H. Thayer: Father of Camouflage," *Leonardo* 21, no. 3 (1988).

5. After the war, Mare founded the Compagnie des Arts Français with Louis Süe and went on to become one of the leading exponents of the style moderne or art deco, as it came to be known. See *André Mare: Cubisme et camouflage, 1914–1918* (Bernay: Musée municipal des beaux-arts, 1998).

6. Marcel Duchamp, the more famous of the brothers, was the least active in the group. Jacques Villon-Duchamp and his brother Raymond Duchamp-Villon essentially founded and were the center of the Puteaux group. Other members of the group included Jean Metzinger, František Kupka, Henri Le Fauconnier, Robert Delaunay, Fernand Léger, Francis Picabia, Walter Pach, Marie Laurencin, Guillaume Apollinaire, Joachim Gasquet, Roger Allard, Henri Valensi, André Mare, André Salmon, Roger de La Fresnaye, and the poet Alexandre Mercereau. See R. V. West, ed., *Painters of the Section d'or* (exhibition catalog, Buffalo, N.Y.: Albright-Knox A.G., 1967). For a discussion of the influence of the Puteaux group in 1920s Paris, see Frédéric Migayrou, "Une cinématique des vecteurs," in *Robert Mallet-Stevens: L'Oeuvre complète* (Centre Pompidou: Paris, 2005), 30–37.

7. Box 9, *Jean Labatut Papers* (Princeton University Department of Rare Books and Special Collections).

8. A. Gleizes and J. Metzinger, *Du cubisme* (Paris: E. Figuière et cie., 1912; Eng. trans., London, 1913).

9. "Hommage à Laloux, de ses élèves américains," *Pencil Points* 18 (1937), 621–30 .

10. Gwendolyn Wright, *The Politics of Design in French Colonial Urbanism* (Chicago: University of Chicago Press, 1991), 15–84.

11. Jean-Claude-Nicolas Forestier especially praised Frederick Law Olmstead's plan for Boston in his *Grandes villes et systèmes de parcs* (Paris: Hachette, 1908).

12. "Princeton Architect Wins Honor in Paris: Prof. Labatut's Design Is One of Nine Purchased by French Capital," *New York Times,* March 13, 1932.

13. Henry A. Jandl, "The School of Architecture and Urban Planning," in Alexander Leitch, *A Princeton Companion* (Princeton, N.J.: Princeton University Press, 1978).

14. Jean Labatut, "Conversations with Jean Labatut."

15. A. Russell Bond, "Foiling U-Boats: Some Methods Used to Overcome Submarines, How They Were Confused by 'Warriors of Paint Brush,'" *Boston Daily Globe,* April 27, 1919.

16. Roy B. Behrens, "The Role of Artists in Ship Camouflage during World War I," *Leonardo* 32, no. 1 (1999): 53–59.

17. Dazzle patterns became a preferred aesthetic for things related to the sea, from food trucks that sold sandwiches on beaches to bathing suits. Journalists reported satirically on the

fashions, noting, "The protective coloring, it is explained, conceals the bathers from sea serpents at tea time and other crucial moments." See "Now It's the Camouflaged Bathing Suit," *Chicago Daily Tribune,* July 6, 1919.

18. Labatut sailed on the *Leviathan* with his bride in 1929. See "Mercedes Terradell to Wed Prof. Labatut: Engagement Is Announced by Mrs. Elliot F. Shepard, Bride Elect's Sister," *New York Times,* May 24, 1929. The *Leviathan,* formerly the *Vaterland,* was captured from Germany by the United States during World War I and converted for troop transport, decommissioned in 1919, and returned to passenger service in 1923. Its "tourist third cabin class" made it popular with students traveling between Europe and America. See "Leviathan" in *Ships of the World: An Historical Encyclopedia,* Houghton Mifflin Online, http://college.hmco.com/history/readerscomp/ships/html/sh_054500_leviathan.htm.

19. The most significant of these houses was the Arthur E. Newbold house, Laverock, Pennsylvania (1919–24), designed when Howe was a partner in Mellor, Meigs & Howe.

20. Henry-Russell Hitchcock and Philip Johnson included the PSFS tower in their 1932 International Style Exhibition at the Museum of Modern Art. Phyllis Lambert has noted that Johnson was inspired by Howe's work in designing the interiors of the Seagram building. Phyllis Lambert, "The Seagram Building and Philip Johnson" (lecture, Columbia University, February 24, 2004).

21. Labatut collaborated with Rolf William Bauhan, a local architect and member of the Federal Works of Art Committee for that district. They produced a conservative Beaux-Arts design involving a 60-foot obelisk atop a 12-foot-tall square base. Bas-relief panels on the base depicted the life of Woodrow Wilson, first as president of Princeton, then governor of New Jersey, president of the United States, and advocate of the League of Nations. Above the panels were to be massed flags of the nations.

22. Jonathan Crary has documented the nineteenth-century prehistory of the discourse that linked aesthetics to the problems of attention and distraction in *Suspensions of Perception: Attention, Spectacle, and Modern Culture* (Cambridge, Mass.: MIT Press, 2001). By the 1920s, a wealth of academic studies appeared that indicated the efficacy of advertising in administering visual experience, enhancing feelings, and helping to focus attention. See, for instance, Howard Kenneth Nixon, *Investigation of Attention to Advertisements* (New York: Columbia University Press, 1926). That literature was the foundation for Labatut's work at the 1939 New York World's Fair and informed his subsequent research into techniques for manipulating visual experience.

23. *Exhibition Techniques: A Summary of Exhibition Practice, Based on Surveys Conducted at the New York and San Francisco World's Fairs of 1939* (New York: New York Museum of Science and Industry, 1940).

24. Sigfried Giedion, "The New Monumentality," in *New Architecture and City Planning,* ed. P. Zucker (New York: Philosophical Library, 1944), 563.

25. The General Motors ride immersed spectators in the collective dream of a modern city networked by highways and pulsating with cars. Its ride over the miniature urban landscapes of Futurama dropped off passengers at a full-scale intersection of the city, giving them the thrilling feeling of having been magically shrunk to the size of the diorama. The fair was really a theater for competing definitions of modern architecture that included Labatut's vision, the restrained classicism inspired by Paul Cret, the international style, and the casual "vernacular" pragmatism of domestic buildings on display in the Town of Tomorrow exhibit, where modernism was simply equated with aesthetic abstraction. The exhibit, built next to the Home Building Center, presented fifteen houses ranging from "traditional" to "transitional," and finally "modern"

dwellings with "severe" abstracted aesthetics. This was an argument for aesthetic pluralism in the domestic built environment, which countered the car industry's monolithic embrace of modernism. In the home, aesthetics were completely divorced from technology. For instance, the Nash-Kelvinator Company promoted the comfort of air-conditioning in every house, regardless of its style. The General Electric Company chose to sponsor a large frame house of traditional style to exhibit all types of modern electrical equipment. See Lee Cooper, "Trends in Homes Displayed at Fair," *New York Times,* May 28, 1939.

26. "'Spirit of George Washington' to Be Portrayed in Giant Fireworks: Spectacle of Fire to Thrill Crowds," *New York Times,* July 4, 1939.

27. Jean Labatut, "Conversations with Jean Labatut," 13.

28. This design method continues to be a favorite of architectural phenomenologists such as Steven Holl, who begins with impressionistic perspectives of spaces that he then translates into building plans.

29. Henri Bergson, *Creative Evolution* (1911; Mineola, N. Y.: Dover Publications, 1998), 306–16.

30. Henri Bergson, *Time and Free Will: An Essay on the Immediate Data of Consciousness,* trans. F.L. Pogson (Mineola, N.Y.: Dover Publications, 2001), 112.

31. Ibid., 115.

32. Ibid., 100.

33. Ibid., 101.

34. For a discussion of how the concept of "cinematic illusion" figures in the work of Bergson, see chapters 1 and 4 of Gilles Deleuze, *Cinema 1: The Movement-Image* (Minneapolis: University of Minnesota Press, 1986).

35. Bergson, *Time and Free Will,* 14–15.

36. Ibid., 15.

37. Jean Labatut, "Conversations with Jean Labatut," 13.

38. Robert Moses, *The Saga of Flushing Meadow, The Valley of Ashes* (New York: Triborough Bridge and Tunnel Authority, 1966), 5.

39. Olin Downes, "Music at the Fair," *New York Times,* August 27, 1939.

40. Raymond Hood, "Architecture of the Night," in *Architecture of the Night,* General Electric Company Bulletin GED-375 (February 1930), as quoted in Kermit Swiler Champa, "A Little Night Music: The Play of Color and Light," in *Architecture of the Night: The Illuminated Building,* ed. Dietrich Neumann (Munich: Prestel, 2002), 23.

41. Kermit Swiler Champa, "A Little Night Music: The Play of Color and Light," in *Architecture of the Night: The Illuminated Building,* ed. Dietrich Neumann (Munich: Prestel, 2002), 16–26.

42. Harvey Wiley Corbett, "The American Radiator Building, New York City: Raymond Hood, arch.," *Architectural Record* 55 (May 1924), 473–77.

43. The phenomenological revision of Panofsky iconography by American scholars like Meyer Schapiro in the 1970s was instrumental in making phenomenology relevant for artists and architects interested in understanding the relationship between artists and their work. Schapiro's study of Paul Cézanne (1970) was particularly influential.

44. Labatut and Russell composed each fifteen-minute show around themes such as "The Garden of Eden," "The World and the Cathedral," and a history of the United States called "The Spirit of George Washington."

45. "'Spirit of George Washington' to Be Portrayed in Giant Fireworks."

46. Jean Labatut, "History of Architectural Education through People," *JAE: Journal of Architectural Education* 33, no. 2 (November 1979): 21–24.

47. Ibid.

48. See Alexander Leitch, *A Princeton Companion* (Princeton, N.J.: Princeton University Press, 1978).

Index

Jorge Otero-Pailos is assistant professor of historic preservation at the Graduate School of Architecture, Planning, and Preservation at Columbia University. He is founder and editor of the architecture and preservation journal *Future Anterior*.